Woodland Indian Educational Programs Presents

The First Peoples of Ohio & Indiana

Written & Illustrated by
Jessica Diemer-Eaton

With Contributions by

David A. Lottes
Author of "Ouabache"

Sheryl Hartman
Author of "Indian Clothing of the Great Lakes 1740-1840"
and "Natives Along the Wabash"

and

Steve Tucker
Retired Art Teacher and Illustrator of
"Natives Along the Wabash"

On the Covers:

Front Cover Left to Right in State Silhouettes
Gourd Container by Perry Riley
Cradleboard Wrappings by Jessica Diemer-Eaton
Heritage Corn and Beans displayed by Jessica Diemer-Eaton

Back Cover Left to Right in State Silhouettes
Wigwam Frame by Jessica Diemer-Eaton and Mark Eaton
Smoking Buffalo Meat exhibited by Jessica Diemer-Eaton
Quillworked Thunderbird by Ralph Heath

Revised 2014 Edition

*To the Native Children Whose Ancestors
Called Ohio and Indiana Home*

And to my Grandparents
Mary and Valentine

About This Book

This Book Offers:

-Supplement material for your classroom lessons and textbook readings. For example, when your students review the Indian Removal Act, this book features question worksheets to use in conjunction.

-Extra classroom lessons and activities. These pages stand on their own as short lessons, such as the reading and puzzle "Historic Woodland Indian Culture," which reviews background cultural information that many textbooks don't address for students.

-Student readings on little known or rarely taught historical facts that connect to other focuses in American history, such as the articles "Iroquois Democracy Inspirers American Forefathers" and "How Native Americans Influenced The Women's Suffrage Movement."

-Multi-subject lessons. Some pages include activities and readings on Native American history that also connect to science (ex. "All About Trees"), health (ex. "Hominy for Heath"), and even math (ex. "The Math of Constructing Woodland Indian Homes").

-Relevant and in-depth cultural background information for teachers, such as, for example, the article "Native American Gender Sociology 101: A "Crash Course" For Teachers & History Enthusiasts in the Basics of Native American Gender Dynamics," which offers explanations of family relationships, mythical matriarchies, and some reasoning as to why certain tasks are assigned to one gender or the other.

-Extra, overlooked historical information often not available to teachers, such as the article "Beyond Popular History: The Other Tecumseh and Tenskwatawa" which reviews Native non-supporters' perspectives of these influential Shawnee brothers.

Pick and choose whatever activities, worksheets, readings, and projects work for your lesson plans.

The pages have been arranged by subject and topic, not by grade levels. The recommended grade levels for each page (if not on the heading of the page) can be found in the book contents list. Because this book has materials for grades 1 through 12, some page topics are duplicated for different grade levels, such as, for example, the handouts on Native American sports (below):

Grades 1-4

Grades 3-6

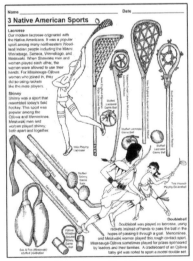

Grades 5-12

The grade levels listed are only a suggestion
It is up to the teacher to decide what learning material is of the appropriate level for his or her students.

About This Book (continued)

How to Use This Book

In order to use this book effectively and repetitively, it is suggested that the physical book pages are not used directly (colored on, written on, cut up), but instead copied for such use. Most pages in this book were made to copy and distribute by select people for educational purposes (IMPORTANT: please review permissions below before using).

Permissions: You are allowed as a teacher, professor, homeschool parent, or youth group leader, to copy and distribute any of the pages that feature the "name" heading:

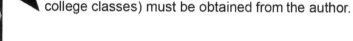

to your students or club members, preschool through college age levels.

Such permissions DO NOT extend to other educational organizations, such as museums, cultural centers, public libraries, nature centers, powwows, historical events, and the like (such organizations can contact the author for special permissions). DO NOT upload these pages electronically for any reason (such as for databases and online resources). County and town school systems ARE NOT authorized to use one copy of this book for multiple schools (whether by circulating the physical book or photocopied pages from the book, or by electronically sharing). Teachers in ONE school may circulate the physical book or keep a copy for teacher use in their library (DO NOT circulate photocopied versions and DO NOT share electronically).

DO NOT copy any page lacking the "name" heading:

Name_____ Date _____

(such as the pages with the ribbon applique borders to the left side of the page). These are not meant for any sort of distribution, and any special permissions to do such (such as by college classes) must be obtained from the author.

About the Illustrations and Photos

Illustrations by J. Diemer-Eaton, unless otherwise noted. Photos by J. Diemer-Eaton and Mark Eaton, unless otherwise noted (such photos are of the author's interpretive work and exhibits). All other illustrations and photos are listed as public domain (Wikimedia Commons) or used by permission and credit is given on the same pages these illustrations or photos appear on.

The author's illustrations have been included in this publication to reflect realistic past Native American life in Ohio and Indiana. The clothing, tools, homes, etc. depicted in the illustrations of this book reflect the the actual historic items utilized and the appearance of the Native peoples from pre-contact times to the mid 1800's.

As part of her commitment to authentic representation of Native American history, there is limited nudity depicted in the form of partially bare breasts and children's backsides. Native women's chests were not traditionally considered a private body area in most Northeastern Native tribes, and therefore it was common for women's chests to be unclothed. Likewise, young Native children were usually without clothing in fair weather (sometimes bare but still wearing belts). The author does not believe in manipulating the image of historic Native culture in a way that threatens the integrity of the cultural history (such as using Plains-style dresses on Woodland women to cover nudity where no such style of dress existed aboriginally). However, the author has placed hair, necklaces, arms, etc. over the details of the exposed chests to make the illustrations appropriate for more grade levels. These illustrations show as much nudity (or less) than many exhibits at reputable museums. It is the teacher's responsibility to pick the worksheets, coloring pages, etc. that are of the level of his or her students.

Please Note: This book includes recommendations of educational websites and books to help further activities or lessons. These are only recommendations, and the author does not endorse these books/sites nor do they endorse this book.

Contents

*"5-8" Suggested Grade Level - It is up to the teacher to decide what lesson, article, worksheet, etc. is appropriate for his or her students.

*"5-8" Suggested Grade Level - It is up to the teacher to decide what lesson, article, worksheet, etc. is appropriate for his or her students.

*"5-8" Suggested Grade Level - It is up to the teacher to decide what lesson, article, worksheet, etc. is appropriate for his or her students.

*"5-8" Suggested Grade Level - It is up to the teacher to decide what lesson, article, worksheet, etc. is appropriate for his or her students.

Introducing Native Americans
Some Tips On Interpreting Native American Subjects To Non-Native Students

Point Out the Similarities

Introduce the Native people and their culture to your students as similar, not fundamentally different. By first pointing out the cultural traits we share, children are given the chance to connect to the Native community on the human level. Introduce similarities - family values, child life, sports, foods (corn, beans, squash, maple sugar, blackberries, raspberries, tree nuts), etc. Students need to view the Native peoples as equal before studying differences such as languages, worldviews, food preserving techniques, tools and technologies, and architecture. Only when we view other people like equals can we learn about another's culture without objectifying it.

Familiar Terminology

When students hear terms they cannot identify with, such as *brave, squaw,* and *papoose,* then children don't value this "category" of people. There is nothing about these terms that equate these individuals' experiences to their own or that of the people they relate to. These terms were historically high-jacked by Euro-Americans, used to both distance Native peoples and label them as inferior. Indeed, many historical texts will solely refer to Native men as *Indians* and Native women as *squaws* in an effort (purposely or subconsciously, depending on the writer) to degrade the Native race. Continuing to use such terminology continues to objectify Native peoples by not allowing them the respect of being described in the same terms we would use to describe our own family members. When we use familiar terms - people terms - such as *husband, mother,* and *child,* then children better value the Native American experience as they would their own.

One Particularly Detrimental Term

The term *squaw* in particular was abused by outsiders, manipulated to label Native women without connecting them to "civilized white women." Native women are, in this practice of labeling, treated as undeserving of the titles of *mother, daughter, sister, wife* or even *woman. Squaw* is not a cute term - the use of *squaw* today in most applications can be considered both racist and sexist. Some Native people have made an effort to reclaim the term for the positive as it was in origin, but until that is successful in mainstream American culture, it is best to avoid its use among students as they have already been exposed to the negatives attached to the word through media. For example, think about the 1953 released Disney movie *Peter Pan,* and how in the song "What Made the Red Man Red?" squaws were equated to female drudgery - female slaves valued only for the menial tasks they preformed, which the animated film makes very clear was work unfit for "valued human beings" such as the all the men or an exceptional looking "Indian princess." If students mentally bring these negatives into a classroom setting all because it's connected to the same term the teacher uses, then they are likely to believe the prior learned negatives as true and factual as your curriculum material (the term acts as a bridge between the real unbias information and the negatively stereotyped imagery). Using better terminology is in an effort to "leave the baggage at the classroom door" so students can really explore Native cultures from a less bias place.

The Dreaded *Indian* Word

So many non-Native individuals question how they should refer to indigenous populations. These are the most common of conversations I have with teachers. They ask me, "Do we say Native Americans or First Nations? Can we say American Indians? I heard that they want to be called by their tribal name." It is the author's opinion that these names matter much less in the classroom than the way in which they are stated. Respect for Native peoples is usually found in the way they are presented, not summed up in what we think is a politically correct term. With that said, feel free to use *Native, Native American, First Nations,* and similar terms, and know that *Indian* is not exactly a bad word. It has undergone positive reclaiming by Native culture to a certain degree of success - although the term was never Native in origin, many Native scholars have pointed out that they feel the term is properly theirs to claim after being forced to live so many centuries labeled as such wrongly.

"People" - A Powerful Term

Indeed, many Native people refer to themselves as *Indian*, but we are more concerned with the delivery of such terminology in the classroom. There is a rather simple practice to transform the term Indian into a constant positive "human" term, and it has to do with the sentence it appears in. For example, the phrase "the Indians" can objectify the Native people in the eyes of young children. One should say instead "the Indian people" so that it feels like the subject is about human beings, not things. *People* is a powerful term; it can change what young students envision from objects to people. *People* is also a familiar term that children can identify with and put value to. Another way to think about this topic: in the way you may choose to say "the Jewish people" instead of just "the Jews" in a classroom setting, is in the same spirit you might choose to say "the Indian people" instead of just "the Indians" in a classroom setting - these terms aren't wrong but there seems to be a devaluing attitude (caused by historic abuse of these terms) that is removed when stated just a little bit differently. That little difference in wording can amount to huge differences in students' perceptions.

The Language of Verbs

Like all peoples around the world, we have bias. Much of our "way of thinking" is many times applied to the interpretation of others. Be aware of this when you teach about Native peoples. For example, I have seen even the most seasoned educator state "Indian men got to go hunting and Indian women had to grow the crops." Using "got" for men's work translates as a positive, while using "had" for women's work translates as a negative, especially in the same sentence or passage. The student perceives from this sentence that men's work is better than women's, or less of a chore and more fun than women's. Because we might value men's work over women's work, hunting over gardening, or assume Native people valued men's work over women's work or hunting over gardening does not mean this is so. When describing gendered work, as in all aspects of Native culture, be sure to use the same verbs (preferably positive). Projecting our own unfounded bias in the classroom is, in a sense, working to undo even the most well intentioned lesson plans about Native Americans.

Understanding This is a History Lesson

It is important to remind students that while they are learning about the historic Native Americans, thousands of Native people are still a part of our American society today. Explain that like all of us, the Native people and their culture change with time. Students need to understand that contemporary Native people live in the same types of homes as themselves and go to jobs just like their parents do. Many Native people are doctors, nurses, scientists, artists, singers, writers, teachers, college students, farmers, truck drivers, pilots, police men and women, etc., just like non-Native people. Your students should understand that Native children today wear the same clothes as they do, and go to school as they do. Students should never think a Native person today must live in a wigwam and wear buckskin as their ancestors did just because they are Native. Students should never suspect that if a Native American person isn't dressed in traditional regalia, that they must not be very "Indian." It is highly suggested that the teacher includes at least one lesson or activity devoted to learning about contemporary Native Americans at the end of any Native American history curriculum.

Notes:

_____

_____

_____

The Original People

Topics Represented in This Section:

Tribal Homelands; Cultural Backgrounds; Post-Contact Tribal Distribution.

The Northeastern Cultural Area

Northeastern Cultural Area:
An area of North America where many Native communities shared the same kind of environment. Similar resources were available from village to village, and many customs and material culture were similar too. For example, houses in all Northeastern Native settlements were covered by bark and reed mats.

MAP 1600–1650

There were many tribes located in the Northeastern United States. We can divide the Northeast up by similar regions. The circles represent regional micro-environments:

1. Great Lakes Region, 2. New England,   3. Mid-Atlantic Region,   4. Ohio River Valley.

Are you located in a Native American micro-environment? If so, which one? Does your state have more than one micro-environment? If so, why do you think that is?

_____

_____

_____

Name _____ Date _____

Tribe Locations in 1600

The above cultural locations for 1600 are based on a mixture of tribal histories, linguistics, archaeological evidence, and/or historic accounts. Some locations are well known for 1600, such as the Delaware in New Jersey, southern New York, and eastern Pennsylvania. They were first met by Europeans in their eastern homelands, and the archaeological record agrees. However some tribes, like the Shawnee and Fox, are mostly theorized to be located at the above areas in 1600, and we don't know for sure if these theorized locations are correct. Some tribes, like the Miami, were first met in Wisconsin as refugees of the Beaver Wars. Their tribal history asserts their homelands to be both Indiana and Ohio, and scholars agree (the Miami returned to their Indiana and Ohio homelands after the threat of Iroquois attacks had subsided). Other nations were formed after the Beaver Wars, such as the Huron and Tionontati refugees that formed the historic Wyandot tribe known to live in Ohio and Indiana in the 18th and 19th centuries. Some Native cultures appear in a lighter gray type - these are societies that dissolved shortly after 1600. Some may have become the historic tribes we know today (such as the Shawnee, which some scholars believe had come from the Fort Ancient culture). **Name 3 tribes that resided in your state historically (between 1600-1900) but claimed homelands somewhere else.**

_____

General Background of the Native American Tribes That Resided Historically in Indiana

Delaware or Lenape
Basics: *Algonquian-speaking people. The Munsee-Delaware (Northern Delaware) were an extensive horticultural people who hunted and gathered, and lived in permanent year-round villages (wigwams and longhouses).* The word "Delaware" is not a Native term. The Delaware were named such after the river many of their society resided on. The river was named after Sir Thomas West, Lord de la Warr (first governor of Virginia). Their name for themselves, Lenni-Lenape, roughly meaning "common people" or "real person," has dropped the Lenni in modern times. The Delaware or Lenape homelands upon European contact included all of New Jersey, eastern Pennsylvania, southern New York, coastal Delaware, and corners of Maryland and Connecticut. Some Delaware may have already passed through Indiana earlier than 1775 while headed to Missouri, and at least one Delaware village was established in southern Indiana by 1776. However, most Delaware who came to reside within the state (on the White River) did so just years later coming from towns in Ohio where they resided in close proximity to the Miami and Shawnee (with the Shawnee in both northern and southern Indiana). By 1821, under American pressure, the Delaware had left Indiana for destinations in the states of Missouri, Kansas (later Oklahoma), Texas, and Wisconsin. There is also a slight possibility that some may have ended up in Mexico (see Kickapoo below).

Kickapoo
Basics: *Algonquian-speaking horticultural people who hunted and gathered, and lived in permanent summer villages and structures (large bark houses: multifamily homes), and semi-permanent winter camps (wigwams: nuclear family homes).** The Kickapoo have one of the most unique "forced migration" histories of any Indiana tribe. Originally from Michigan (west of Lake Erie), they were met by Europeans in Wisconsin in the late 17th century. They lived in Indiana (on the Wabash River near Lafayette), Illinois and Missouri until the early 19th century when they moved to Kansas. Disillusioned by the government's handling of their Kansas lands, the Kickapoo moved south in 1864 to Arkansas and then Texas (where they stayed with some Shawnee, Delaware, and Cherokee) before they were forced to move (this time by Texan settlements) to Oklahoma. However, some Kickapoo broke away and headed south instead to Mexico where it is believed that a few hundred Kickapoo still reside (about 400 in 1905).

Mahican
Basics: *Algonquian-speaking people who were extensive horticulturalists who hunted and gathered, and lived in permanent year-round villages comprised of longhouses.* The Mahican, sometimes spelled Mohican, are not the same people as the Mohegan (a completely different group in southern New England, related to the Pequot). Mahican homelands upon European contact included western Vermont, Massachusetts, Connecticut, and eastern New York. Very few Mahicans came to live in Indiana (when compared to other Native communities represented) and those who did melded with the Delaware because they tended to live in the same villages with their old neighbors from the east (and share much the same culture as the Munsee-Delaware). As early as 1669 some Mahican had been exploring the Midwest. In 1721, part of the Mahican came to settle among the Miami on the Kankakee River (two bands of Mahican had been living among the Miami since 1680). In 1818, the Stockbridge (a branch of the Mahican) arrived on the White River, just in time to learn that the Delaware and Miami had sold those very lands. Many of the Stockbridge and some Delaware ended up moving to Wisconsin where their descendants still reside today known as the Stockbridge-Munsee.

Mascouten
Basics: *Algonquian-speaking horticultural people who hunted and gathered, and lived in permanent summer villages and structures, and semi-permanent winter camps.** The

Mascouten are placed in Michigan at the time of European contact, and in 1679 the Mascouten lived in areas all around the bottom of Lake Michigan including northwestern Indiana. After 1735, many Mascouten lived with the Kickapoo, especially near Lafayette on the Wabash. By 1800, they seemed to have melded in with the Kickapoo who were vacating the Indiana-Illinois border by 1820. Unfortunately, the Mascouten may be arguably the least known tribe to have inhabited Indiana during the historic period which is why they have been under-represented in general publications and text books.

Miami
Basics: Algonquian-speaking people who were extensive horticulturists. They also hunted and gathered foods. They lived in permanent summer villages and structures (possibly large bark houses: multifamily homes), and semi-permanent winter camps (wigwams: nuclear family homes). Considered Indiana's original people, the Miami (or Myaamia in the Miami language) were first met near Green Bay, Wisconsin as refugees from the Iroquois Wars. Compared to their Fox (Meskwaki) neighbors in Wisconsin, the Miami seemed "out of place," and unable to deal with northern weather patterns that inhibited their hunting (as Miami seemingly made no snowshoes aboriginally). This was because the Miami probably didn't practice deep snow hunting as their culture placed a great importance on horticulture and their Indiana homelands provided large harvests of crops to get them through deep snow seasons. Indeed, the Miami were noted for their miles and miles of cornfields that surrounded their villages during the historic period. By 1680, the Miami had begun to filter back into their homelands of Indiana and Ohio. The Miami tribe included six major sub-groups: Atchatchakangouen, Kilatika, Mengakonkia, Pepikokia, Piankeshaw, and Wea. The Miami proper (excluding the Wea, Pepikokia, and Piankeshaw) inhabited central Indiana east into Ohio during the 18th century. The later three groups had separated into two distinct tribes and retained their status as such for the majority of the historic period (see Piankeshaw and Wea). The Miami proper was a constant presence in Indiana during the post-historic period. Most were removed by American troops in 1846 to Kansas, then Oklahoma where most still reside (Oklahoma Miami). Some Miami were able to resist or compel the United States to not remove them, and their descendants continue to live in Indiana today (Indiana Miami).

Nanticoke
Basics: Algonquian-speaking people who were extensive horticulturalists who also gathered (especially fishing and clamming) and hunted. They lived in villages comprised of multifamily longhouses. The Nanticoke homelands encompassed eastern Maryland, western Delaware, and a small corner of Virginia. Like other tribes of the east, the Nanticoke experience in the historic period included necessary migrations away from encroaching white settlements. When last holdouts in Maryland were threatened, they removed to Pennsylvania, usually living among other refugee Native groups, especially the Delaware. Later many Nanticoke moved up to New York to live with the Iroquois, but a faction went west with the Delaware. By 1805, this Nanticoke community established a village on the White River in Indiana, and by 1818, they removed west of the Mississippi, where they resided in Kansas for a period before ending up in Oklahoma.

Ojibwa or Chippewa
Basics: Algonquian-speaking hunters and gatherers (especially wild rice and fish), who also gardened (depending on their location for full growing seasons to cultivate corn). They resided in seasonal villages and camps comprised of multi-family homes and single family homes (dome, conical, and a-frame wigwams) – those who farmed lived in summer villages. The southern Ojibwa homelands most probably extended from the Georgian Bay, west along the north shore of Lake Huron, to the Upper Peninsula of Michigan. With the Huron (many

of whom became Wyandot) being routed in the mid 17th century by the Iroquois, the Iroquois then began putting pressure on the Ojibwa. Since then, conflict and the fur trade had encouraged the movement of many Ojibwa communities all over the Great Lakes stage, including south to Ohio and Indiana. Some had come to reside for a time in Prophetstown in the early 1800's. While most tribes of the region were removed west of the Mississippi, most Ojibwa have remained in the Great Lakes region until present – their higher populations can be found in Minnesota, Wisconsin, Michigan, and adjacent areas in Canada. By 1970, about half of the Ojibwa population resided in urban centers.

Ottawa or Odawa
Basics: Algonquian-speaking fishing people who hunted, gathered, and cultivated crops. They lived in permanent villages comprised of longhouses, and utilized conical wigwams during hunting and fishing trips. At the time of European contact, the Ottawa were located on Manitoulin Island and the adjacent Bruce Peninsula (lands and shores just northeast of Lower Michigan on the other side of Lake Huron). They moved around and expanded their areas into more Canadian county, Ohio, Michigan, Illinois, Wisconsin, and small sections of Indiana's borders with Michigan and Ohio during the historic period (up to 1839). Groups of Ottawa (Odawa) and closely related Chippewa (Ojibwa) also took up residence in Prophetstown (in Battle Ground near Lafayette, 1808-1811), however, most left after one severe winter (some Ottawa returned later). Today, larger Ottawa populations reside in Ontario, Michigan, and Oklahoma.

Piankeshaw
Basics: Algonquian-speaking extensive horticulturists who hunted and gathered. They lived in permanent summer villages and structures (possibly large bark houses: multifamily homes), and semi-permanent winter camps (wigwams: nuclear family homes). The Piankeshaw are a faction of the Miami, who separated and maintained separate tribal status in the historic period (until 1854 when they formally joined some Illinois and the Wea, creating the Confederated Peoria). The Piankeshaw, like their Miami cousins, were the original people of Indiana. From 1725 they inhabited southwestern Indiana and part of southeastern Illinois until 1814 when they removed to Missouri in response to white expansion and pressure. Today, the Piankeshaw are no longer a separate entity, and Piankeshaw descendants identify as the Peoria, one of the Illinois groups they merged with in the 19th century.

Potawatomi
Basics: Algonquian-speaking horticultural people who hunted and gathered, and lived in permanent summer villages and structures (large bark houses: multifamily homes), and probably dispersed into semi-permanent winter camps (dome wigwams: nuclear family homes). Potawatomi homelands were situated in the southwestern quadrant of Lower Michigan (which might have possibly dipped into northwestern Indiana). By 1701, the Potawatomi had established a village on the Indiana-Michigan border. By 1768, Potawatomi residence had expanded to include the whole northern border of Indiana and by 1810, they established villages further south along the Wabash River. In 1830, the Potawatomi had several villages in northern Indiana including on the Eel, Tippecanoe, and Wabash Rivers. The 1838 removal of the Potawatomi in northern Indiana to designated areas west of the Mississippi became famously known to modern Indianans as the "Trail of Death" (not to be confused with the "Trail of Tears" - referring to the Cherokee and Southeastern Indian removal journey – although they were all carried out under the same Indian Removal Act). These Potawatomi communities were eventually removed to Kansas and Oklahoma, where many still reside today. Some Potawatomi had also removed to Ontario between 1837 and 1840, where they are usually counted with the Canadian Chippewa and Ottawa communities today. Some Potawatomi remained in Indiana and Michigan, and their

descendants continue to reside within the two states.

Shawnee
Basics: Algonquian-speaking, horticultural people who hunted and gathered, and lived in permanent summer villages and structures (large bark houses: multifamily homes), and semi-permanent winter camps (dome wigwams: nuclear family homes).* The Shawnee homelands are usually thought to be southern Ohio and adjacent areas in West Virginia and Kentucky (possibly associated or directly descended from the Fort Ancient complex). They are known for their extensive movements during the historic period (pre-removal), inhabiting at one point the states (east of the Mississippi) of Pennsylvania, Ohio, Indiana, Illinois, Maryland, Kentucky, Tennessee, and even Georgia and Alabama. Shawnee villages were built in southeastern Indiana along the Ohio River by 1670. By 1788, the Shawnee established villages on the lower White River and near the Miami and Delaware near Fort Wayne. They continue to establish villages throughout Indiana, but especially in the southern half of the state (with Delaware towns along the Ohio River and near Beck's Mill in Salem), until a small portion of Ohio Shawnee founded Prophetstown in 1808 (in Battle Ground near Lafayette). Prophetstown, while founded by the Shawnee renegade war leader Tecumseh and his brother The Prophet, was not a Shawnee "tribal" village. It was a pan-Indian village for believers of any Indian nation, and most Native Americans of the time did not agree with or support the village or brothers and their movement. However, it was the establishment of Prophetstown that would in fact attract some sympathizing Winnebago from Wisconsin to live in Indiana for a short period (see Winnebago). After the credibility of The Prophet was destroyed at the Battle of Tippecanoe in 1811, Tecumseh's Shawnee followers went with him to Ontario but later ended up in Kansas. Today, three federally recognized Shawnee tribes reside in Oklahoma, while a few groups identifying as Shawnee still reside in Ohio.

Wea
Basics: Algonquian-speaking extensive horticulturalists who hunted and gathered. They lived in permanent summer villages and structures (possibly large bark houses: multifamily homes), and semi-permanent winter camps (wigwams: nuclear family homes).* The Wea (and the Miami sub-group Pepikokia who were probably absorbed by the Wea in about 1742) are a faction of the Miami, who separated and maintained separate tribal status in the historic period until 1854 when they formally joined some Illinois and the Piankeshaw, creating the Confederated Peoria. The Wea, like their Miami cousins, were the original people of Indiana. From 1700 they inhabited west-central Indiana and part of eastern Illinois until 1820 when they removed to Missouri in response to white expansion and pressure. Today, the removed Wea are no longer a separate entity, and removed Wea descendants identify as part of the Peoria, one of the Illinois groups they merged with in the 19th century. There do however exist individuals of Wea heritage who have re-identified as a Native community along the Indiana-Illinois border.

Winnebago or Ho-Chunk
Basics: Siouan speaking horticulturalists who hunted and gathered. They lived in large, rectangular bark structures in their summer villages, while also utilizing dome wigwams (presumably during winter), which soon replaced the larger structures as the preferred year-round dwelling during the historic period.* The Winnebago homelands were located in the lower half of Wisconsin and on the northern Illinois border. During the span of Prophetstown, some Winnebago came to live there as believers, supporters, and fighters (some of Tecumseh's warriors included Winnebago men). The population of Winnebago people at Prophetstown may have led to some of today's misunderstandings of "Sioux" people from the "west" in Indiana, which then led many to believe that Plains peoples with tepees were in Indiana. The accounts are actually speaking of the Winnebago who are Siouan and from the Old Northwest - they were not Plains people who lived in tepees. The Winnebago are a part of the Northeastern cultural area

and led the lifestyle of such; they lived in large bark houses and dome wigwams like their Woodland Indian neighbors. Removal for the Winnebago included residency in the states of Minnesota, Iowa, South Dakota, and Nebraska (Nebraska Winnebago), although a faction remained in Wisconsin (Wisconsin Winnebago).

Wyandot (Refugee Huron & Tionantati/Petún)

Basics: Iroquoian-speakers were extensive horticulturalists who hunted and gathered (especially fishing). They lived in permanent year-round villages comprised of multifamily longhouses. This most likely gave way to smaller homes (wigwams) while fleeing war during historic times. The term Wyandot, for historians, is not just another word for the Huron tribe, as popularly believed. It is a Huron word ("Wendat") that is applied by historians to a faction of Hurons and refugee Iroquoian peoples (including the Tionontati or Petún and possibly some Erie) who went to Detroit in 1701, and their community thereafter. While the French referred to the tribe as "Huron," this refugee faction was known to the British as the "Wyandot." The Wyandot made their way from their Huron and Iroquoian homelands in the eastern Great Lakes to the western Great Lakes while fleeing the Iroquois Five Nations (Haudenosaunee) during the "Iroquois Wars" (1641-1701). By 1811, a Wyandot village was established in Indiana by Prophetstown, where an area of pro-British Indian peoples were residing during the War of 1812 (other Wyandot were located in Ohio and Michigan at this time). Their influence probably reached farther than this single village in the northern part of the state, as legends of their residence and refugee hideouts in southern Indiana gave way to naming natural features in the state (like forests and caves) after the Wyandot.

Visitors to Indiana

Unquestionably, there were individuals of other tribal backgrounds who visited Indiana Indian towns for formalities and politics, or came to live individually as members of tribes established in Indiana, melding into the larger communities. One such example was the couple dozen Creek men who came to Prophetstown after being invited by Tecumseh to become part of the pan-Indian movement to resist American expansion. Some Meskwaki (Fox) also came to stay for a couple weeks at Prophetstown. Native people of other tribal backgrounds would have passed through Indiana to their destinations either east or west of the state.

*Terms in Context
Permanent village and structures - villages and bark-covered homes lasting 10 or more years in one location before a settlement is moved.

Semi-permanent winter camps and wigwams - camps used for 2-3 months and returned to year after year; the structure framework was always permanent (ex. dome wigwam frames are permanently secured in the ground and never moved, but the cattail mat coverings may be removed and taken away, then placed back on when returning next winter).

A Note About Native Camps: All Native people of Indiana, whether they resided in their villages year-round or most of the year, did take "family trips" to fishing and/or hunting and/or maple sugar camps. Their time spent at these locations amounted to anywhere from 4 -7 weeks a year. After spending a few weeks at a camp, they returned home to their village. This is not nomadic, nor living at "temporary" camps. These camps can be thought of in the same way one would think of a vacation home or hunting cabin; the location a family may return to each year for a couple weeks or so - most of their belongings staying at home, not coming on the trip. If we do not think of this as "living on the move," then we should not apply it to the Native people who did the same.

Sources:
-Kraft, Herbert C. 2001. The Lenape-Delaware Indian Heritage: 10,000BC – AD2000. Lenape Books.
-Sturtevant, William C. and Bruce G. Trigger. 1978. Handbook of the North American Indians. Vol. 15 – Northeast. Smithsonian
     Institution.
-Tanner, Helen Hornbeck. 1987. Atlas of Great Lakes Indian History. Norman: University of Oklahoma Press.

The Historic Native American Tribes of Indiana

1681 Shawnee Mahican
1679? Miami Mascouten
1810 Potawatomi
1720-1759 Miami Potawatomi
1768 Potawatomi
1781 Miami
1810 Potawatomi
1810 Potawatomi
1733-1752 Miami
1788, 1790 Shawnee
1752 Miami
1781, 1787, to 1792 Delaware
1810 Potawatomi

1768 Kickapoo & Mascouten
1830 Potawatomi

Potawatomi
to 1812 Miami
to 1812 Miami
to 1812 Miami
1830 Miami

to 1812 Winnebago
Wyandot
1808 Ottawa
1810 Delaware
1810 Delaware
1790 Miami Delaware
1810 Delaware

1735-1752 Mascouten, Kickapoo
1803-1811 Shawnee Potawatomi Kickapoo
to 1791 Wea
to 1733 Miami

1811-1816 Nanticoke

1768 - Miami (Piankeshaw & Wea)
1810 Delaware

to 1814 Wea
1744-52 Kickapoo, Mascouten

1810 Delaware

to 1670 Shawnee

1768 Shawnee

1791 Delaware

Piankeshaw

Delaware Shawnee

Above Illustration: Miami Woman Pounds Corn Into Meal, 1810.

to 1811 Delaware Shawnee

1670-1830

11

Historic Native Indiana Crossword Puzzle

Words Pool:

Adena
Andersontown   mussels
Angel Mounds   Piankeshaw
chert   Potawatomi
copper   Prophetstown
corn   Shawnee
cradleboard   Wea
Delaware   wigwam
earthenware   Wyandot
~~Indiana~~
Miami
mica
Mississippian

A Potawatomi mother makes maple sugar while her son eats all the sugar he can.

Down

1. A community founded by The Prophet in 1808.
3. A term that refers to a small Native home.
5. ~~A state named for its historic Native American population of many tribes.~~
7. A stone material traded to Indiana from the southern Appalachians.
9. Tribe that separated from the Miami, known for their occupation near Vincennes.
11. Early mound building society whose earthworks can be seen at Moundsville (SHS).
13. A metal used by Native people to make tools and jewelry - most was traded to Indiana from large deposits located around Lake Superior.
15. A crop grown by Indiana's tribes - this plant accounted a for large part of the Native diet.
17. Gathered for food from Indiana's rivers.
19. A type of pottery made by the Native people that was strong enough to cook in.

Across

2. A tribal community that stayed in Indiana until removal on the "Trail of Death."
4. The Native society responsible for the earthworks at Angel Mounds (SHS).
6. A tribe named after a major river that separates New Jersey and Pennsylvania.
8. This tribe claims Indiana for their homelands.
10. A historic town named after a Delaware leader - the city still bears his name today.
12. A baby carrying device used to transport and keep infants safe and comfortable.
14. Referred to as the "Southerners," this tribe's homelands are not well known but thought to be Ohio.
16. A group separated from the Miami, known for their historic villages along the Wabash.
18. A site once occupied by the Mississippian.
20. A rock material used to make tools from.
21. A group of people from the Huron tribe.

General Background of the Native American Tribes That Resided Historically in Ohio

Abenaki

Basics: Algonquian-speaking hunters and gatherers (many were especially fishers), many of whom also gardened. They lived in seasonal residences: those villages utilized in the summer were comprised of dome-shaped wigwams, elongated dome-shaped wigwams, and/or small longhouses. They preferred the conical wigwam for winter living. The Abenaki (sometimes spelled Abnaki) are usually spoken of in two groups: the Western Abenaki (which includes the Penacook) and the Eastern Abenaki (which includes the Penobscot). Together, their homelands included Vermont, New Hampshire, most of Maine, adjacent areas in Canada, eastern border of New York, and northern border of Massachusetts. While the Abenaki are a specific tribe, it should be noted that when the Miami extended invitations to the eastern Algonquian-speaking peoples, including Abenaki, Mahican, and the Delaware, they commonly referred to them all as "Abenakis" as to say "Easterners." This term is actually very appropriate as the Abenaki derive their name from their own language meaning "dawn land people" or just "easterners." Although their homelands were in the east, some of the St. Francis Abenaki did come to reside within the state of Ohio, especially in the mid-18th century multi-tribal villages in present day Cleveland. Most Abenaki peoples today reside in Canada, New Hampshire, and Vermont.

Delaware or Lenape

Basics: Algonquian-speaking people. The Munsee-Delaware (Northern Delaware) were an extensive horticultural people who hunted and gathered, and lived in permanent year-round villages (wigwams and longhouses).. The word "Delaware" is not a Native term. The Delaware were named such after the river many of their society resided on. The river was named after Sir Thomas West, Lord de la Warr (first governor of Virginia). Their name for themselves, Lenni-Lenape, roughly meaning "common people" or "real person" has dropped the Lenni in modern times. The Delaware or Lenape homelands upon European contact included all of New Jersey, eastern Pennsylvania, southern New York, coastal Delaware, and corners of Maryland and Connecticut. Delaware villages had been established within the state by 1740, and they remained a constant influence in Ohio until the early 1800's. After this point, most Delaware were already in Indiana or further west across the Mississippi, however, a small reserve designated as Delaware existed until 1828 within the state. During their occupation, they resided both in tribal villages and Christian Indian towns. Such towns like Schonbrunn and Gnadenhutten were constructed under the direction of Moravian missionaries. Unfortunately, while the Delaware were generally treated well by this religious faction, their white, non-Moravian Christian neighbors were usually less friendly. One of the most famous incidents that came from such hostilities was the Gnadenhutten Massacre, where over 90 innocent and unarmed Moravian-Delaware men, women, and children were slaughtered by a Pennsylvania unit. The Delaware moved on to establish villages in Indiana, but by 1821, under American pressure, the Delaware had already left Indiana for destinations in the states of Missouri, Kansas (later Oklahoma), Texas, and Wisconsin. There is also a slight possibility that a few may have ended up in Mexico when traveling with a group of Kickapoo.

Erie

Basics: Iroquoian-speaking who, like their Iroquoian neighbors, were probably extensive horticulturalists who relied also on fishing and hunting. They resided in large, multi-family longhouses. The Erie resided in northeastern Ohio along the coastal region of Lake Erie up to the mid-17th century when warfare with the Iroquois Confederacy wiped them out. Erie survivors were most likely absorbed by enemy Iroquois and allied Huron societies. Some also theorized they may have gone to the coastal southeast or up north to Canada. Some Seneca of Oklahoma and Kansas claim Erie ancestry.

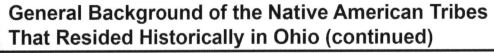

Mahican

Basics: Algonquian-speaking extensive horticulturalists who hunted and gathered, and lived in permanent year-round villages comprised of longhouses. The name Mahican, commonly spelled Mohican, is not to be confused with Mohegan (a completely different group in southern New England related to the Pequot). Their homelands upon European contact included western Vermont, Massachusetts, Connecticut, and eastern New York. As early as 1669, some Mahican had been exploring the Midwest. From about 1740-1760, Mahicans resided in the multi-tribal villages on the Cuyahoga River at present day Cleveland, and in 1760, a Mahican residence was established at Mahican Johns village with the Delaware. In 1792, Ohio Mahicans come to reside within largely Delaware Christian towns. In 1818, the Stockbridge (a branch of the Mahican) crossed into Indiana to reside on the White River, just in time to learn that the Delaware and Miami had sold those very lands. Many of the Stockbridge and some Delaware ended up moving to Wisconsin were their descendants still reside today known as the Stockbridge-Munsee.

Miami

Basics: Algonquian-speaking extensive horticulturalists who hunted and gathered. They lived in permanent summer villages and structures (possibly large bark multifamily homes), and semi-permanent winter camps (nuclear family wigwams).* While Ohio and Indiana are considered Miami homelands, the Miami were actually first met by Europeans near Green Bay, Wisconsin as refugees from the Iroquois Wars. Compared with their Fox (Meskwaki) neighbors, the Miami seemed "out of place," unable to deal with northern weather patterns that inhibited their hunting as the Miami made no snowshoes. This was because the Miami probably didn't practice deep snow hunting as their culture placed a great importance on horticulture and their Ohio and Indiana homelands provided large harvests of crops to get them through deep snow seasons. Indeed, the Miami were noted for their miles and miles of cornfields that surrounded their villages in the historic period. By 1680, the Miami had begun to filter back into their homelands. The Miami tribe included six major sub-groups: Atchatchakangouen, Kilatika, Mengakonkia, Pepikokia, Piankeshaw, and Wea. The Miami proper (excluding the Wea, Pepikokia, and Piankeshaw) inhabited central Indiana east into Ohio during the 18th century. Their residency within the state of Ohio was on and off, as conflicts forced the Miami west over the Indiana border, only to return to Ohio due to population growth (the Miami invited displaced tribes like the Delaware, Kickapoo, and Mascouten to live as neighbors on Miami lands). By 1800, the Miami were once again pressed back across the Indiana border where they remained up until removal in 1846; they were removed to Kansas, then on to Oklahoma where they still reside (known as the Oklahoma Miami). Some Miami were able to resist or compel the United States to not remove them, and a community of their descendants continue to live in Indiana (known as the Indiana Miami).

Mingo (Mixed New York Iroquois and Ohio Valley Algonquian Communities)

Basics: Iroquoian-speakers (however, because Algonquian individuals also came to identify with the community, some may have also spoken their native Algonquian languages). They were originally extensive horticulturalists who supplemented their diets with hunting and gathering. Traditionally, they lived like their Iroquois ancestors, in permanent longhouse villages. While in Ohio, they probably lived in smaller homes like wigwams or smaller bark cabins. The Mingo were splinter groups from Iroquois tribes who established residences in Ohio in the 18th century. Most Mingo were of Seneca, Cayuga, and Mohawk descent, and some also had Susquehannock, Delaware, and Shawnee backgrounds. Some Mingos even lived in Miami and Shawnee villages. In the mid-18th century, the Mingo resided in villages in eastern Ohio, and by 1780, they established villages in north-central Ohio, especially at Sandusky and on the Scioto River (including at the site of modern day Columbus), with more Seneca and Cayuga communities. They remained in Ohio (labeled "Seneca" in this period of time in Ohio) on reserved lands at Sandusky until 1831 when they were removed to Kansas. Years later, they were once again relocated by the government, this time to Indian Territory in Oklahoma. Today, many of their descendants reside as the Seneca-Cayuga Tribe of Oklahoma.

Nanticoke (and Piscataway)

Basics: Algonquian-speaking horticultural people who gathered (especially fishing and clamming) and hunted. They lived in permanent villages comprised of multifamily long-houses. The Nanticoke and Piscataway are closely related by language. The Nanticoke homelands encompassed eastern Maryland, western Delaware, and a small corner of Virginia; Piscataway homelands are thought to be on and around the Potomac River. Like other tribes of the east, the historic Nanticoke and Piscataway experienced necessary migrations away from the encroaching white settlements. When last holdouts in Maryland were threatened, they removed to Pennsylvania, usually living among other refugee Native groups, especially the Delaware. Later many Nanticoke and Piscataway moved up to New York to live with the Iroquois, but a faction went west with the Delaware to Ohio where they were known to have resided in the multi-tribal villages at The Glaize in 1792. In 1805, the Nanticoke relocated to the White River in Indiana, and by 1818, they had removed to west of the Mississippi, where they resided in Kansas for a period before ending up in Oklahoma. Some Piscataway descendants live among the Six Nations; those who either stayed in Maryland or found their way back became a part of a new Piscataway culture built upon relationships to the local African-American community. Today, there are three state-recognized Piscataway communities in Maryland, and many descendants have both Native American and African-American heritage.

Ojibwa (Mississauga-Ojibwa)

Basics: Algonquian-speaking hunters and gatherers who gardened. They lived between permanent villages and seasonal camps comprised of dome and cigar-shaped wigwams, and conical and double-conical wigwams. Southern Ojibwa homelands were most likely the northern shores of Lake Huron west to Lake Superior (including the most northern reaches of Michigan). Those Ojibwa that came to reside in Ohio did so in the northeastern section of the state, including in the multi-tribal villages located in present day Cleveland. Today, many Ojibwa still reside in the Great Lakes region, with larger populations in Michigan, Wisconsin, Minnesota, and Canada.

Ottawa or Odawa

Basics: Algonquian-speaking fishers who hunted, gathered, and cultivated crops. They lived in permanent villages comprised of longhouses, and utilized conical wigwams on hunting and fishing trips. At the time of European contact, the Ottawa were located on Manitoulin Island and the adjacent Bruce Peninsula (lands and shores just northeast of Lower Michigan on the other side of Lake Huron). They moved around and expanded their areas into more Canadian country, Ohio, Michigan, Illinois, Wisconsin, and small sections of Indiana's borders during the historic period. Within Ohio, they established residency in the northern part of the state on the Cuyahoga River at present day Cleveland from about 1740 until 1760, and in the northwestern part of the state along the Maumee River after 1760. They resided in Ohio up to the 1830's. Today, larger Ottawa populations reside in Ontario, Michigan, and Oklahoma.

Shawnee

Basics: Algonquian-speaking horticultural people who hunted and gathered, and lived in permanent summer villages and structures (large bark houses: multifamily homes), and

15

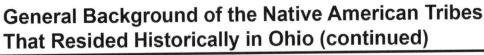

semi-permanent winter camps (dome wigwams: nuclear family homes).* The Shawnee homelands are usually thought to be southern Ohio and parts of West Virginia and Kentucky, and possibly associated to or directly descended from the Fort Ancient complex. First European contact was made with the Shawnee in the states of Ohio, Illinois, and Maryland. Shawnee villages were built in southwestern Ohio before 1670. Major Shawnee occupation was established on the Scioto and Muskingum Rivers before 1778, and due to threat of war by neighboring white settlements, they relocated to the Great Miami River. Shawnee villages were also established along the Mad and Little Miami Rivers. These villages attracted a few distant Cherokee tribesmen from the south who came to reside with the larger Shawnee population (see "Native Visitors to Ohio"); after Benjamin Logan's expedition, many Shawnee relocated to the Tennessee River on the Alabama-Georgia border to live with the Chicamaugua Cherokee. They were also known to reside with the Creeks while staying in these southeastern villages (Tecumseh and The Prophet's mother was reportedly Creek). The Shawnee are known for their extensive movements during the historic period (pre-Indian Removal Act), with a history of inhabiting many states east of the Mississippi including Ohio, Pennsylvania, Indiana, Illinois, Maryland, Kentucky, Tennessee, Georgia and Alabama, and some even crossed the Mississippi in 1784 to Spanish Louisiana. By 1788, many Shawnee established villages across the border in Indiana, however, a couple Shawnee villages were established within the same time period at The Glaize - an area known to house residents of several different tribal backgrounds within the larger Miami, Shawnee, and Delaware villages. The Shawnee Prophet made Greenville in Ohio his base of opposition from 1802 to 1807. After, with the urging of a Potawatomi leader, he and his brother Tecumseh moved their village to the Tippecanoe River in Indiana. After the credibility of The Prophet was destroyed at the Battle of Tippecanoe in 1811, Tecumseh's Shawnee followers followed him to Ontario but later ended up in Kansas. Their complicated dispersal ultimately split them once again, this time into three independent tribes: the Absentee Shawnee, named such as they were not residents of the Shawnee reservation in Kansas at the time it was formed; the Cherokee Shawnee, who are descended from part of the tribe that had remained in Ohio, and then, being forced west, joined the Cherokee Nation in their territory and settled under the name Cherokee Shawnee; and the Eastern Shawnee, who residing with a Seneca community in Oklahoma by 1831 (formally known as Mixed Band of Shawnee), had separated from the Seneca in 1867 and took the new title Eastern Shawnee. A few communities identifying as Shawnee still reside in the state of Ohio, including the United Remnant Band of the Shawnee Nation and the Piqua Sept of Ohio Shawnee.

Wyandot (Refugee Huron & Tionontati/Petún)

Basics: Iroquoian-speaking extensive horticulturalists who hunted and gathered (especially fishing). They lived in permanent year-round villages comprised of multifamily longhouses. This most likely gave way to smaller homes (wigwams) while fleeing war during historic times. The term Wyandot, for historians, is not just another word for the Huron tribe as popularly believed. It is a Huron word ("Wendat") that is applied by historians to a faction of Hurons and refugee Iroquoian peoples (including the Tionontati or Petún and possibly some Erie) who went to Detroit in 1701, and their community thereafter. While the French referred to the tribe as "Huron," this refugee faction was known to the British as the "Wyandot." The Wyandot traveled from their homelands to the southwestern Great Lakes region while fleeing the Iroquois Five Nations (Haudenosaunee) during the "Iroquois Wars" (1641-1701). By 1652, the Tionontati (before joining up as Wyandot) had established a village near Toledo. As part of the Wyandot, they established residency in present day Cleveland by the 1740's, an area known for its multitribal population. The Wyandot established numerous villages in the north portion of the state and along the Muskingum River. They were, however, increasingly becoming more restricted to northwestern Ohio as white settlement encroached further west from Pennsylvania and north from Kentucky. Land transactions, like the Greenville Treaty of 1795, gave away southern sections of Ohio, and by 1817, the last large track of land, the northwestern section of the state, was ceded to the United States. However, some Wyandot remained in on small "reserves" in Ohio up until 1840, at which point they were removed. The Wyandot, like their Miami neighbors in Indiana, were extremely reluctant to leave. The US government failed to secure the Wyandot's Grand Reserve at Upper Sandusky with a bribe of alcohol in 1838. It wasn't until 4 years later the US acquired the reserve and the Wyandot were removed to Kansas. Wyandot descendants are found today largely in Kansas, Oklahoma, Michigan, and Canada.

Native Visitors to Ohio

The previous text highlights the cultures with numerous citizens that called Ohio home. This is not to say that Native people of other tribal backgrounds never stepped foot in the state during these times. In fact we know others did, like the Cherokee. Some Cherokee delegates and warriors came to the state for tribal government business, while very few Cherokee families probably stayed for an extended period in some Ohio Shawnee villages. The Shawnee themselves had many citizens of Creek backgrounds, since they previously stayed with some of their tribe while residing in areas further south. A Mohawk woman living as a Shawnee lived at "The Glaize" in northwestern Ohio, and although many surviving Susquehannock came to reside with the Iroquois in New York, some probably came to live among the Mingo and Delaware in Ohio. Of course others traveling from the direction of New York and Pennsylvania toward Indiana, and vice versa, traveled through the state.

Meaning of Terms in Context

Permanent village and structures - villages and bark-covered homes lasting 10 or more years in one location before a settlement is moved.

Semi-permanent winter camps and wigwams - camps used for 2-3 months and returned to year after year; the structure framework was always permanent (ex. dome wigwam frames are permanently secured in the ground and never moved, but the cattail mat coverings may be removed and taken away, then placed back on when returning next winter).

A Note About Native Camps: All Native people of Ohio, whether they resided in their villages year-round or most of the year, did take "family trips" to fishing and/or hunting and/or maple sugar camps. Their time spent at these locations amounted to anywhere from 4 -7 weeks a year. After spending a few weeks at a camp, they returned home to their village. This is not nomadic, nor living at "temporary" camps. These camps can be thought of in the same way one would think of a vacation home or hunting cabin; the location a family may return to each year for a couple weeks or so - most of their belongings staying at home, not coming on the trip. If we do not think of this as "living on the move," then we should not apply it to the Native people who did the same.

Sources:

Kraft, Herbert C. 2001. The Lenape-Delaware Indian Heritage: 10,000BC – AD2000. Lenape Books.

Sturtevent, William C. and Bruce G. Trigger. 1978. Handbook of the North American Indians. Vol. 15 – Northeast. Smithsonian Institution.

Tanner, Helen Hornbeck. 1987. Atlas of Great Lakes Indian History. Norman: University of Oklahoma Press.

Notes:

_____

_____

_____

_____

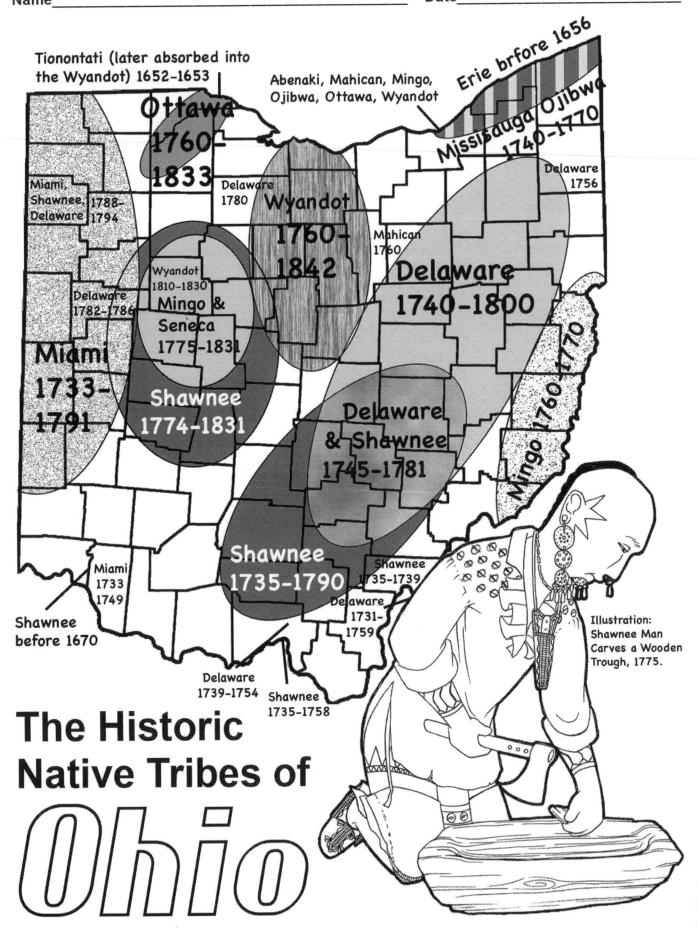

Tionontati (later absorbed into the Wyandot) 1652-1653

Abenaki, Mahican, Mingo, Ojibwa, Ottawa, Wyandot

Erie brfore 1656

Ottawa 1760-1833

Missisauga Ojibwa 1740-1770

Delaware 1780

Delaware 1756

Miami, Shawnee, Delaware 1788-1794

Wyandot 1760-1842

Mahican 1760

Wyandot 1810-1830

Delaware 1740-1800

Mingo & Seneca 1775-1831

Delaware 1782-1786

Shawnee 1774-1831

Miami 1733-1791

Delaware & Shawnee 1745-1781

Mingo 1760-1770

Shawnee 1735-1790

Shawnee 1735-1739

Miami 1733 1749

Delaware 1731-1759

Shawnee before 1670

Illustration: Shawnee Man Carves a Wooden Trough, 1775.

Delaware 1739-1754

Shawnee 1735-1758

The Historic Native Tribes of Ohio

Historic Native Ohio Crossword Puzzle

WORDS POOL

canoe
chert
copper
corn
cradleboard
Delaware
earthenware
Fort Ancient
Gnadenhutten
Hopewell
Miami
Mingo
~~Ohio~~

Ottawa
Serpent Mound
Shawnee
snowshoe
St. Clair's Defeat
wigwam
Wyandot

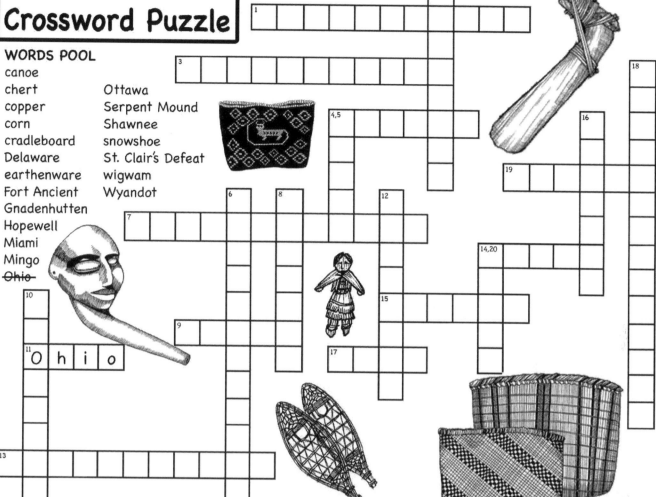

11. **O h i o**

Across

1. A baby carrying device used to transport and keep infants safe and comfortable.
3. A type of Native pottery that food was cooked in.
5. A type of metal that was used by Native people to make some tools and jewelry. Most of this metal came from quarries around Lake Superior.
7. A Christian Indian town built by Native people and Moravians. It was the site of the _____ Massacre.
9. A Native American boat created from bark sheets or a hollowed log.
~~11. A state that takes its name from an Iroquoian word that refers to the large river that flows along its southern border and bares the same name.~~
13. A culture of Native people named after a hilltop fort that was actually built by the Hopewell.
15. A term that refers to a small Native home.
17. The most abundant crop the Native people grew.
19. A tribe closely related to the Ojibwa who once resided in a few villages in northern Ohio.
20. Iroquois-mix group of people who resided in Ohio.

Down

2. Mounds like the Newark Earthworks and Mound City are attributed to this Native American culture.
4. A stone material used to make sharp-edged tools.
6. This Native American earthenwork is thought to resemble a snake with an egg in its mouth, or a comet with a tail trailing behind.
8. Referred to as the "Southerners," these people's homelands are not well known but thought to be possibly in the state of Ohio.
10. The _____ was used to distribute the wearer's weight so that he or she didn't sink while traveling in deep snow.
12. A tribe named after a major river that separates New Jersey and Pennsylvania.
14. This historic tribe claims northwestern Ohio and most of Indiana as their homelands.
16. A group of refugee people of Huron origin who filtered into Ohio.
18. The largest American defeat by Native American forces.

Social Culture

Topics Represented in This Section:

Anthropological Terms & Definitions; Family Relationships; Government; Clan Membership; Cradleboard Usage; Growing Up; Marriage; Gender Roles; Death; Captives; War Armor; Conduct of Councils; Wampum Belts; Sports & Games; Storytelling; Music.

Worksheets: Historic Woodland Indian Culture Crossword Puzzle & Reading

Subjects: Social Studies (American History, Cultural Studies)
Grades 4-8

Students will read about historic Woodland Indian culture and learn anthropological concepts and terms, and complete the related crossword puzzle. Copy and distribute the next four pages to your students and read together. Then distribute the crossword puzzle and have students complete either as classroom work or homework. **Answers for crossword: 1.culture, 2.customs, 3.clan, 4.matrilocal, 5.artifact, 6.spokesperson, 7. patrilineal, 8.patrilocal, 9.reciprocity, 10.war chief, 11.women's council, 12.pan-Indian, 13.matrilineal, 14.extended, 15.village, 16.tribe, 17.village leader, 18.nuclear.**

Take It Further
Activities Relating to the Worksheets

Activity: Become an Anthropologist (relating to the terms *culture, customs, & artifact*)

Have each student look at his or her own family as if they were an anthropologist staying with a host family of another culture. Have students answer specific questions. Some might be:

-How is each person related to each other (parents, step-parents, grandparents, sons, daughters, brothers, sisters, etc.)?

-Does each child have his or her own bedroom, or do they share rooms with siblings?

-What is their usual ritual after school? Do they have sports or club meetings? Is homework or play first?

-Describe the homes their families live in. Is it a house or an apartment? Does it include a small backyard or rooftop garden, or do they live on a farm?

-Does the family have animals? Are they pets or livestock? What kind of animals and why?

-What is the material culture of the families (electronics, furniture, clothing, etc.)?

-What kind of foods do their families cook and/or enjoy most? Is it ethnic (Mexican, Italian, Greek, Polish, Irish, Korean, Southern American, etc.)? Is it local based foods (from their gardens or farms, or from local producers or other countries)? Do their families eat out more or prepare meals in their homes more?

Activity: Study the Components of the Powwow (relating to the term *Pan-Indian*)

Invite a person of the powwow community (dancer, drummer, arena director) to come into your classroom and answer questions regarding powwow culture -or- have groups of students research the subject online and present the research to the class. Questions to explore may include:

-Where does the word powwow come from and what does it actually mean (clue: powwow was a verb and a noun in its original usage)?

-What is a powwow today, and why do so many Native people participate in them?

-Why is there a drum group? How many drum groups participate in a powwow? Drummers also provide the song (they sing)... do these songs have words?

-The big drum groups with multiple beaters is another "pan-Indian" practice... with what tribe(s) or region did this drum style originate?

-What is the difference between an arena director and MC? What is Grand Entry?

-With what tribe is it believed the Jingle Dress Dance originated? What about the Grass Dance and Fancy Dance?

-Most powwows invite other entertainers to perform such as flutists and hoop dancers. Was the Native flute originally played for public gatherings? Where does the Hoop Dance originate from?

-The dancers always go around the dance arena in one direction. What direction is that and why? Is there any exception to this and why?

-Why is the public (non-Native non-participants) invited to dance with the Native dancers sometimes but not at other times?

-What are some rules visitors should follow to be respectful of a powwow and its participants?

Historic Woodland Indian Culture: Inroduction

What is Culture?
When we are studying the Native American people of the past, we are not just learning about American history, we are learning about another culture of people. **Culture** is the shared beliefs, manners, values, and practices of a group of people. You are a part of a culture too. As citizens of the United States, you all share some of the same values and customs. When you and your classmates say the Pledge of Allegiance to our flag, you are showing you respect and share your country's values with other Americans (freedom, equality). The act of pledging with your classmates at the start of a school day is a custom among your culture. **Customs** are the usual practices, behaviors, and activities of a culture. Name another custom you and your classmates might share.

_____

_____

_____

_____

_____

_____

The Things We Make and Use
The clothes you wear, the computers you research your school papers on, the mode of transportation you use to get to school, and the foods you eat are all a part of your material culture. Any object a person makes and/or uses is called an **artifact**. List 5 cultural artifacts that you use daily.

_____

_____

_____

_____

Trading More Than Objects
Whether we trade, gift, sell, or purchase, this exchange of goods or services is referred to as **reciprocity**. All cultures exchange goods. Like it is for us, reciprocity was a big part of historic Woodland Indian life. Many European traders had to learn that Native trade was a personal exchange that made strangers into family. Smart traders who understood the Native cultures they traded with knew to first give gifts when meeting possible "customers." When a trader gave gifts before conducting business, it signified to the Native people that he was looking to forge a relationship with them, and relationships fostered trust. When trading took place, it was expected that all parties were fair, that no one trader was trying to gain bargains at the expense of the other traders.

Like Time, Culture Can't Stand Still
You may be learning about the Native American people who historically lived in your area, however, Native American people still live in your state. It just so happens that they are not dressed in the same clothes as their ancestors, those who you are learning about. This is because culture changes with time.

When the Native people were forced west because of American expansion, many Native tribes and communities with different cultures started living in close quarters. The different cultures began to share their differences, and their differences became less as they adopted each others' cultural traits. This mixing of cultures created something we call a **pan-Indian** culture. One pan-Indian custom is the powwow - a Native American gathering that includes music, dancing, traditional clothing, and beliefs of many different tribal origins being shared by all.

Historic Woodland Indian Culture: Community

The Native Community

A **tribe** is a group of people who are identified as being related to each other. They usually share the same culture and the same language (though there may be different dialects).

What tribes lived near you?

_____

_____

The Tribal Truth

The term "tribes" was applied to the Native American communities by Europeans and later Americans. This meant that many Native people did not actually identify themselves in these "tribes."

Example:

The Delaware (Lenape) may or may not include the Wappinger people. We don't know whether we should identify them as Delaware because they are so similar in culture, or if we should keep them separate since they are a separate community. In all reality, many Delaware communities grouped into this "Delaware tribe" never did identify with each other or have a central government. Each village governed itself, and Delaware villages in New York probably knew little of day-to-day operations of Delaware villages located along the coast of southern New Jersey, who in turn, functioned independently from the Delaware villages of eastern Pennsylvania.

In the late 1700's and early 1800's, as the Delaware migrated west into Ohio and Indiana, the "tribe" was actually identified as 2 separate tribes by Europeans and Americans: the "Delaware" and the "Munsee." Munsee actually refers to the northern Delaware who spoke the Munsee dialect. At least three dialects were found in the Delaware language, which points to some sort of division among these communities. Today the Delaware are identified by their separate communities, although we still use a common "tribal" identity to lump these groups together, whether right or wrong.

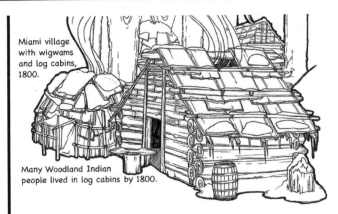

Miami village with wigwams and log cabins, 1800.

Many Woodland Indian people lived in log cabins by 1800.

A **village** is a town, a cluster of human settlement. Woodland Indian villages could be small with about 50-75 people, or large with several hundred. Either way, a village identified together and governed together.

Do you know of any past historic or pre-historic Native American villages near your location? What culture or tribe occupied that village?

_____

_____

_____

Different Villages for Different Communities

The Miami inhabited their villages from spring to fall, especially while they planted, tended to, and harvested their crops. Their village structures were permanent and stayed intact even when the residents were away. A village usually lasted 12 to 15 years before a new village was built in a new location to take advantage of new resources. Like the Miami, Wyandot villages were permanent too, however, the Wyandot stayed in their villages all year round. Their villages consisted of large bark longhouses. Like the Wyandot, the northern Delaware also had year-round villages, but Delaware villages consisted of both longhouses and smaller wigwams.

Historic Woodland Indian Culture: Family

The Family Unit

The **Nuclear Family** defines a basic family unit of parents and children. An example may be a mother, a father, and their son and daughter. Many modern Americans live in nuclear family units - each nuclear family living in one home or apartment.

Many Woodland Indian families did live in single family wigwams, however, they did not always live as nuclear family units. The Native people lived near and relied on their relatives in daily life. They lived in extended family networks. **Extended Family** is a family categorized by several nuclear families related to each other. These could be aunts' and uncles' families, and grandparents. They could all share the same clan name. They lived close together, or sometimes even in the same home - in a longhouse.

Example: Seneca (Iroquois) families were known to live together in large longhouses. Some longhouses were longer than a football field! This size of longhouse may have housed about 125 family members of the same clan (with exception to fathers and husbands of different clans).

Above Illustration: Delaware (Lenape) boys, who are cousins related by their mothers, work together to collect maple sap at the maple sugar camp, 1750.

The Family or Clan Name

A **Clan** is a group of family members that share the same ancestry or lineage. So how does a person inherit their clan or family name? This depends on the tribe.

Which Side of The Family?

Matrilineal Descent: When a person belongs to the same descent group as his or her mother. Clan membership comes from their mother's side of the family. Titles and property may also be passed through the family along female lines.

Ex. The Delaware (Lenape) are matrilineal. When a child is born to a mother of the Turtle clan and a father of the Turkey clan, the child will be of the Turtle clan, like his or her mother.

And so **Patrilineal Descent** must be:

_____

_____

_____

_____

_____

Whether a society was matrilineal or patrilineal depended on the tribe.

Living With Extended Family

Patrilocal Residency: When a married couple lives in or near the husband's parent's home.

So **Matrilocal Residency** must mean:

_____

_____

_____

_____

Historic Woodland Indian Culture: Government

Native Roots of Democracy

Benjamin Franklin, Thomas Jefferson, and others who helped to form our government were influenced by Native American societies. While their classical training (school) taught them of historic Greek society's ideals of democracy, it was the present and working democracies of people like the Iroquois that really showed patriots that democracy was possible. Benjamin Franklin essentially said at one time, if the Indian people can do it, why can't we. Thomas Jefferson was also quoted in his admiration of Native American democracies. Even Iroquois delegates sent to the colonies to make treaties suggested that they (the colonists) ought to learn from them (the Iroquois) and the way they govern. Equal representation in government was always a part of most Native American governments.

Who's In Charge?

This was a common question that early explorers posed to Native communities. It was Europeans' way of thinking that many times gave us the wrong impression of Native leaders. Native leaders or chiefs (a term of French origin) usually never ruled like a European king. They had no real authority (power) to order or command. As an early observer once noted, Delaware leaders did only what the citizens wanted. This is quite true of Woodland village leaders, who many times acted more as spokespeople in international affairs, as teachers who offered their advice to those who needed it, and judges to decide the outcome of disputes. **Village leader,** or peace time leader, was usually a job passed down family lines (through matrilineal descent for the Delaware), however, a village leader could never be such if the people did not approve of him. Lineage was not enough to be a leader. A leader had to be well-liked - the popular candidate among his community.

Women Leaders

Although most chiefs were men, many women leaders were noted early on during first European contacts. In the 1700's a female chief was recorded among the Ottawa. Some women leaders even provided warriors for battles, such as the two famous female 'sachems' of southern New England, and a legendary Ojibwa female war chief.

Dual Leadership

While village leaders were usually consulted in all large matters, another type of leader was ready to defend the community in the threat of danger. These leaders, known as **war chiefs**, helped to take care of affairs in war and lead parties of warriors into battle. War chiefs came into leadership not by hereditary, but by popularity. A war chief gained the respect of his community by leading warriors on raids and into battles, and returning with all of his men unharmed. It was better to return having lost the battle with all of your warriors than return victorious with even just one warrior lost. A war chief originally had limited authority to represent his community, which was done only in wartime. This changed during interactions with the Europeans, who made no distinction between war chiefs and village leaders.

Equal Representation

Native American citizens were allowed to voice their opinions and have councils that represented their position in governmental affairs. This included women. **Women's councils** were present in many Native communities so that women had their views and votes represented during times of decision making. Most councils had a **spokesperson** to voice their position on the matter at hand. A spokesperson had to be an eloquent speaker who would only state what the council wanted him to, even if he disagreed with them.

Historic Woodland Indian Culture
Crossword Puzzle

Word Pool:
artifact
clan
~~culture~~
customs
extended
matrilineal
matrilocal
nuclear
pan-Indian

patrilineal
partrilocal
reciprocity
spokesperson
tribe
village
village leader
war chief
women's council

Down

1. A set of shared beliefs, customs, and values of a group of people or society.
3. A group of family members who share the same ancestry and family name.
5. Any object a person makes and/or uses.
7. When people inherent their clan names from their fathers, they are inheriting their clan membership through _____ descent.
9. The act of giving, trading, and receiving goods and services from others in your community.
11. A group of people who represent the women of a community, and their positions and votes.
13. When people inherent their clan names from their mothers, they are inheriting their clan membership through _____ descent.
15. People and their homes clustered together in one location; a community or settlement.
17. A respected person whose leadership and guidance is called upon during peace times.
18. A mother, father and children are a _____ family unit.

Across

2. Usual practices, behaviors, and activities of a culture.
4. When a husband moves into or near his wife's family's home, this is _____ residence.
6. A _____ speaks on a group's behalf.
8. When a wife moves into or near her husband's family's home, this is _____ residence.
10. A person who gives guidance during times of outside threat, and leads warriors on raids against enemies.
12. _____ culture is created from the beliefs, values, and material culture of several tribes, forming a singular 'Indian' culture and identity.
14. Groups of nuclear families that are related is an _____ family unit.
16. A label applied to separate and categorize Native American cultures and/or societies.

Name _____   Date _____

Native American Analogies
Directions: Circle the word that best completes the statement.

Example:
Wampum is to quahogs (clams) as quillwork is to _____.
a. beavers   b. porcupines   c. feathers

---

1. Mussels are to river as deer are to _____.
a. earth   b. lake   c. forest

2. Canoe is to water as sled (toboggan) is to _____.
a. hill   b. snow   c. sand

3. Bow is to hunting as hoe is to _____.
a. gardening   b. gathering   c. trapping

4. Knife is to sheath as arrow is to _____.
a. arrowhead   b. quiver   c. bow

5. Moccasins are to feet as leggings are to _____.
a. arms   b. wrists   c. legs

6. Chert is to flintknapping as hides are to _____.
a. painting   b. weaving   c. hide-tanning

7. Pumpkin is to vine as corn is to _____.
a. stalk   b. root   c. corn husk

8. Corn is to hominy as deer is to _____.
a. corn bread   b. antlers   c. venison

9. Mats are to cattails as bark sheets are to _____.
a. leaves   b. trees   c. wigwams

10. Longhouse is to extended family as wigwam is to _____.
a. clan family   b. nuclear family   c. grandparents

11. Miami is to patrilineal as Delaware is to _____.
a. patrilocal   b. matrilocal   c. matrilineal

12. Wyandot is to the Iroquoian language family as Shawnee is to the _____.
a. Algonquian language family   b. Siouan language family c. Munsee dialect

Three Woodland Indian longbows
and a close-up of a bow notch.

The Delaware Clan System:
A Branch of the Turtle Family Tree

For most Native Americans, clan membership was passed down on only one side of the family. You were either the same clan as your father, or the same clan as your mother. When the clan name is passed through the men of your family, you are inheriting it through *patrilineal* descent. When the clan name is passed through the women of your family, you are inheriting it through *matrilineal* descent.

The Delaware trace their clan lineage through matrilineal descent. The diagram to the right shows three generations of Turtle Clan members (shown in black). Use this diagram to answer the following questions.

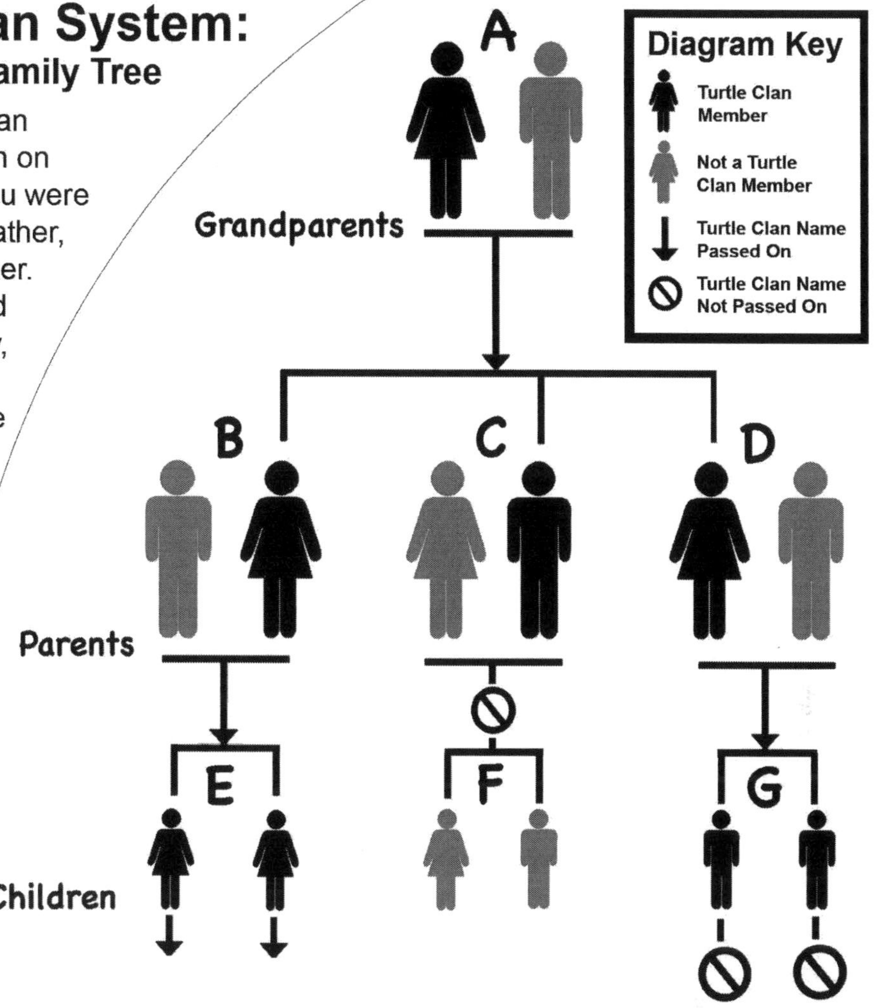

Diagram Key

- Turtle Clan Member
- Not a Turtle Clan Member
- Turtle Clan Name Passed On
- Turtle Clan Name Not Passed On

Grandparents — A

Parents — B   C   D

Children — E   F   G

Questions

1. Grandma (A) belongs to the Turtle Clan. Why are her grandchildren in bracket F not the same clan as her?

_____

_____

2. The children in bracket E and G belong to the turtle clan. Why can E pass along their clan name to their future children but G can not?

_____

_____

3. The boys in bracket G will need to be taught male skills as they get older so they may become productive citizens. Both boys will be taught these skills not just from their father (D) but also by their uncle (C). Why do you suppose their uncle teaches them just as much as their father?

_____

_____

_____

Name _____ Date _____

The Native American Family

A New Baby

Everybody was happy when a baby was born. The father carved the cradleboard out of wood for his new baby to be carried and kept safe in. The mother decorated the cradleboard so her new baby would look special. Grandparents, aunts, and uncles provided the new baby and proud parents with presents. **Does this sound like something we do today? What do we do?**

_____

_____

_____

_____

Baby in a cradleboard.

Family Relationships

Aunts and uncles acted like parents. They helped to teach and guide their nieces and nephews as if they were their own children. Cousins had the same close relationship as brothers and sisters. Brothers and sisters were suppose to have a very strong bond.

Children play house.

How Did Children Learn?

Children learned by doing. They helped the older children and adults at their work. Parents even made little play tools for their children. **Did you ever play with a toy that was made to imitate an adult tool or item? If so, what was it?**

_____

_____

_____

_____

The Cradleboard: Feeling Safe & Being Safe

Board

Bow

Ear Joint

Charms & Toys

Wrappings

Strap

Foot-board or Cradle

The cradleboard provided a tight, cozy niche for infants, which may have helped to curb crying fits. Babies cry at times because they feel vulnerable and want to be held and soothed. The cradleboard provided the same sensation as being held by a person for for ten or more hours a day.

The cradleboard was a safe environment from which a baby could observe his or her world. Cradleboards allowed even the smallest infants to view family members from an upright position, instead of just staring up while laying down most of the time. This allowed the infant more chances to interact with others, as well as begin to learn by watching others for extended amounts of time. The cradleboard was portable, and a mother could even wear it on her back suspended by a strap from her head or shoulders. It featured a removable bow that protected the child's head. In a way, the cradleboard was like a car-seat because it protected the baby inside by acting like a shell that never separated from the child in the event of an accident.

Ojibwa woman, child, and baby in in cradleboard, 1830.

Cut & Fold Cradleboard Page 1 of 2

Directions: To make this paper model cradleboard, color the wooden components below and cut these 3 pieces out. Take the cradle hoop and bend it into a U shape, then bend back the tabs to the inside of the U, and attach the tabs to their corresponding letters on the board with tape (the shape following the big U outline on the board). Next, take the head bow and fold it in the two spots that have dotted lines. Then fold tabs back and attach to board where the corresponding letters are.

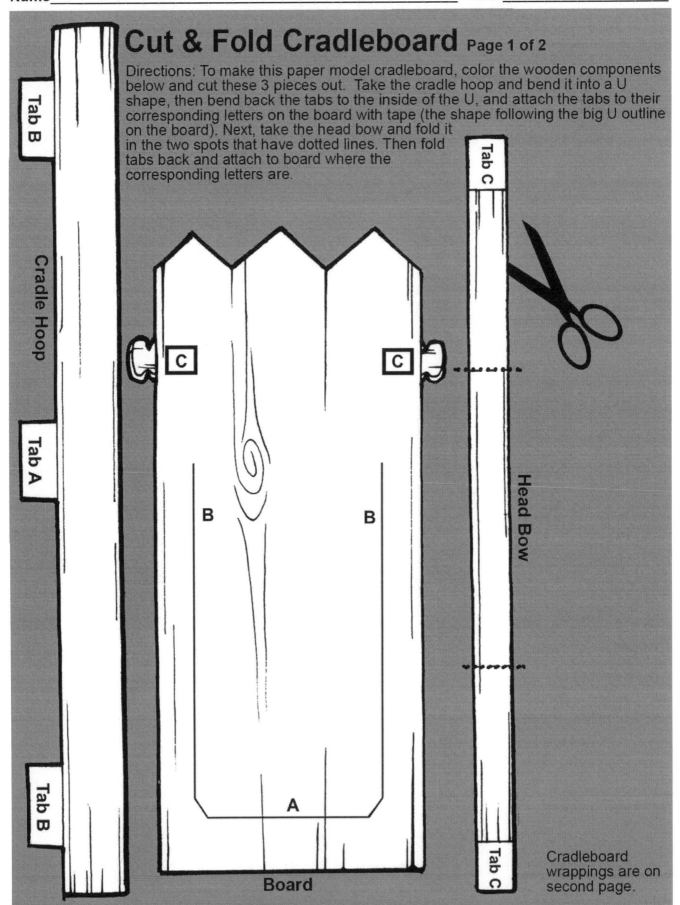

Tab B

Cradle Hoop

Tab A

Tab B

Tab C

Head Bow

Tab C

C

C

B   B

A

Board

Cradleboard wrappings are on second page.

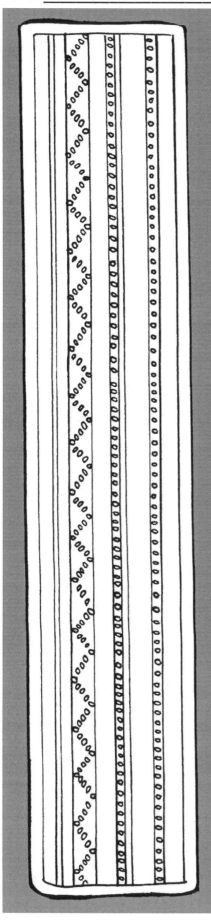
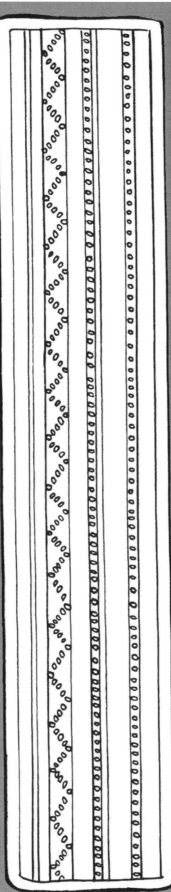

Cut & Fold
Cradleboard Page 2 of 2

Directions continued: Color the 2 cradleboard covers in bold colors, then cut them out. Attach by wrapping around the cradle under the bow (1 higher, 1 lower). These wrappings are what kept the baby inside the cradle.

Cradleboard Covers or Wrappings

A boy hands his cousin back her doll.

Growing Up & Getting Married

Young boys and girls enjoyed playtime with toys and objects they used as toys. Both were given similar tasks and small jobs by their mothers. As they grew older, they were given harder jobs, and they began to imitate their adult relatives. It would not have been unusual for a little girl to be given a small ax so she could help break up firewood with her mother. Boys were given toy bows and arrows when they were old enough. Most boys first practiced shooting their bows under the direction of their mothers in the gardens, where their job was to shoot at and scare away thieving animals.

Around the time of puberty, boys and most girls were to participate in a vision quest. This included separating themselves for many days, taking little food and water, (fasting), praying, and waiting for a "vision." A vision was considered to be spiritual communication to the supernatural world - it created a personal bond between the person and spirits that guided the environment. Girls and boys usually sought their visions in different ways; even tribes that did not have a female vision quest (in the way we define it) still sought visions during their first menses seclusion, which was in a manner their vision quest.

Young men and women were guided through their vision quests by an older family member or spiritual leader. They helped them connect to the spirit world, sought to their health while they were fasting, and gave advice as to how to be a good citizen and a future spouse.

When old enough, they were eligible to get married. Marriageable partners were sometimes suggested by mothers and fathers, but they usually did not press an unwanted marriage upon their children. Sometimes the young men and women picked their own partners, and if accepted by both families, the couple courted for a while before officially getting married. Much gift-giving back and forth from the bride's and groom's families solidified the marriage. This didn't mean they "bought" their bride or groom - both were free to divorce if unhappy in an undesirable marriage.

Although there was much gift-giving, the actual marriage ceremony wasn't very formal. Usually it included the couple eating from the same bowl, or as in the case of some, publicly sitting next to each other announced their formal union.

This groom courted his sweetheart by playing the flute for her. Flute music was said to sing to a woman's heart.

Native American Gender Sociology 101

A "Crash Course" For Teachers & History Enthusiasts In the Basics of Native American Gender Dynamics

Mutual Goals

Gender relations is another subject usually shrouded in a cloak of misinformation. So many think of genders as opposites, which is far from true. Native American gender realms were not opposite (oppose each other), they were complimentary (worked together). Gender realms such as male and female should be thought of as offense and defense playing on the same team to score goals -- not on separate teams looking to win at the expense of the other. The word opposite insinuates the latter, which is destructive thinking when applied to Native American lifeways. Men and women did not battle it out, like a war of good versus evil. Native American gender roles were supportive of each other, and genders respected each other's roles. Without all gender roles fulfilled, not only would the physical, earthly work not be accomplished, but for many Native societies, it may not satisfy the supernatural world that demanded balance (a reason many had special social places for "two-spirited" persons – a "two-spirited" person was a person who identified with the other gender (ie woman identifying as male or man who identified as female) or identified with a gender in between the spectrum of masculine and feminine).

Dividing the Work

Many assume the work assigned to men and women was based mostly on physical strength. Indeed, usually men biologically have more strength, however, gendered work was less based on strength as most tend to believe. The two more predominant reasons for assigning certain tasks to men or to women had to do with reproduction.

First, women tended to have jobs that allowed them to have their young children nearby. This meant tasks that tended to be closer to home (unless the family as a whole traveled), and such tasks could be completed while taking care of young children. Why? Well not because men weren't able to take care of their own children or because men are "inherently" not nurturers - men of some cultures are routinely expected to be caretaker to their children in the absence of their mothers (both in developed countries and tribal cultures). We know today that men are as "in-touch" with the needs of their children as mothers are, that is if given the chance to be a primary nurturer (ie "mother's instinct" is also found among fathers and male caregivers). There is only one biological truth that places women as more necessary to be in close quarters with their young children, and that is because of nursing. Only women have the biological capability to nurse their children (or the children of others), and in many cultures (including Native cultures) children are nursed not for months, but for years (these children are weaned completely around the age of two or three). In societies where formula didn't substitute breast milk well (arguably it never has), young children relied upon their lactating mothers (or wet nurses) for the nutrition they needed. Women had to be able to contribute to their family and society in tasks that were suited for children to be near. The cries of children would scare the game from a hunter, but the cries of children didn't inhibit farming tasks. Also, children are a precious resource of any society, and keeping children safe to ensure they grow to adulthood was also factored into the tasks that were assigned women. For example, warfare and hunting dangerous game were far too risky for young children to be near, so women's tasks tended to be those that posed less threat to life. And this concept of avoiding dangerous jobs is related to the second reason for assigning certain tasks or not assigning certain tasks to women, and it has to do with women's potential children.

The second reason for assigning certain tasks to men and certain tasks to women was based on reproductive value. Women's reproductive capabilities are considered more valuable then men's. Why? Well women who average one child per pregnancy, each lasting nine months, makes her reproduction frequency rather limited when compared to men. Extended nursing common in Native cultures further delays the frequency of pregnancy (many Native cultures didn't believe in pregnancy until the lastborn was weaned, which could be two to three years after the last birth). To illustrate this point, if a group of 30 men went to war and 20 were killed, that would be a tragic event, however, the village's ability to produce new generations wouldn't be very stunted. If though those 30 warriors were women, and 20 had died in the same manner, the continuance of the community may be impeded for the next several years. It is interesting to note that many of these Native societies felt a woman's life was worth twice that of a man's, and that in the event of a murder, a female victim demanded more compensation than that of a male victim. The reasoning seems to be in the fact that women bore children, and if a woman was murdered, so were all her potential children (this was even more of a stronger belief in matrilineal societies as only women passed the clan name, and so women were important to the survival of the clan).

In Equal Standing

Likewise, genders were thought of as equal in many Native worldviews. A foreign concept to us, we insist that genders (like any practice of "categorizing") must be placed in the same line, in some sort of order or hierarchy -- one better than the other. For example: the way we insist "equal" must be the "same," such as men and women must do the "same" job to be equal. Our modern movements for sex equality is fought by opening up jobs traditionally dominated by men to women, yet part of the fight, less popularly known, must address assigning due respect to traditional women's work to begin with. This is because we feel we cannot give equal status (respect) to two different jobs; one "must be better than the other" according to our cultural beliefs. We have no concept of judging two different activities on one scale like many historic Native American cultures did (some still do), and so we tend to project our judging methods on Native American concepts of gender roles, believing "they" must think the same way "we" do.

"Gendered" Work

It is true, as with all Native activities, there were gender roles, but gender roles are not black and white. Gendered activities are usually more misleading in their categorization of being "gendered." In most informational outlets (books, museums, films), Native American warfare is exclusively assigned to the male gender. While fighting was usually physically executed by men, the realm of warfare was incomplete without the female presence, whether it be spiritual, authoritative, supportive, and/or celebratory (not to mention the rights of women to participate with the war party based on spiritual, cross-gendered, or reasons to personally deliver justice). It would be wrong to think of warfare as simply male, as if to insinuate elements of Native societies as simple, able to be summed up in one word - male, female. Likewise, the act of hunting may have been a skill usually assigned to the male gender role, however, the female role of providing hunters their provisions, setting up traps near the village, and female ownership of the spoils of the hunting cannot be overlooked (nor can the role of "independent women" or "hunting women" be discounted). In another example, horticultural activities may be aligned with female prerogatives, but in all truth it was male work that cleared the fields and created female garden tools, and in some societies, men were called upon to help harvest and break soil along side of their female kin. He too celebrated the harvest and prayed for the cooperation of the weather, and for the safety of his family in the fields. Male participation cannot be devalued in lieu of the fact that we as modern Americans have categorized historic Native gardening as being in the female realm. Absolutely no gendered activity was exclusively the realm of one particular gender. In fact, because Native work was not highly segregated on the basis of gender (as commonly mistaken), the Moravian missionaries had a hard time attracting many Delaware converts because they (the Moravians) practiced a very gender segregated daily lifestyle that was foreign to Delaware culture.

Crossing Genders

Native American gender roles were not as exclusive as many history outlets and textbooks might lead you to believe. While the majority of men performed male-gendered work, and women performed female-gendered work, there were, in many tribes, men who performed female-gendered work and women who performed male-gendered work. Among the Miami, Ojibwa, Winnebago, Potawatomi, and Iroquois, some men were recorded as preferring women's work and living their lives as feminine men. Likewise, some women among the Ojibwa and Illinois (related to Miami) were recorded as taking up the pursuits of men full-time. These women who joined the hunt were referred to as "hunting women" in the Illinois, and such "independent women" among the Ojibwas tended to do both the jobs of men and women to care for their households. The role of civil chief was sometimes fulfilled by women (such as one late 18th to early 19th century Ottawa woman chief). It should also be noted that women in some Native societies (including Miami, Ojibwa, Winnebago) had the mobility in their gender to participate in war (whether as warriors, spiritual leaders, or even war captains), without giving up their female status. More examples of women warriors and leaders exist east of Indiana and Ohio from the 17th and 18th centuries. It is obvious that with more time for European influences to take hold, a sharp decline in women leaders follows.

Matrilocal and Patrilocal Residence

Matrilocal residence is when a husband moves into his wife's family's home, or near her family's location (ex. her clan's longhouse, or her hometown village). Patrililocal residence is when a wife moves into her husband's family home, or near his family's local. Many Indian societies stuck to practicing one or the other as custom. Some Native cultures were known to have practiced a "honeymoon period" matrilocal residence that could last a few years before the couple moved to the groom's family's home or village. And still others never committed to a sanctioned social pattern of residency. For these folks, living among the bride's or groom's family was just a matter of personal preference for the couple and their relatives. And please note: just because a society practices matrilocal residence does not mean they are automatically matrilineal (same with with patrilocal and patrilineal). These practices are not codependent, although many do go hand-in-hand.

Matrilineal is Not the Same as Matriarchal

It is a common misconception that Native American societies whose clan membership through the women's lines are matriarchal. This does not mean they are matriarchal, however, this does mean that this society is matrilineal. Matrilineal descent is when clan membership, property, and/or hereditary titles are passed in the family from mother to child. As one might guess, when clan membership, property, and/or hereditary titles are passed from father to child, this is called patrilineal descent (also does not mean patriarchy). Both matrilineal and patrilineal practices may be found in one Native community, for example, while clan membership may be passed from father to child (patrilineal), the title/position of village leader may be passed through the women's lines (nephew becomes elected because his mother's brother or father was the previous statesman) such as was practiced in the Winnebago culture.

The Myth of Matriarchal Tribes

A common myth is that the Native American tribes of our region were "matriarchal." While many, like the Iroquois (and Mingo), Wyandot, Delaware, Mahican and such were quite egalitarian, they were not matriarchal. Why? Well, there are three markers a society must comply with to be categorized as such. We will use the Iroquois for example (as they are most likely to be categorized as a matriarchy than any other nation): The first marker is the society's ability to give women positions in the highest of formal authority roles. The Iroquois pass this as only women are eligible for the position of Clan Mother (which has more power than the position of Chief), and they can stand in the role of Chief when necessary (their constitution allows such). The second marker is is the wanting of daughters over sons. Their is limited evidence that speaks to the Iroquois of wanting female babies to carry on the name of the clan, and one such account that points to the families being even more delighted when a daughter is born than a son. The third marker is the society's oppression of the "other" sex and gender (in patriarchal societies, it is the oppression of biological women and the female gender). This is where the Iroquois fall short as they never penalized biological men or those who identified as male for their sex or gender. In fact, men and those who identified as male were celebrated as much as women and those who identified as female in the Iroquois culture. With these factors in mind, the Iroquois were not a matriarchy but were instead a more egalitarian society. Their neighbors and all the tribes within our region were, as well, not matriarchal, but instead, more egalitarian in their social practices.

Social Status Based on Relation
A woman in a male-dominated society was usually judged more or less important based on her relation to respected and powerful men. A large part of our society seems to inherently assume other cultures do the same. We have partly misunderstood the real workings of matrilineal relationships in Native societies because many have not explored these networks on their own terms. The truth is a man who receives his title through female lines would be without influence had it not been for his mother's lineage (not his father's). A man's inherent status, in a matrilineal society, was based on his relationship to the women of his family.

Unlike Europeans of the time, many Native societies of the northeast did not practice inheriting titles or status through marriage. An Iroquois matron's husband had no special place based on her position – he was of a different clan, and his ability to gain a title was solely based on his mother's family. While these spouses were undoubtedly respected, and indeed may have helped their partners entertain diplomats and help see to their community's needs too, they never became leaders with power just because they married a leader as was practiced by Europeans.

Marriage and The Strongest of Bonds
Many of us think of our spouses as our "better half," and our marriages the strongest bonds we will ever make with another person. We expect a spouse newly widowed to be the most pained member of the grieving family. We feel our bond to be "natural" and therefore universal, but in truth, relationships and even aspects of love are culturally influenced. Not all peoples think or "feel" the way we do in the same situations. Marriage among the Native people was, many times, not considered the strongest relationship two people could have. As one Fox (Meskwaki) widow recalled, she was very sad after the death of her husband, and publicly morning her loss was no problem, as she was seriously distraught. However, she mourned too much. She couldn't help her feelings. She mourned so much she had to hide it because people began to talk. They said she was disgraceful morning so much, too much mourning as if she had lost a brother. Indeed, in her culture, the loss of a sibling was considered to be the loss of a closer bond than a spouse. Sisters and brothers were of the same clan, and their relationship was considered to be emotionally stronger than that of a wife and husband.

Fathers, Father Figures, and Matrilineal Societies
A boy learning to use a bow and arrow may drum up an image of a father patiently teaching his son learning to hunt. There is nothing wrong with this image as fathers were teachers to their children, and especially important in a young man's upbringing. Men taught boys how to become good husbands and fathers, providers and protectors, and admirable, well-minded persons who respected both natural and supernatural beings. The only miss here is that it was not just fathers who played the fatherly role in matrilineal societies. When clan membership passed down from mother to child, a father and son were not of the same clan, however, a boy and his maternal uncle(s) were both of the same clan. For many, this meant that uncles and nephews (mother's brothers) of the same clan were considered "closer" than fathers and sons of different clans. It

Native American Gender Sociology 101 (continued)

was not unusual for uncles to teach their nephews life skills just as much as the boys' fathers. This also meant that a man had duties to not only raise his children, but also help raise his sister's children (such as was found in Iroquois, Wyandot, Delaware, and other cultures). This practice helped to reinforce clan relationships, and established stability for children (ex. divorces were not as devastating, and children were still well provided for in the case of a parent's death, which was certainly not the case of many Euro-American widows who needed to remarry just to feed their children). Native societies relied more on extended family than many Europeans and white Americans who lived a "pioneering" lifestyle. This offered more security for children, so that in the case of parents' deaths, they would not become orphaned, which was definitely a threat for many white children of the times.

Notes:

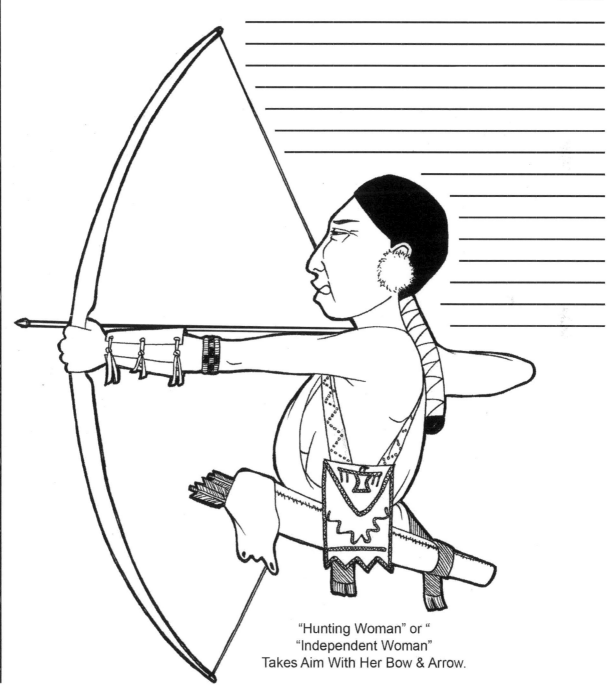

"Hunting Woman" or "
"Independent Woman"
Takes Aim With Her Bow & Arrow.

Student Article: Grades 8-12

Native American Fathers of the Northeastern Woodlands

A man proved his worth and maturity in many ways: by accomplishing a vision quest, going to battle and bringing home captives to his mourning relatives, carrying out hunting activities for days at a time to bring meat home to his female kin, and then getting married and securing a residence for his bride (or melding well into his mother-in-law's home). While these accomplishments certainly added to his good character and proved him as a productive citizen, it was the act of raising children that turned "just a man" into a father whose voice would be taken seriously in communal affairs. Not unlike the women of his community, becoming a parent was becoming a "real" adult - the most important right-of-passage for a Native American man.

The coming of his child was a reason to rejoice. The Delaware husband sought to his pregnant wife's needs, including her cravings. "Squirrels, ducks, and other like delicacies, when most difficult to be obtained, are what women in their first stage of pregnancy generally longed for. I have known a man to go forty or fifty miles for a mess of cranberries to satisfy his wife's longing (Heckewelder, 1876:159)." More than satisfying his wife's wishes, he took such painstaking care to also satisfy the needs of his growing unborn child.

Like his pregnant wife, he too had to follow certain taboos to ensure the baby would be born healthy and the mother's life kept safe in the delivery. Not only did he watch his actions to not negatively affect his unborn child, in some societies it was believed the fetus could actually affect fathers-to-be. A Delaware man may feel the child's playful spirit was inhibiting his hunting activities by scaring the animals away. He might make a toy bow and arrow to wear on his person for the amusement of the child's spirit. If his luck in hunting did not change, he might then suspect the unborn child to be a girl

and suspend a miniature mortar and pestle from his clothes.

Daughters were, contrary to popular (Western) belief, just as much reason for a father to celebrate as having a son. In many Northeastern societies, the birth of a girl child signaled a continuance of the family, and for a matrilineal people (Iroquois, Huron, Delaware, Mahican, etc.), girls ensured the clan and family lineage would continue. "They rejoice more in the birth of a daughter than a son (Axtell 1981:8)." Only in the northern regions of the Northeastern cultural area did the birth of sons seem favored.

Even if a Native father had all daughters and no sons, he did not miss out on instructing boys in how to become good men. A man was still compelled to teach other adolescent boys (from his clan and community) the skill sets of the male gender. Especially if he was in a matrilineal community, he would have obligations to help raise the children of his sister(s). He shared the same clan name as his nieces and nephews, making the position of "maternal uncle" more of a second father to his nephews. A Winnebago man, while a part of a patrilineal clan system still had special obligations and a close relationship to his sister's children (possibly because of a recent matrilineal system replaced by patrilineal during the fur trade). He was called upon to discipline his nieces and nephews, he teased with his nieces and nephews, and he was obliged to take his nephew on his first battle. A man could also teach one or more of his daughters some male duties such as hunting and trapping while on hunting expeditions, as some Ojibwa fathers of the western Great Lakes did. Gender roles were not as strict as many today believe, and these girls who preformed men's work could continue to do so in adulthood or switch to female work -- it was just that easy and acceptable (in most Woodland Indian societies). And for the man who had a son, he had

Native American Fathers of the Northeastern Woodlands (continued)

much reason to look forward to time spent instructing him and creating the kind of bond he and his father (and uncles) had before. This was his chance to pass on the values every Native man should follow and exemplify.

In anticipation of the birth of his child, the Micmac father took it upon himself to create the cradleboard. Woodworking was a male pursuit in all Northeastern Indian societies, and the father took great care in carving and assembling the wooden components that created the cradle frame his child would be laid upon and secured to. Later he would carve the bowls and spoons his child would eat from and create miniatures of adult tools for his child to play with. The Delaware father would also carve wooden dolls for his daughter to dress, decorate, and care for.

Should disaster strike and the mother of his child die or become too ill to nurse, he created a "formula" of corn juice, cornmeal soup, animal fat, and/or nut broth to feed his baby, presumably until he could get his child to a nursing woman back in his village or a relative's village. To feed his baby he simulates breastfeeding as best as he possibly can. A Huron father "fills his mouth with it [the "formula"], then putting the child's mouth against his own makes it [the infant] take and swallow the liquid, and this is to make up for the lack of the breast and of the pap (Axtell, 1981:6)."

A father spent his time away from home working to provide the basics for his child, and spent his time at home indulging his beloved son or daughter. "Men and their wives do not in general trouble themselves with each other's business; but the wife, knowing that the father is very fond of his children, is always prepared to tell him some diverting anecdote of one or the other of them, especially if he has been absent for sometime (Heckewelder, 1876:156-60)."

To be a good man was to be many things, but one male attribute was usually overlooked or ignored by Western observers wanting to demonize or degrade the Native peoples - his relatable role as a father. The Native man showed affection to his children (Bragdon, 1996:174).

Sources:

"American Encounters. Natives and Newcomers From European Contact to Indian Removal, 1500-1850." Edited by Peter C. Mancall and James H. Merrell

"Captured by the Indians: 15 First Hand Accounts." Edited by Frederick Drimmer

"Chippewa Customs." By Frances Densmore

"Handbook of the North American Indian: Volume 15 - Northeast." Edited by William C. Sturtevent, and Bruce G. Trigger

"History, Manners, and Customs of the Indian Nations Who Once Inhabited Pennsylvania and the Neighbouring States." By Rev. John Heckewelder

"Iroquois Women: An Anthology." Edited by W.G. Spittal

"Men as Women, Women as Men: Changing Gender in Native American Cultures." By Sabine Lang

"Mythology of the Lenape. Guide and Texts." By John Bierhost

"Native People of Southern New England 1500-1650." By Kathleen J. Bragdon

"The Lenape-Delaware Indian Heritage. 10,000BC to AD2000." By Herbert C. Kraft

"The Indian Peoples of Eastern America: A Documentary of the Sexes." Edited by James Axtell

Mourning The Loss of Loved Ones

In Native American cultures, family and community members mourned the death of their loved ones and fellow villagers, often in a very public manner. For some, mourning may last only a few days, and for others, mourning could last for a year. During this time, they would wear old, dirty clothes, not comb their hair, and rub dirt and ashes on their faces, all to show how hurt they were over such a loss. Some even chopped their hair short. The duration and intensity of the mourning depended on the mourner's relationship to the deceased. Some Native people also "hired" professional mourners, or people (usually women) who would put on public displays of heart-wrenching anguish during the funeral services. Just because these people were given gifts in exchange for their services does not mean that they were "faking" grief. These mourners were conveying the deep sadness of family members, and demonstrating how beloved the deceased persons were. There was no acting needed for such, especially in tight-knit communities where everybody knew everybody else. These mourners may have freed up closer family members to grieve in their own way, and follow taboos during the funeral process.

Packing For The Afterlife
Most deceased Native persons were buried with some of their most loved possessions. The custom of placing items into the grave translated to preparing the deceased for their journey to the afterlife. It gave comfort to those family members to know the deceased had their favorite or essential items with them.

Student Reading: Grades 7-12

The Funeral of a Delaware Woman, 1762
A Historical First-Hand Observation

John Heckewelder, a Moravian missionary to the Native American people, witnessed first-hand the funeral of a beloved Delaware village woman. Being a missionary to their town, he was considered a part of the community, and was even asked to participate. The passages that follow is his account of the funeral customs he observed, along with additional commentary concerning certain Native beliefs and practices to help the reader understand the historical text.

Announcing Her Death

"Women...are not treated after their death with any less respect than a man,... I was present in the year 1762, at the funeral of a woman of the highest rank and respectability, the wife of a valiant Delaware chief Shingask... At the moment that she died, her death was announced through the village by women specially appointed for that purpose, who went through the streets crying, "She is no more, she is no more!" The place on a sudden exhibited a scene of universal mourning; cries and lamentations were heard from all quarters; it was truly the expression of the general feeling for a general loss (Heckewelder: 269-70)." While being the wife of a leader will gain respect, most women in a matrilineal society (like the Delaware) were of "higher rank" usually based on their birth family or clan membership (which was not the same as her husbands). It is possible at this time that Native society placed a "rank connection" between husbands and wives as European culture influenced Native cultures with more and more contact.

Dressed in Her Finest

"The next morning,... we...proceeded to the house of the deceased, where we found her corpse lying in a coffin...dressed and painted in the most superb Indian style. Her garments, all new, were set off with rows of silver brooches, one row joining the other. Over the sleeves of her new ruffled shirt were broad silver arm-spangles from her shoulder down to her wrist, on which were bands, forming a kind of mitten, worked together with wampum, in the same manner as the belts which they use when they deliver speeches. Her long plaited hair was confined by broad bands of silver, one band joining the other, yet not of the same size, but tapering from the head downwards and running at the lower end to a point. On the neck were hanging five broad belts of wampum tied together at the ends, each of a size smaller than the other, the largest of which reached below her breast, the next largest reaching to a few inches of it, and so on, the uppermost one being the smallest. Her scarlet leggings were decorated with different coloured ribands sewed on, the outer edges being finished off with small beads also of various colours. Her

mocksens were ornamented with the most striking figures, wrought on the leather with coloured porcupine quills, on the boarders of which, round the ankles, were fastened a number of small round silver bells, of about the size of a musket ball. All these things, together with the vermillion paint, judiciously laid on, so as to set her off in the highest of style, decorated her person in such a manner, that perhaps nothing of the kind could exceed it (270-1)."

Grave Goods

"...A number of articles were brought out of the house and placed in the coffin, wherever there was room to put them in, among which were a new shirt, a dressed deer skin for shoes, a pair of scissors, needles, thread, a knife, pewter basin and spoon, pint-cup, and other similar things, with a number of trinkets and other small articles which she was fond of while living. The lid was then fastened on the coffin with three straps, and three handsome round poles, five or six feet long, were laid across it, near each other, and one in the middle, which were also fastened with straps cut up from a tanned elk hide; and a small bag of vermillion paint, with some flannel to lay it on, was then thrust into the coffin through the hole cut out at the head of it. This hole, the Indians say, is for the spirit of the deceased to go in and out at pleasure, until it has found the place of its future residence (271)."
"It is always customary, when an Indian dies, of whatever rank or condition he may be, to put a number of the articles which belonged to the deceased in the coffin or grave, that he may have them when wanted (275)."

The Procession

"Everything being in order, the bearer's of the corpse were desired to take their places. Mr. Calhoon and myself were placed at the foremost pole, two women at the middle, and two men at the pole in the rear. Several women,... now started off, carrying large kettles, dishes, spoons, and dried elk meat in baskets, for the burial place, and the signal being given for us to move the body, the women who acted as chief mourners made their air resound with their shrill cries. The order of the procession were as follows; first a leader or guide,... Next followed the corpse, and close to it Shingask, the husband of the deceased. He was followed by the principle war-chiefs and councilors of the nation, after whom came men of all ranks and descriptions. Then followed the women and children, and lastly two stout men carrying loads of European manufactured goods upon their backs. The chief mourners on the woman's side, not having joined the ranks, took their own course to the right, at the distance of about fifteen or twenty yards from us, but always opposite to the corpse. As the corpse had to be carried by the strength of our arms to the distance of about two hundred yards,... we had to rest several times by the way, and whenever we stopped, everybody halted until we moved on again (271-72)." So much of the Delaware culture at this time has Christian influences... we can see it in the coffin usage, outstretched corpse positions (which had been prior to European contact fetal positions), and possibly in the procession that also seems to mimic Christian practices. Still, so much is Delaware, such as the woman's family walking at a distance (she would have been of her mother's clan name – women did not take on the husband's clan name, so her family would have been considered closer in relation). While close family members dressed and prepared the corpse, there seems to be a pattern of the closest family members (her family and husband) purposely putting distance in between themselves and the corpse after the funeral started (the widower's custom of distance will be illustrated later in this account).

Quiet Reflection

"...At the grave, we were told to halt, then the lid of the coffin was again taken off, and the body exposed to view. Now the whole train formed themselves into a kind of semi-lunar circle on the south side of the grave,... the disconsolate Shingask retired by himself to a spot at some distance,

where he was seen weeping, with his head bowed to the ground." "In this situation we remained for the space of more than two hours; not a sound was heard from any quarter, though the numbers that attended were very great; nor did any person move from his seat to view the body, which had been lightly covered over with a clean white sheet. All appeared to be in profound reflection and solemn mourning."

Funeral Mourners Apply Their Trade

"...Six men stepped forward to put the lid upon the coffin, and let down the body into the grave, when suddenly three women mourners rushed from their seats, and forcing themselves between the men, loudly called out to the deceased to "arise and go with them and not to forsake them." They even took hold of her arms and legs... crying out all the while, "Arise, arise! Come with us! Don't leave us! Don't abandon us!" At last they retired, plucking at their garments, pulling their hair, and uttering loud cries and lamentations, with all the appearance of frantic despair. After they were seated on the ground, they continued in the same manner crying and sobbing and pulling at the grass and shrubs, as if their minds were totally bewildered and they did not know what they were doing (272-3)."

"...Those who had rendered the greatest services received the most valuable presents, and we were much pleased to see the female mourners well rewarded, as they had, indeed, a very hard task to perform." "When the heirs of the deceased cannot afford to hire female mourners, the duty is performed by their own immediate relations and friends. But "mourning over the corpse" is a ceremony that cannot be dispensed with (274-5)." This might seem very unusual to the reader, but professional mourning is actually common practice in many cultures. Some might wonder why the immediate family members didn't just take on the role themselves in all cases instead of "hiring" mourners if they could afford to do so. Maybe it was because close family members were to stay at a particular distance during the funeral while professional mourners could get close to the corpse. Or maybe it had something to do with freeing up family members to grieve in their own way so that they didn't have to worry about not showing enough grief outwardly. Having such mourners put on public displays of extreme grief was by no means "fake" – it was done to reflect the grief of the family, the general sadness of a community, and pay respect to the deceased by putting on such a show.

The Widower's Walk

"They let down the coffin into the earth, and laid two thin poles about four inches in diameter... lengthwise and close together over the grave... Then the husband of the deceased advanced with a very slow pace, and when he came to the grave, walked over it on these poles, and proceeded forward in the same manner into an extensive adjoining prairie... (273)" In short, the widower (no one else) seemingly walked away from the grave steadily at the proper time, probably not looking backwards. Although Heckewelder did not say why this was done, and we don't know if he knew why himself, we can use cross-cultural references to possibly find the reasoning for this

custom. In fact, we know through a widowed Meskwaki (Fox) Indian woman (Meskwaki is another Woodland Algonquian-speaking tribe located in the western Great Lakes) that was interviewed in 1918 by an anthropologist, that widows and widowers in her tribe were suppose to *"walk towards the East. They continue to go any place in the bush... They are to never look backwards."* "If she [the Meskwaki widow] had obeyed the tribal custom of walking far into the brush away from her husband's grave without looking back, she could have successfully hidden from his departing soul (Axtell: 224-5)." Could it be that the Delaware had a similar belief, that the spirits of spouses could attach to a widow or widower, which could in turn make it impossible for the surviving spouse to move on with his or her life? Is it possible that a similar Delaware belief may have been the reason the widower walked away a great distance?

The Grave Marker
"When the widowed chief had advanced so far that he could not hear what was doing at the grave, a painted post, on which were drawn various figures, emblematic of the deceased situation in life... was brought by two men and delivered to a third, a man of note, who placed it in such a manner that it rested on the coffin at the head of the grave, and took great care that a certain part of the drawings should be exposed to the East, or rising of the sun; then, while he held the post erect and properly situated, some women filled up the grave with hoes, and having placed dry leaves and pieces of bark over it, so that none of the fresh ground was visible, they retired, and some men, with timbers fitted beforehand for the purpose, enclosed the grave about breast-high, so as to secure it from the approach of wild beasts." For the Unami-Delaware, there is a pattern of putting the corpse's head toward the east and feet toward the west, however, not all Delaware practiced such. The proto and historic Munsee-Delaware graves, for example, many times featured the heads to the west or southwest. The reasoning for the difference is unclear (Kraft: 345).

The funeral was followed by a communal meal, and the items the two men brought to the gravesite on their backs were distributed. A local trader/shop keeper estimated the goods handed out during the funeral at a value of about $200 (back in 1762). Every man, woman, and child were given at least a token gift for their presence. The most well compensated were the professional mourning women, each of whom took home new ruffled shirts, blanket, leggings, and "stroud" (referring to a wool wrap skirt or extra wool fabric). Such widespread distribution of gifts and goods during both happy celebrations and sad occasions was the heart of Native American reciprocity.

Sources:
Axtell, James. *Indian Peoples of Eastern American: A Documentary History of the Sexes.* Oxford University Press: New York, New York, 1981.

Heckewelder, John. *History, Manners, and Customs of the Indian Nations Who Once Inhabited Pennsylvania and the Neighbouring States.* Philadelphia: Historical Society of Pennsylvania, 1876.

Kraft, Herbert C. *The Lenape-Delaware Indian Heritage: 10,000BC-AD2000.* Lenape Books, 2001.

Extra Credit: Define "Reciprocity"

_____
_____
_____
_____
_____
_____

Taking Captives

The Native people practiced "mourning warfare." This was the practice of raiding enemies to take retribution for deaths. This retribution was gained in deaths of enemies to revenge deaths of loved ones, or in the form of captives to "replace" deceased loved ones. Native women were especially known to request warriors to perform raids to bring home captives for their families. Although the word captive might bring to mind the image of one who will suffer at the hands of their captors, this was not true from what most adopted captives of Native societies experienced. Captives were to become family members, not slaves. Young children and women were usually adopted with little violence. Men and older boys, on the other hand, were usually put through a gauntlet even if they were marked for adoption. In a gauntlet, the captive would run in between two lines of men, women, and children as they beat on the captive with sticks and clubs. When the adopted captive reached the end, he was promptly given medical care by the people who beat him. Many went through symbolic baths to "wash away" their previous identities. Once adopted, a captive man, woman, or child had the same inalienable rights as any citizen born into the tribe that adopted them.

This Shawnee warrior has taken an enemy girl to be adopted by his sister. He treats this captive no different than a blood niece.

Some Euro-American women, captured in their adult age, were convinced being captive women in Native societies afforded them more rights than being a woman in their own culture. *"As an Indian woman I was free. I owned my home, my person, the work of my own hands... I was better as an Indian woman than under white law."*
-Alice Fletcher: 1888, from the perspective of Indian women

This included not just other Native captives, but also adopted Anglo-Americans and African-Americans. Such children captured young and raised in Indian families only knew their Indian families. At certian times in history, Euro-American governments demanded such children be returned, but most of these captive children were scared to be taken away from the only parents they recognized. Some Native parents even hid their adopted children in fear they would be taken from them. Though taking others' children wasn't fair for the blood parents, we can't deny the Native parents' love for their children, blood related or not.

A Delaware uncle entertains his two nieces with stories while cleaning his musket. One niece is a Euro-American captive.

47

Native Armor

Did you know some Native Americans wore armor? They did. Some cultures like the Miami, Delaware, Potawatomi, and Ottawa made shields out of wood, bark, and rawhide. Others like the Wyandot (Huron) wore rod- or slot- wood armor in the form of chest plates, arm guards, and leg guards. Some wore pointy helmets made of woven materials, and others wore helmets made of wood. Their armor worked well to block most stone and bone tipped arrows and the powerful blows of war clubs, however, it didn't protect the wearer from European musket balls. Even worse, it didn't allow the wearer to flee fast enough in battle, which put his life in danger. Native armor became ineffective and so was discontinued, just the same as European metal armor disappeared with the introduction of better firearms.

Native American Warriors in 1600

Quotes From *"Of the Order the Hurons Observe in Their Councils"*
By Jean De Brébeuf, 1636 - Jesuit Missionary to the Huron

"All having arrived, they take their seats each in his own quarter of the cabin, those of the same village or of the same nation near one another, in order to consult together. If by chance some one is absent, the question is raised whether, notwithstanding this, the assembly would be legitimate; and sometimes, from the absence of one or two persons, the whole gathering is dissolved, and adjourns until another time. But if all are gathered, or if, notwithstanding, they think it their duty to go on, the council is opened. It is not always the leaders of the council who do this; difficulty in speaking, unwillingness, or even their dignity dispenses them from it."

"After salutations, thanks for the trouble taken in coming, thanksgivings rendered,… that every one has arrived without accident,... in brief, that every one has arrived happily, all are exhorted to deliberate maturely. Then the affair to be discussed is brought forward, and… the councilors are asked to give their advice."

"At this point the deputies of each village, or those of one nation, consult in a low tone as to what they will reply. Then, when they have consulted well together, they give their opinions in order, and decide according to the plurality of opinions, in which course there are some things worthy of remark. The first is in the manner of speaking, which, on account of its unlikeness (to common speech), has a different name and is called *acwentonch*; it is common to all savages; they raise and quaver the voice, like the tones of a preacher in olden times, but slowly, decidedly, distinctly, even repeating the same reason several times. The second remarkable thing is, that the persons giving their opinions go summarily over the proposition and all the considerations brought forward, before giving their advice."

"It is true that their speeches are at first very difficult to understand, on account of an infinity of metaphors, of various circumlocutions, and other rhetorical methods."
"In short, it is in these places they dignify their style of language, and try to speak well. Almost all their minds are naturally of very good quality; they reason very clearly, and do not stumble in their speeches; and so they make a point of mocking those who trip; some seem to be born orators."

"After some one has given his opinion the head of the council repeats… what he has said; consequently, matters must be clearly understood, so often are they repeated."

"Each one ends his advice in these terms, *coxdayauendi ierhayde cha nonhwicwahachen*: that is to say, "*that is my thought on the subject under discussion*" then the whole assembly responds with a very strong… "*haau.*" I have noticed that when any one has spoken to their liking, this haau is given forth with much more effort."

Another "remarkable thing is their great prudence and moderation of speech; I would not dare to say they always use this self-restraint, for I know that sometimes they sting each other, — but yet you always remark a singular gentleness and discretion. I have scarcely ever been present at their councils; but, every time I have been invited, I have come out from them astonished at this feature."

A council spokesman recites a speech with the help of wampum strands used as a memory device.

Activity: Hold a Native American Style Council Debate

Subjects: Language Arts (Public Speaking, Debate), Social Studies (American History, Cultural Studies)
Grades 5-12

Goals:

Students will understand that Woodland Indian societies were democratic in nature, relying on councils and wishes of citizens to make large decisions that affected their whole communities. Students will recognize the importance Native people placed on the art of public speaking. Students will learn that public speakers worked to communicate the messages of their councils whether they agreed or disagreed with the views they presented (and that leaders too put their personal feelings aside to do as his or her community wanted). Students will acknowledge the elements of Native debate: restraint, respect, listening to understand, and eloquent speaking. Students will hone their own critical thinking skills and public speaking skills during this activity.

Activity Background:

Usual Conduct of Council and Treaty Meetings

The historic Native people of the Northeastern Woodlands followed customs that showed speakers, leaders, councils and civilians present at government debates respect. Councils were composed of individuals charged to represent the general public's best interest.

Speakers were elected to represent the positions of councils in government affairs. The spokesperson had to present the views of the people they represented, even if they themselves did not agree. Iroquois leader Red Jacket was at one time the spokesman for the Women's Council (Iroquois), and in one government transaction he did not agree with the women's decision to sell certain tracts of land. He had to put his feelings aside and continue to "speak" for the women's wishes (1).

When one spoke, others listened (the "one speaks at a time" custom, especially in government affairs, was more Native American in mannerisms than European). Time was given before the next speaker started, whether the next speaker, or the council he or she represented, agreed with the last perspective or not. This was time to think about what a speaker had just presented. The point of these debates were not to confront but more to persuade. It was not unusual for spokespersons to break to consult the councils they represented. Because of their attention to making sure their citizen's prerogatives were represented correctly, it was not unusual for government meetings to last for days, even weeks (an issue to many Euro-Americans who wanted fast treaty proceedings). Important matters were never taken lightly among the Native people, and they followed formal procedures and customs in all government affairs.

The Eloquent Speaker

"Indian men trained their sons in oratory -- Huron men teased each other if they made a slip of the tongue or mistake, and accorded the eloquent speaker praise and honor" (2). The position and delivery of a council's perspective rested on the shoulders of the spokesperson. Usually, honing oratory skills and becoming a spokesperson was a man's activity and duty, although women were never banned from such an occupation, and some women speakers were noted. Women's councils even elected spokesmen to represent their opinions in council. Becoming an eloquent speaker was perhaps much more important than being a successful warrior in Northeastern Native societies upon European contact. "I know enough to instruct my son," said an Algonquian [man] -- "I'll teach him to give speeches" (3).

Activity Procedure:

1. The Dilemma - Pose a question to your students, one that affects school. Ideas could include:
-Should we institute uniforms?
-Should the school switch to a 4-day school week schedule?
-Should the school day be extended by 1 hour, and in return, no homework will be assigned?

Activity: Hold a Native American Style Council Debate

Subjects: Language Arts (Public Speaking, Debate) Social Studies (American History, Cultural Studies)
Grades 5-12

Continued

2. Formulate an Opinion - After the question is posed, split students into 2 councils (probably based on students initial position on the question). Have both councils discuss the reasoning and pros to their position and the cons of the other council's position.

3. Nominate a Spokesperson - A spokesperson must be able to persuade an audience to think the same as their council does. Students will vote a member of their council be the spokesperson for their perspective. Students should pick this person only for their speaking skills. *Tip: Throw your students a TWIST, and switch the spokespersons to speak for the other councils. The spokespeople have to be not only good public speakers, but they must be able to put their opinion aside to sell their new council's opinion to the rest of the class. The councils will then brief their new spokesperson on all the points they want him or her to present in favor of their position.*

4. Present And Defend Your Position - Have each spokesperson present the position of the council they represent. Spokespeople are the only ones who can speak for their council. When the spokesperson is finished, the other council will get time to formulate questions and relate the questions to their spokesperson for him or her to ask. Spokespeople can only say what they have been briefed on. Any questions posed to the spokesperson by the other council's spokesperson can be answered only if they have been told that point by the council previously. If they don't have the answer, they cannot give an answer as it would only be the spokesperson's opinion. They will have to remember (or write down) the question(s) and meet with their council and be told what to reply with. Time will be given for the answering council to brief their spokesperson on the reply. He or she will then formally answer all questions. It was this type of protocol that encouraged Native council meetings to last for days, but it also saw to it that what was being represented was the true perspectives of the councils. For example, although some Iroquois treaty meetings with Europeans and Americans might be attended by mostly men (when at a distance from their villages), the spokespeople still had to consult the women's council; it was not unusual for negotiations to halt and recess so spokespeople could meet with the councils they represented. *Tip: When asking or answering questions, spokespeople should remember they are there to persuade others listening to agree with their council's views. Answers might sound like... Council A: "By wearing uniforms, it gives one less thing students could be singled out for by bullying. We feel that if we could eliminate bullying from our school we would do it." Council B: "The other council might have you believe that uniforms will stop the negative singling out of students, but who's to say that matching clothes will eliminate a problem as large as bullying. Bullying will continue because there are so many things that make us unique that matching clothes cannot cover. Bullying itself is a psychological problem that is not based on what there is to make fun of; it is based on the fact that they must bully to feel better about themselves. Why sacrifice our individuality through what we wear to supposedly stop bullying, which it will not. Isn't that just bullying us from expressing ourselves?" Council A: "Individuality is much deeper than clothing. The other council has just said "there are so many things that make us unique." We express ourselves in so many more important ways than clothing..."*

5. The Final Decision - This historic Native American style debate may last a few classes. In reality, Native meetings on important matters could take days and days because the spokespeople had to relate the meeting information to the councils (who may not be present for meetings unlike your students), and the councils had to relate their answers, replies, and new developments to the spokespeople. At the end of the debate, when both sides have addressed all they could, take a private vote (on paper - no names) to see if the councils and spokespeople did their jobs to persuade others to agree with their views. Maybe a popular decision had been reached.

Activity: Hold a Native American Style Council Debate

Subjects: Language Arts (Public Speaking, Debate) Social Studies (American History, Cultural Studies)
Grades 5-12

Continued

Alternative Procedures:

Instead of dividing your class into two councils debating one question, divide your class into four councils debating two separate questions (Group A vs. Group B, Group C vs. Group D), this way, half the class (not debating) can play the role of the civilians looking to be swayed in one direction or the other. Take a vote to see which council they agreed with, and see if students changed their minds as a result of the debate.

-or-

Have your class hold their council debate for other classes of the same grade. The other classes will represent the general village population, while your class represents two councils of different opinions. At the end of the council, take a vote among the other classes to see which side most of the "village" agrees with. See if any students changed their vote because of the council debate.

Take It Further:

Complete Lesson: Share *Iroquois Democracy Inspires American Forefathers* on page 167 with your students, and explore how Native American governments, especially the Iroquois, influenced the formulation of the United States and The Constitution.

Sources of Quotes & Examples:

(1) Iroquois Women: An Anthology edited by W.G. Spittal, 1996:13,19
(2) and (3) *American Encounters* edited by Peter C. Mancall and James H. Merrell, 2000:106

Notes:

_____
_____
_____
_____
_____
_____
_____
_____
_____
_____
_____
_____
_____
_____
_____
_____

Project: Make a Classroom Wampum Belt

Subjects: Art (Cultural Arts), Social Studies (American History, Cultural Studies)
Grades 1-5

Background

Many Northeastern Native societies used wampum belts to solidify treaties, transactions, alliances, and other government formalities. They were used in extending invitations as much as they were used as binding contracts. Wampum belts recorded speeches and history in the same spirit written languages did for other societies. With this in mind, have each one of your students design a section of the classroom wampum belt - a wampum belt that commemorates your class unity during the school year.

Materials

-Student Copies of Worksheet (provided
     on next page)
-1 Copy of Belt Ends (this page)
-Crayons or Colored Pencils
-Scissors
-Tape or Glue

Procedure

Copy the wampum belt worksheet (on the next page) for every student. Let them color in and cut out their wampum sections. Make sure they keep the tab attached. Next assemble the belt by gluing or taping the tab on the left side of one to the right underside of the next wampum section. Finish the belt by attaching the ends (provided on this page). Display the belt in your classroom or in the hallway.

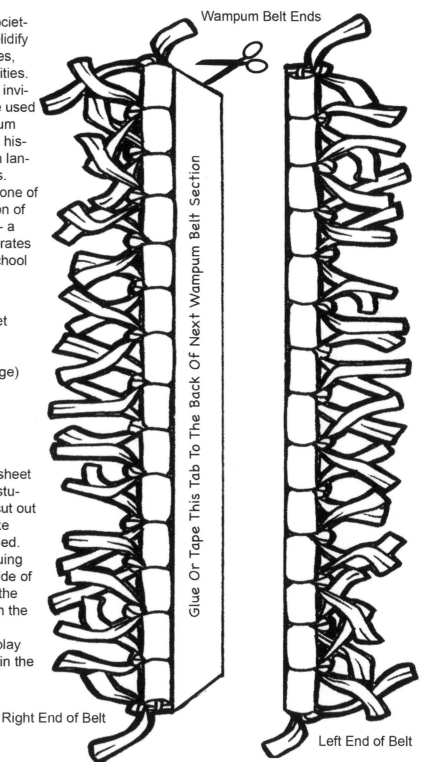

Wampum Belt Ends

Glue Or Tape This Tab To The Back Of Next Wampum Belt Section

Right End of Belt

Left End of Belt

Design a Section of the Classroom Wampum Belt

The term 'wampum' usually refers to white and purple beads made of east coast seashells, especially clams called quahogs. These beads were traded from coastal tribes to inland tribes. Wampum beads were used for many purposes, including being made into 'strings' to remember speeches and made into belts to solidify treaties.

Directions: Design, color, and cut out the wampum belt section below. The belt will then be attached to other wampum belt sections colored by your classmates to make a large classroom wampum belt.

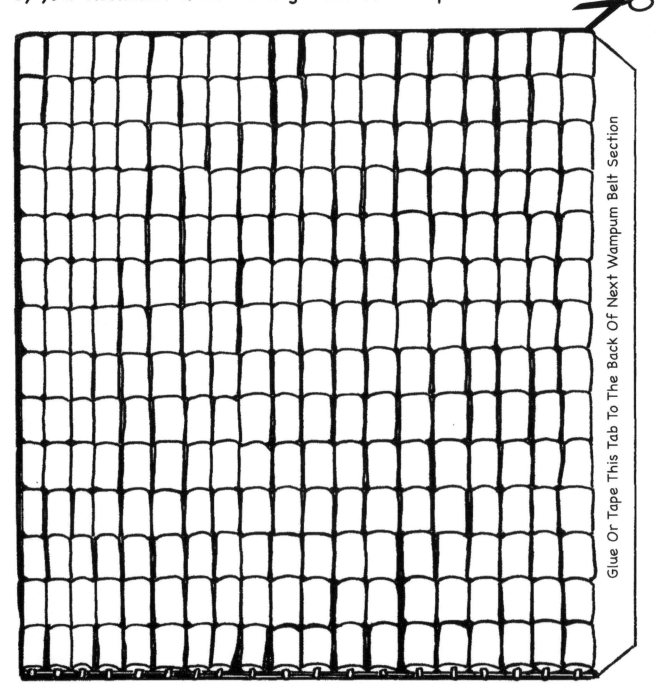

Glue Or Tape This Tab To The Back Of Next Wampum Belt Section

3 Native American Sports

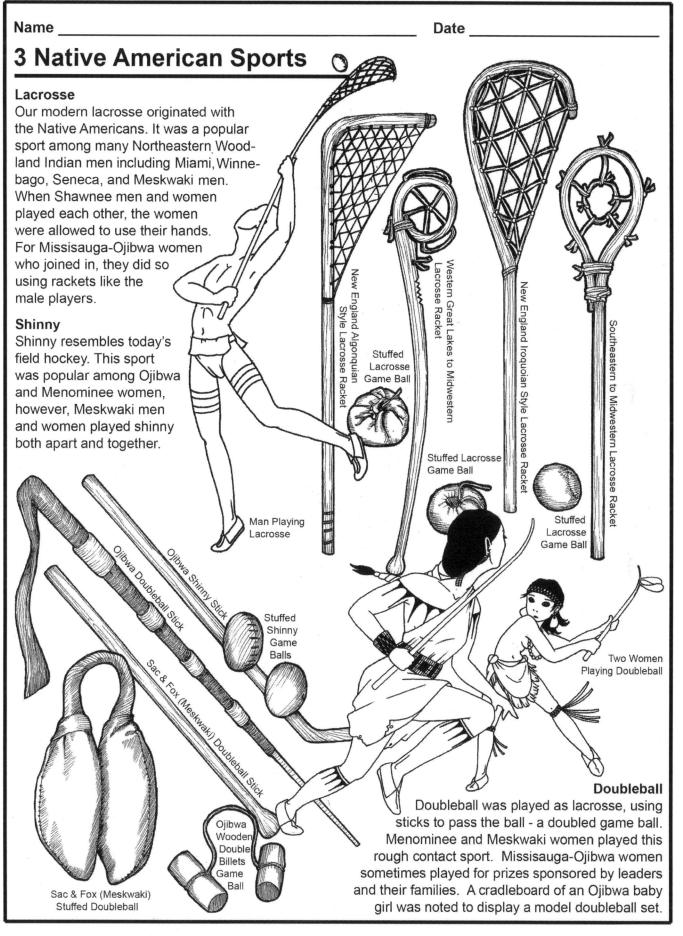

Lacrosse

Our modern lacrosse originated with the Native Americans. It was a popular sport among many Northeastern Woodland Indian men including Miami, Winnebago, Seneca, and Meskwaki men. When Shawnee men and women played each other, the women were allowed to use their hands. For Missisauga-Ojibwa women who joined in, they did so using rackets like the male players.

Shinny

Shinny resembles today's field hockey. This sport was popular among Ojibwa and Menominee women, however, Meskwaki men and women played shinny both apart and together.

New England Algonquian Style Lacrosse Racket

Western Great Lakes to Midwestern Lacrosse Racket

New England Iroquoian Style Lacrosse Racket

Southeastern to Midwestern Lacrosse Racket

Stuffed Lacrosse Game Ball

Stuffed Lacrosse Game Ball

Stuffed Lacrosse Game Ball

Man Playing Lacrosse

Ojibwa Doubleball Stick

Ojibwa Shinny Stick

Sac & Fox (Meskwaki) Doubleball Stick

Stuffed Shinny Game Balls

Two Women Playing Doubleball

Ojibwa Wooden Double Billets Game Ball

Sac & Fox (Meskwaki) Stuffed Doubleball

Doubleball

Doubleball was played as lacrosse, using sticks to pass the ball - a doubled game ball. Menominee and Meskwaki women played this rough contact sport. Missisauga-Ojibwa women sometimes played for prizes sponsored by leaders and their families. A cradleboard of an Ojibwa baby girl was noted to display a model doubleball set.

Activity: Lacrosse

Subjects: Physical Education, Social Studies (American History, Cultural Studies)
Grades 5-8

Background

Lacrosse was originally a Native American sport. As it is today, lacrosse was a contact sport in which two teams attempted to score more points by hitting their respective goals (in the past, these goals were usually poles which the game ball had to strike or be hurled past). In the Indiana and Ohio region, Algonquian rackets were not shaped like the popular Iroquois-style "shepherd's cane" rackets (which modern lacrosse adopted), rather, these Midwestern rackets' pockets were round in shape, like a hoop. Every player has a racket to catch, throw, and carry the ball with; no hands were allowed to touch the ball. Lacrosse was played usually by men, however, some social games included women. Missisauga women sometimes engaged in lacrosse where they too used rackets to play. The Shawnee were noted to even play men versus women, and the women, unlike the men, could use their use hands instead of rackets. Besides the Shawnee and Missisauga, other local tribes that traditionally played lacrosse included the Ojibwa (Chippewa), Miami, Menominee, Fox (Meskwaki), Huron (Wyandot), Seneca, and probably the Delaware (Lenape).

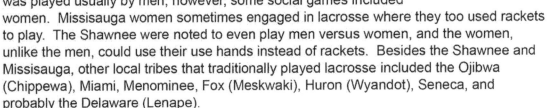

Description

Students will play catch using Midwestern Native hoop style lacrosse rackets.

Materials Needed (To Make One Set)

-2 yard long, 3/4" diameter wooden dowels (can be found at home improvement stores)
-2 sets of 4-5" diameter needle point wooden hoops (wider frames)
-Decorative net (can be found at craft stores by sea shore theme decor)
-Bag of small, dry beans
-New child size sock
-Needle and coat strength thread
-Jute or cotton string
-Hot glue gun and glue sticks
-Scissors

Preparation: Make The Lacrosse Rackets and Ball

Cut 2 circles from the decorative net about 3" larger that the diameter of the needle point hoops. Trap and stretch the cut net circles between each needle point hoop. Secure the net further by tying the net and hoop at 4 or more points around the hoop with the jute or cotton string. Take the netted hoops and attach them each to a dowel. They should be attached 2" from the end. Secure it in place first with string, then pump hot glue to the attached section part. Use a very generous amount. When dry, finish by wrapping the string over the glued areas. Make the play ball by stuffing the toe end of the sock with beans until it forms about a 2" diameter sack. Sew shut and cut the excess off the sock ball.

Procedure: Game Play

Have students stand at a distance from each other and play catch with the rackets and ball. Use the racket to catch and throw the ball. Do not use the rackets to pick the ball up from the ground as the hoops are not strong enough for that kind of stress. Make sure all onlooking students are at about a 15 foot distance. A player with a racket may swing it or jump in one direction in order to catch the ball which can put students closer than 15 feet at risk of being accidently hit by the racket.

Shawnee Lacrosse

Although lacrosse was usually played by Shawnee men, in social games men and women played together. Men had to go by the usual rules of using only a racket to catch and pass the ball, but women were allowed to use their hands.

Two teams strived to get the game ball to their respective goals. The team with the most goals won. Such games were probably played during celebrations. Spectators had just as much fun watching as players did playing.

Activity: Doubleball

Subjects: Physical Education, Social Studies (American History, Cultural Studies)
Grades 1-8

Background

Doubleball, also known as the Maiden's Ball Game among the Missisauga Ojibwa, was a sport usually played by women. The basic game involved two teams and two goals. The objective was for a team to score the most goals. Goals were located at a great distance from each other, sometimes up to a mile apart. Up to a hundred or more women could play at once. The game ball could not be touched by hands, rather, it had to be thrown and caught using a game stick, and it took much skill to do this. Doubleball was also a contact sport, played in the same manner as lacrosse. Goals were defended, and it was not unusual for women  to get very hurt playing this game. Prizes were sometimes awarded the winning team players; such prizes were usually sponsored by leaders or chiefs, and other influential individuals and families. Spectators, including male kin to the players, enjoyed placing bets on the outcome of the game. Doubleball was played by Great Lakes tribes such as the Menominee, Ojibwa, and Fox (Meskwaki).

Description

Students will play catch using the doubleball sticks to pass and throw the doubleball.

Materials Needed (for 4 players at one time)

-4 one yard long, 3/4" - 1" diameter dowel sticks
-Bag of dry, small beans
-New tube sock
-Needle and thread

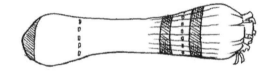

Preparation: Make the Doubleball

Fill the toe of the tube sock with 3/4 cup of beans. Sew that end shut about 3" up from the toe. Then fill the sock again with another 3/4 cup of beans. Sew the tube sock opening shut. Push all the beans from the second filling to the sewn shut tube sock opening. Sew 3" above the opening to trap the beans equally on the other side of the doubleball.

Procedure: Game Play

Have 4 students stand at a distance from each other, as if each were on the corner of a square. Pass the doubleball in one direction. Have them throw and catch the doubleball only using their sticks. Switch players so every student has a chance to try. Make sure all onlooking students are standing at least 15 feet away so they are not hit by a stick. Never allow 2 or more players to play in swinging distance of each other.

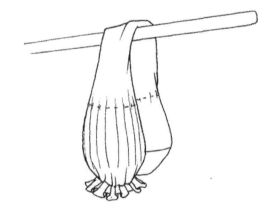

Native American Games and Sports

Like you, the Native American people enjoyed
playing games. Men and women both played a
game called the bowl game. The bowl game used
a bowl and flat, 2-sided dice. The dice were
flipped using the bowl. The score was given by
which side the dice landed on. This was a favorite
game of the Native American people. Players could get
prizes for winning, and those watching would bet on the
outcome too. Another favorite game of both adults and
children was the ring and pin game. The ring and pin
were connected by a string. Players had to swing the
ring up and catch it on the pin to win. Both the ring and
pin game and the bowl game were played at annual
celebrations. The games could go on for days, just as
long as the festival. **What kinds of games do you play?**

Girl playing double-ball.

_____

_____

Boy playing lacrosse.

They didn't just play games, they also played sports.
Adults played racket ball games like lacrosse and doubleball. Both games are played the same way.
They had 2 teams. Each team had to score
by hitting goals on the opposite team's side
with the ball. Players could not touch the game
ball with their hands. They had to throw it and catch
it using their rackets. Like football, the players could
block the players of the other team. Lacrosse was usually
played by men, and double-ball was played by women.
The Native American people had games for children and
adults, and sports for both men and women. **What kinds
of sports do you play?**

_____

_____

Activity: Make a Ring & Pin Game

Subjects: Social Studies (American History, Cultural Studies)
Grades 2-5

Background

The ring & pin game is a minor amusement enjoyed by both children and adults. The basic ring & pin game consists of a pin: the pin was a stick made of wood or bone; and the ring: the ring could be a hoop or piece of leather with holes that could be caught by the pin, bone or hoof beads which the pin must catch, or a bundle of pine needles or grass which the pin must pierce.

Description

Students will each make and play with their new ring & pin game.

Materials

-12" long 1/2" diameter dowel for each student
-Project foam sheets (brown or tan to look like leather)
-Multicolored plastic pony beans
-Yarn
-Scissors
-Paper hole punch
-Cardboard

Procedure

Make cardboard stencils of the "ring" pattern below. Have each student trace the cardboard "ring" stencil on flexible project foam sheets, and cut it out (including the holes to catch the pin/dowel in). Use a paper hole punch to punch out a hole in the corner of the "ring" to attach one end of a 14" - 18" long piece of yarn to this hole. After attaching the string, thread 10 plastic pony beads onto it and tie the other end of the yarn off to the middle of the dowel. The ring & pin game is ready to play! Swing the "ring" up and attempt to catch on the end of the dowel.*

*Important: Make sure you give a safety talk before playing with the game. It can be easy to poke another classmate while playing, so students need to keep a distance from each other while playing with their ring & pin games.

"Ring" Stencil

Punch hole for string on the black dot.

Activity: Bowl Game Math

Subjects: Math, Social Studies (American History, Cultural Studies)
Grades 1-4

Background

The bowl game was a form of dice game popular among adults. Potawatomi and Ojibwa (Chippewa) men and women played this game, however, women more frequently played. The bowl game is also noted to be played among the Delaware (Lenape), Ottawa (Odawa), Kickapoo, Menominee, Missisauga, Nipissing, Huron (Wyandot),Seneca, and Fox (Meskwaki). While considered to be a game of chance, the players were said to use much skill in flipping the dice and catching them in a way that would benefit the players' scores. For most, even those dice that missed their target and fell to the ground were counted (however you may want to enforce a rule among your students that dice don't count unless they are caught in the bowl, in order not to encourage throwing items chaotically in the classroom). The bowl game was more than just a way to pass time; among some it was a necessary part of certain celebrations (as a specific dance or song would be), and gambling on the outcome by both the players and onlookers was usual. Scores were kept by counting sticks. It was a very festive and competitive game.

Description

Students will break up into smaller groups and play each other in the bowl game, and tally their scores to see who won using basic addition skills.

Materials (Enough For 4 Groups)

-4 Bowls (thin-walled wooden salad bowls or plastic dishes work well - no breakable bowls)
-20 - 1" Diameter Wooden Circle Chips (found in the wood crafts section at craft stores)
-Red and Black Acrylic Paint or Permanent Markers
-200 or more ice cream pop sticks

Preparation

1. Paint or color one side of chips: 4 chips (dice) with black parallel lines, 4 chips with a black X, 4 chips with a red X, and 8 chips with one half colored in red. Divide each kind of 'dice' equally between the 4 bowls.

2. The ice cream pop sticks are counting sticks to keep score. Take 40 sticks and give them a black marking on both sides; these sticks will count for 5 points each. Take another 40 sticks and give them a red marking on both sides; these sticks will count for 10 points each. The blank 120 sticks will represent one point each. As students play, they will keep these sticks to see who wins.

Procedure

Devise a scoring system and write the key up on the blackboard (ex. blank side=0, parallel lines=2, black X=3, red X=4, half colored=5). Divide students into 4 groups and have them play in turns, flipping and catching the 'dice' using the bowl to see which side they land on, keeping score of each student's turn. Whichever student reaches 40 points first (or whatever score you have agreed on) in their group wins.

Native women playing the bowl game, 1820.

Native American Bowl Game Math

The bowl game was a dice game Native Americans played. They used the bowl to toss the dice, and what dice side landed right-side-up gave the players their scores.

Directions: Using the scoring key, figure out the scores in problems 1-4.

Scoring Key: =3 =2 =0   These values only apply to dice that land in the bowl. Dice outside the bowl = 0.

1.

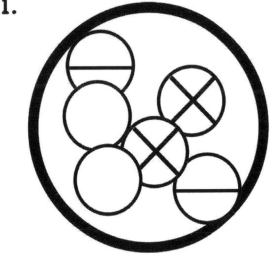

__+__+__+__+__+__=__

2.

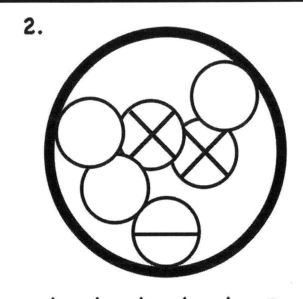

__+__+__+__+__+__=__

3.

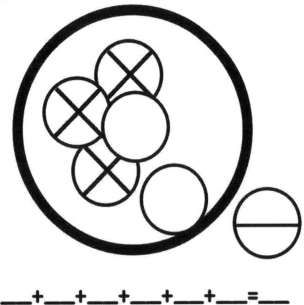

__+__+__+__+__+__=__

4.

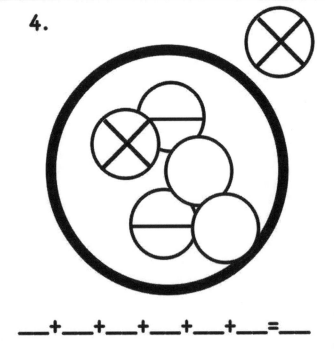

__+__+__+__+__+__=__

The Native American people enjoyed
telling jokes and funny stories.

By listening to stories, young people learned about their history and beliefs, and many life lessons.

Music & Dance

Young woman applies face paint before attending a dance.

Celebrations and times of giving thanks were usually accompanied by music and dance. Native American dances were usually of two types: the ceremonial and the social. Ceremonial dances were usually performed by certain people, for example, maybe persons who belonged to secret medicine societies. This type of dance can be thought of as a form of prayer. Social dances, on the other hand, were usually open for all to join. As the name implies, social dances were very social. Young unmarried people especially took advantage of such dances to get to know potential suitors. Dances were an occasion to dress up. Both young men and women wore their best clothes and jewelry, styled their hair, and even applied paint to their faces and bodies.

Man, painted black, dances with his otter skin medicine bag, dew claw rattle in hand, and deer hoof garter rattles below his knees.

Seneca snapping turtle shell rattle and Delaware male/female manitou drumsticks for unique Delaware folding drum.

Musical Instruments

Drums and rattles were the predominant instruments used to make music. Both made rhythmic beats that dancers could time their steps with. Drums were usually small, hand-held drums. One variety was the water drum. The hollowed inside was filled with water to change the pitch of the drum. It was not the level of water that changed the drum's sound - it was actually the act of turning the drum over to soak the drum face, then pulling the wet leather face tight while it dried that gave the drum its high "ping" sound. Other small drums used rawhide for their faces. Hand rattles were made of wood, bark, gourds, and turtle shells filled with pebbles or similar materials that created noise when they shook. Some turtle shells were tied to the legs so dancers would make sound when they danced. Other dancers used deer hoofs and dew claws dangled from their garters and rattles to create such rhythmic sounds. Another Native instrument, the wooden flute, was used usually only when men courted women in private.

65

Material Culture

Topics Represented in This Section:

Wigwams & Longhouses; Reed Mats; Containers; Earthenware; Farming Culture; Native Dishes & Nutrition; Maple Sugaring; Fishing; Hunting; Bows & Arrows; Flintknapping and Stone Tool Technology; Copper Tools & Jewelry; Hide-Tanning; Native Clothing (Pre-Contact & Historic); Quillworking; Fingerweaving; Silk Ribbon Appliqué; Wampum Jewelry.

Traditional Miami, Shawnee, and Delaware Homes

The Wigwam

The wigwam was a home designed to house a single, nuclear family (sometimes 2 families would live in one large wigwam). The pole framework of a dome shaped wigwam could be bent at only one time of the year, from late spring to mid summer. The base of the wigwam frame (poles) was secured permanently in the ground.

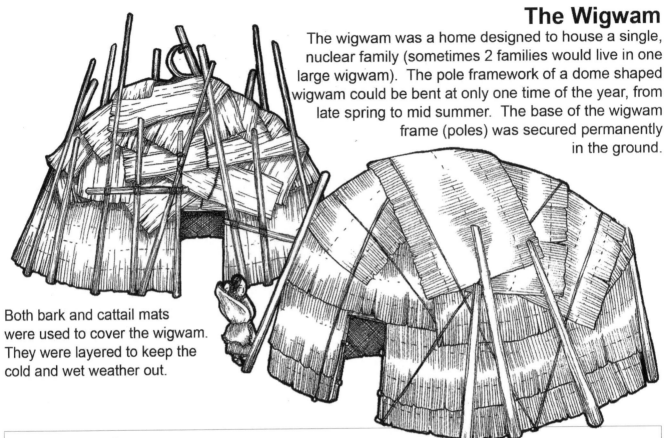

Both bark and cattail mats were used to cover the wigwam. They were layered to keep the cold and wet weather out.

The Longhouse

The longhouse was a multi-family home built usually in the same manner as a wigwam in both materials and method. For some, the longhouse was just an extension of a wigwam. Excavation sites have shown such alterations, where the sides of smaller homes were torn down and the home extended. Most longhouses or multifamily homes were built to last 10 years or longer. Some longhouses were built in excess of 100 feet in length, with ceiling peaks more than 20 feet tall. Longhouses were usually covered with bark, however, mats could be fixed to the interior walls for insulation.

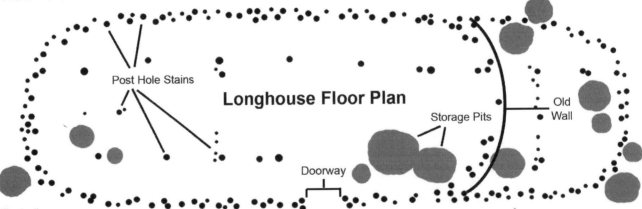

Illustration:
Post holes discovered by archaeologists reveal a Delaware longhouse located in their homelands along the Atlantic coast. The stains in the ground show the layout (door, sleeping platforms, and storage pits), and that the longhouse was added on to, possibly to accommodate a growing family. Posts are doubled to create an outer frame to hold bark covers (in between the inner and outer frame).

Student Article: Grades 5-12

The Wigwam: A Traditional Native American Home

The dome-shaped wigwam was a nuclear family home utilized by the Delaware (Lenape), Miami, Potawatomi, Kickapoo, Shawnee and other local historic tribes. This type of home was large enough to fit a nuclear family comfortably, averaging about 10 to 12 feet in diameter with about an 8 foot peak. The traditional dome-shaped family wigwams were not little huts used for camping while traveling; the traditional dome-shaped wigwam was the family cabin, either utilized half the year in winter residences (like the Miami practiced), or year-round in villages (like the Delaware/Lenape practiced). For those who lived in their wigwams fulltime, the wigwam structure could last over a decade with minor repairs and maintenance. The start of a sound and long-lasting wigwam structure began with its construction.

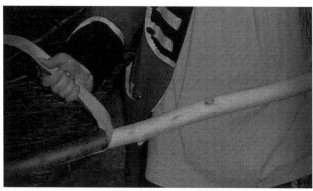

Constructing The Dome-Shaped Frame

Poles selected to construct these round house frames were obtained from hickory, chestnut, cedar, or other kinds of tree saplings. It was generally the job of men to harvest and collect poles used in home building, as men tended to be the major woodworkers of the family. Saplings selected for vertical posts in the framework had to be around 2-3 inches in diameter at the base. These small trees were cut near the ground with axes (stone axes in earlier times and trade metal axes during colonial times). The saplings were then stripped of their bark, and the thin bark was probably saved for later to be used as cordage in securing the framework. Doing this added to the lifespan of the frame as bark would only hasten wood rot, trapping moisture and bugs in between the bark layer and inner wood.

The domed wigwam frames were permanent and secured in the ground. Dome wigwam frames were not transported – they stayed where they were built. Securing the frame to the ground could be accomplished by digging holes or trenches, however, some archaeological evidence shows minimal ground disturbance around posthole stains which suggests a possible different method than just digging to make the holes. It is likely that men hammered stakes into the ground to mold the holes instead, and then the vertical frame poles were thrust into the cavities to a depth of 12 to 18 inches under the surface. Vertical poles were usually placed about 12 inches apart, with exception to the home's entrance.

Upper Right: The bark is striped from saplings before the pole is used to build the frame. Lower Left: Vertical poles were place about a foot a part in the ground.

The vertical poles secured in the ground were then bent inward at the top to form the dome roof of the home. Each vertical pole end was secured to another vertical pole end on the opposite side of the wigwam. Saplings had to be used and bent within a day or so of being cut down; any longer and the dead trees would start to loose their flexibility and become more likely to break under the tension of bending the barrel roof. Dome wigwam frames were to be constructed during the spring to summer seasons, when the saplings were much more flexible and able to bend into the desired dome shape.

Once all vertical posts were in place, horizontal poles were added. This added strength to the frame by creating a latticework. Cordage was used to secure the horizontal poles in place; finer cord was made from the inner layer of mature barks, and rougher cord from the entire bark of young trees, such as the bark that was previously stripped off the saplings. Cordage-making was generally the job of women, and most likely, men and women worked together to tie down the poles. The latticework had to be secured at most points where each sapling passed another in order to make the wigwam frame solid. These frames had to be strong enough to carry hundreds of pounds of bark, as well as a snow load.

Before the coverings were added, the interior sleeping platforms and shelves were probably built. These were constructed also from saplings. Wigwams usually featured platforms along most sides of the walls, enough space to sleep the whole family and extra space for visitors. Some wigwams also had a covered entrance; such porches were constructed of sapling poles.

Covering the Wigwam Frame

Two traditional materials were used to cover wigwams in our region: bark sheets and reed mats. During the historic period, canvas provided by Euro-Americans was also used, usually in conjunction with bark and reed mats. Animal hides were rarely used as a primary material in covering homes, such as it was for the tipis of the Plains area. When wigwams where noted using some hide coverings, they were usually the residences of refugees - communities just uprooted from war or threat of violence, many times leaving behind their homes just burned by encroaching armies and enemies. Hides and any sufficient materials were employed in making living quarters after the loss of their villages. Canvas, hides and other materials were also employed during times of confinement caused by the loss of land and forced migrations during Indian Removal.

Lower Left: The sleeping platform made of sapling poles is installed. Upper Right: The dome wigwam frame is complete. Lower Right: Beginning to cover the wigwam; the bark sheets are attached to the frame starting from the bottom up.

Although canvas and other materials were utilized in poor times, bark sheets and reed mats were much more desirable; bark and reeds were the traditional materials utilized in home construction, valued for their availability and effectiveness in making a comfortable indoor living space in inclement weather.

Harvesting Bark Sheets For Wigwams

Bark was traditionally used to cover Northeastern Native American wigwams. From spring to summer, many deciduous trees yielded their bark layer with little resistance. The reason for this lies with the annual growth of the tree, in which a new layer or ring is added to the sapwood just under the bark layers. Later in the year, the bark layer and sapwood will "fuse" together or become very hard to separate, making the window to harvest bark only when the new annual layer is being grown with substantial sap activity.

The historic Native peoples perfected their method of bark harvesting by employing tools that cut into and wedged the bark off in a skillful manner that minimized the risk of splitting the bark sheets. Stone axes and later trade metal hatchets were employed in the cutting of the bark layer while wooden wedges helped to peel back the large sheets of bark. Heavy, thick bark was taken from mature trees while they were still alive and standing, usually a job reserved for able-bodied men. Such men would girdle or cut into the bark layer of the tree as high as they could (possibly using ladders at times), and from their cuts begin to peel the bark layer off the tree trunk.

The living tree being stripped of its full bark layer cannot survive, which is why trees not coveted for their nuts or sap, or trees standing in areas where future cornfields were to be located were stripped. Presumably, trees uprooted by spring and summer storms were targets for their bark too, as working from the ground level not only made it easier but allowed for the whole trunk to be peeled of its bark. These trees would have been stripped within days of coming down, as bark needs to be separated and flattened within days of a tree's demise.

Once bark was peeled, it was laid out flat on the ground so it might loose its natural cylindrical curve, or it was used right away, being secured to the house frame so it might take on the shape of the wigwam walls. Bark sheets were shingled on the home, bottom to top, so they would shed water. An opening was left at the top of the wigwam so smoke from the interior fire could escape. The bark was secured most likely with cordage, and many times with a second or outer framework of poles. An outside frame compressed the bark between it and the home's interior frame, keeping it flat and in place. This is an important feature as medium to heavy bark sheets can curl and warp in moist weather with so much force that cordage alone may not be sufficient to keep the bark in place.

Upper Left: A Hickory tree, blown down in a spring storm in Indiana, is striped of its bark layer. Lower Right: Red Oak and Hickory bark sheets are weighted down with rocks to dry flat.

Many trees yielded bark suitable to cover wig-wams including Poplar, Ash, Hickory, Elm, and Chestnut. Some mature bark sheets used on wigwams were up to an inch thick. These barks were too heavy to transport and so were permanent with the wigwam frame. The only bark that Native peoples transported as build-ing materials was Paper Birch bark, however, most of our area being south of the main native Paper Birch tree region, the Native peoples here did not rely this thin bark the way their neighbors to the north did.

Utilizing Reed Mats For Insulation
While bark sheets worked well to shed water, they did not provide adequate insulation against cold weather. This was instead the job of reed mats. Woven interior mats were made to hang on the inside of the wigwam, such as the many bulrush mats woven carefully with striking decorative patterns. These interior mats added air space and insulation between the outer bark wall and the interior living space. Women were the artisans of such works and were presumably in charge of arranging the in-terior mats.

By Harvey Barrison.   Creative Commons Attribution-Share Alike 2.0 Generic license.

Other mats were made to be house coverings with or without the help of bark sheets. These exterior mats were usually made of cattail leaves sewn together, each leaf side-to-side. These mats did shed most water and when the exterior cattail mats were soaked by rain, the leaves of the mats expanded ever so slightly, creating a seal between each leaf, which then stopped the water from seeping through to lower layers of mats that covered the wigwam. Three to five layers of these mats made a wigwam toasty warm inside even in the coldest winters.

Cattail mats were also lightweight and able to roll, making them the perfect house coverings to transport to temporary hunting, fishing, and maple sugar camps. Women, who generally owned the home and most of the household goods, could transport several mats bundled on their backs. While their parcel may have been bulky, it was deceivingly lighter than it looked.

Upper Left: This mature tree can yield a bark layer up to 1 inch thick. Upper Right: Cattails grow in shallow water. Lower Right: A finished cattail mat.

Furnishing the Interior of the Wigwam

Interior reed mats were not only hung along the inside walls, but were also used as a carpeting of sorts. The floor was covered in mats to walk on, sit on, and work on around the fire. The sleeping platforms along the sides of the walls were covered with mats and furs for mattresses. The space under the platforms could store firewood, pumpkins, and other items. Clothing, utensils, and tools were packed away on shelves and hung from the walls and ceiling. Even certain foods could be dried and hung inside the house, as well as be packed away on shelves or underground in storage pits. Storage pits could be located outside or inside the home. The wigwam didn't offer any more indoor area than a small one-room cabin, but it did provide a cozy and workable space out of the elements.

Upper Left: A dome wigwam measuring 14 x 14 ft. with a 9 ft. peak. It is covered with bark, reed mats, and trade canvas. Lower Left: A sleeping area inside the wigwam; the decorative interior mats help to insulate the home. Upper Right: Interior wall of wigwam. Middle Right: A small hole lets in a little light and offers an escape for smoke produced by the fire (Lower Right).

The Math of Constructing Woodland Indian Homes

Directions: Answer the following 5 questions.

1. If a longhouse that measures 24 ft in length needs about 56 poles to build one long-side wall frame, how many poles will a longhouse twice as long need to build both its long-side wall frames?

Answer:_____

2. If a Poplar tree gives about 54 sq ft of usable bark, how many Poplar trees will be needed to make a longhouse with 1,250 sq ft of walls to cover?

Answer:_____

3. If a cattail mat measures 5 x 11 ft, then how many sq ft does this mat cover?

Answer:_____

4. If all the cattail mats measure 5 x 11 ft, then how many of them are needed for a wigwam that has 850 sq ft to cover?

Answer:_____

5. To stay warm and shed rain, a wigwam must be covered with at least 3 layers of cattail mats. How many cattail mats are now needed to cover the same wigwam from question 4?

Answer:_____

Illustrations: Top: Men cut down sapling poles to build a house frame with.
Left: Father and son peel a large piece of bark to use as house coverings.

Lesson: All About Trees
Subjects: Science (Environmental Science)
Grades 4-10

Because Native people harvested bark sheets from trees to utilize as house building materials, this topic lends itself to introducing or reviewing tree layers with your students.

Review Vocabulary Terms:
annual rings
cambium
cell
heartwood
outer bark
phloem
sapwood
tracheids (conifers)
vessels (deciduous)
xylem

Questions for Students:
1. What layers are found in a tree trunk?
2. What sub-layers are a part of the bark layer?
3. Which layer can you see from the outside?
4. What is each bark layer responsible for?
5. Why do you suppose Native people collected bark from deciduous trees in the spring to summer season (clue: annual rings)?
6. Why would this annual action separate the bark layers from the sapwood?

Take it Further:
Activity 1: Have students make a cross-section diagram of the layers of a tree.
Activity 2: Find cross-cut log sections (6" or larger in diameter, about 2" thick, with outer bark intact), one for each student, and have students mark the tree layers on their cross-cut sections.

Left: The bark layer on Hickory, Poplar, Ash, Oak, Maple, Elm, and other trees were harvested for home coverings. Mature trees could yield up to inch thick bark. Right: The author has peeled off the bark layer of this Poplar tree in Indiana.

Cut & Fold Wigwam

The dome-shaped wigwam was a nuclear family home. This wigwam is covered in cattail mats to insulate against cold winter weather. Although the mats could be removed, the wigwam frame was permanent and didn't move.

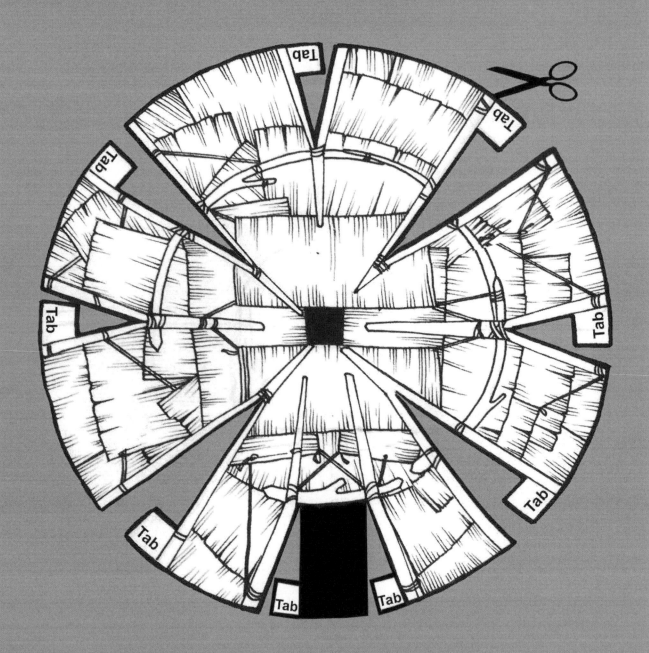

Directions:
Color and cut out the wigwam, keeping tabs attached. Match each slit to its matching side and fold the tab under the matching side and tape in place (underneath). Tip for coloring: Cattail mats were generally tan in color. Use this wigwam in a diorama project or a model village.

Cut & Fold Bark House

Page 1 of 2

These large multi-family homes, sometimes called longhouses, were usually built in summer villages. Covered in thick bark, these homes were permanent structures.

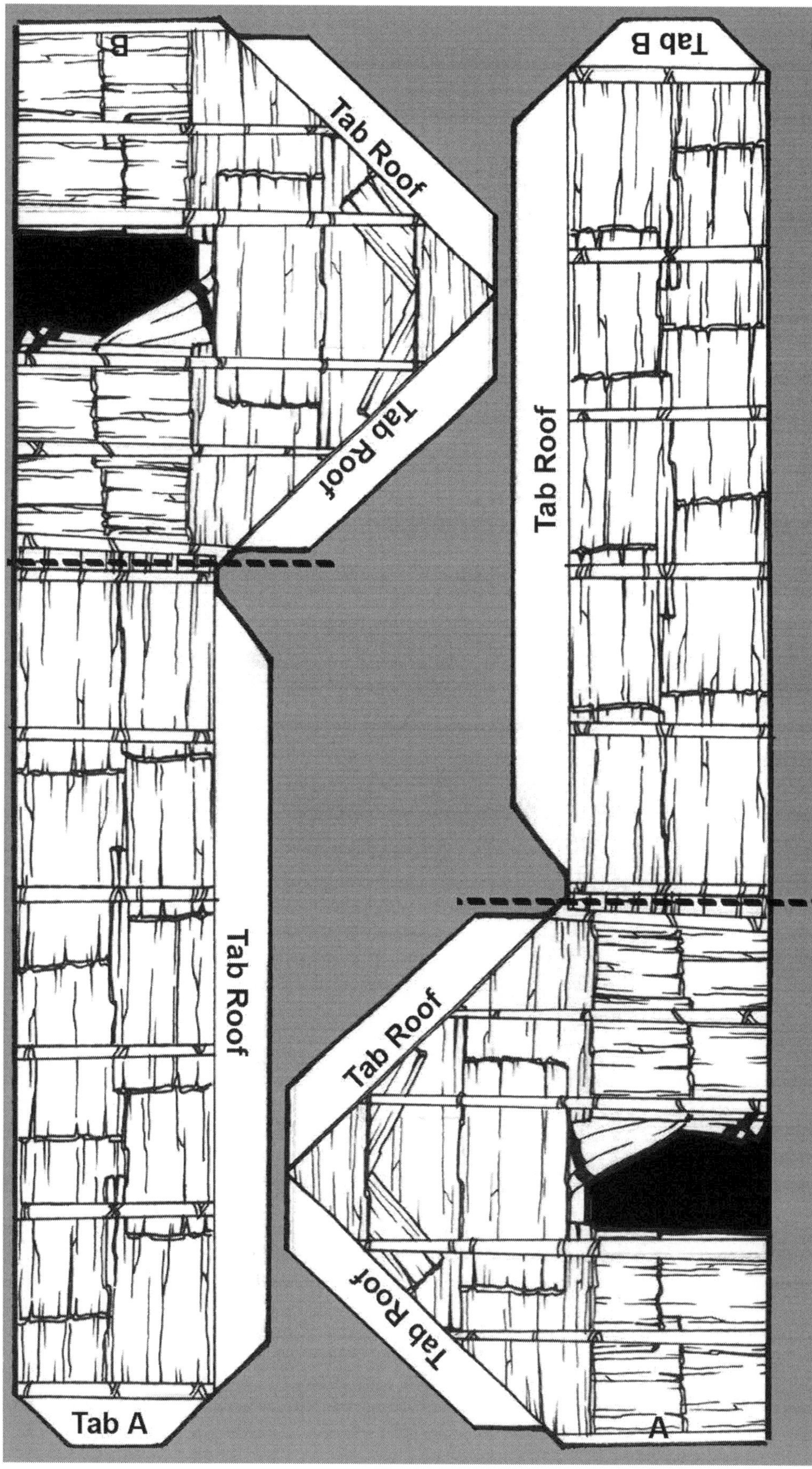

Tab Roof

Tab Roof

Tab Roof

Tab Roof

Tab Roof

Tab Roof

Tab B

Tab B

Tab A

A

B

Directions:
Color and cut out the walls of the bark house, keeping tabs attached. Fold at the dotted lines to create 4 walls. Fold tab A under and attach to side A on opposite wall cut-out, and tape. Repeat for tab B. Fold roof tabs under and tape to the underneath of the roof (on second page). Use this bark house in a diorama project or a model village.

Cut & Fold Bark House
Page 2 of 2

These large multi-family homes, sometimes called longhouses, were usually built in summer villages. Covered in thick bark, these homes were permanent structures.

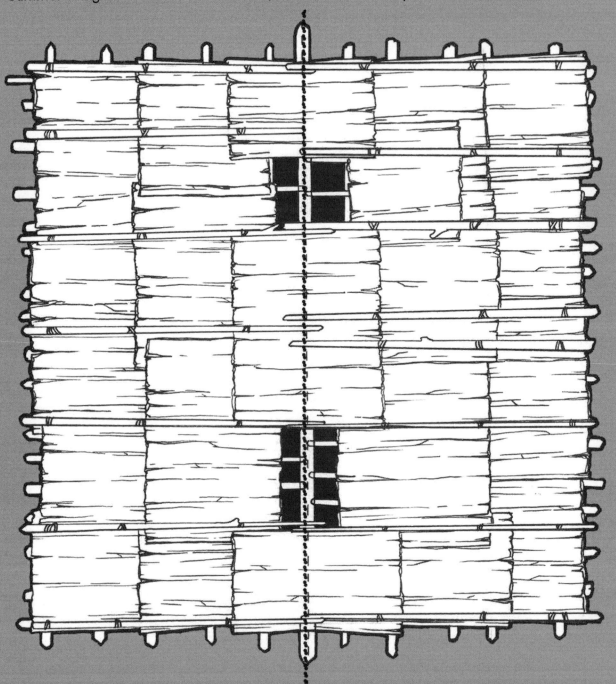

Directions: Color and cut out the roof of the bark house. Fold at the dotted lines to create the roof peak. Attach to bark house walls cut-outs from the previous page to make the structure (roof will overhang on all sides). Use this bark house in a diorama project or a model village.

First-Hand Historical Observation:

Coo-coo-chee's Bark Cabin, 1792

In the early 1790's, the Maumee River in northwestern Ohio was the main "highway" of several Native American villages, including those established near the mouth of the Auglaize River; this area where the two rivers met is also referred to as The Glaize by historians. At The Glaize was established one Miami village, two Delaware villages, three Shawnee villages, and an Indian-friendly European trading town. It has been estimated that the population at The Glaize was probably about 2,000 persons. These residents had recently relocated to The Glaize after being attacked by American troops in their previous villages (including Kekionga) located at present day Fort Wayne, Indiana, in 1790; there, Josiah Harmar's expedition burned down about 300 Native homes and destroyed an estimated 20,000 bushels of corn (keep in mind this was only the food they couldn't save before evacuating – it is believed they took quite of bit of food stores with them before the advance of American troops). These residents rebuilt their villages at the new location at The Glaize.

One resident of The Glaize was Coo-coo-chee – an older Mohawk woman who came to live among the Shawnee. Her bark cabin was situated in between a Miami and Shawnee village, but the language of her home was Shawnee. In the cabin lived herself, her granddaughter, her grandson, and the family dog. In 1792, a white-American captive by the name of Oliver Spencer came to also live in Coo-coo-chee's home. It is from him we have this detailed account of the Mohawk woman's bark house he resided in:

> "Covering an area of fourteen by twenty-eight feet, its frame was constructed of small poles, of which some, planted upright in the ground, served as posts and studs, supporting the ridge poles and eve bearers, while others firmly tied to these by thongs of hickory bark formed girders, braces, laths, and rafters. This frame was covered with large pieces of elm bark seven or eight feet long and three or four feet wide; which being pressed flat and well dried to prevent their curling, fastened to the poles by thongs of bark, formed the weather boarding and roof of the cabin. At its western end was a narrow doorway about six feet high, closed when necessary by a single piece of bark placed beside it, fastened by a brace, set either within or on the outsides the occasion required. Within, separated by a bark partition were two apartments, of which the inner one, seldom entered but by the old [woman], was occupied as a pantry, a spare bedroom, and at times as a sanctuary,..."
> The other room "having on each side a low frame covered with bark and overspread with deerskins serving both for seats and bed steads, was in common use by the family, both as a lodging, sitting, cooking, and eating room. On the ground in the center of this apartment was placed the fire; and over it, suspended from a ridge-pole in the middle of an aperture left for the passage of the smoke, was a wooden trammel for the convenience of cooking (Spencer: 83-84)."

Sources:

Spencer, Oliver M. *The Indian Captivity of O. M. Spencer.* Milo M. Quaife, ed. The Lakeside Press: Chicago, 1917.

Tanner, Helen Hornbeck. *The Glaize in 1792: A Composite Indian Community.* In *American Encounters: Natives and Newcomers from European Contact to Indian Removal, 1500-1850.* Peter C. Mancall and James H. Merrell, ed. Routledge: New York, 2000.

Questions for the Reading "Coo-coo-chee's Bark Cabin, 1792"

Directions: Use the previous text to answer the following history and math questions. You will need to reference other sources to answer questions 1,2,7 and 8.

1. Josiah Harmar's campaign, although succeeded in destroying the abandoned village of Kekionga, mostly failed its mission. His army suffered major defeats, making his expedition the third largest American defeat by Native American forces (in Indiana). The second largest American defeat by Native American forces was The Battle of Little Bighorn in Montana. What was the largest American defeat by Native American forces (clue: it took place in Ohio)?

_____

2. What did Chief Little Turtle have to do with both the third and first largest American defeats by Native American forces (clue: before Little Turtle was a tribal chief, he was an acting _ _ _ chief/captain)?

_____

3. If each bushel of corn destroyed by Harmar's troops equaled 8 dry gallons of shelled corn, how many gallons of corn kernels were being stored by residents in the vicinity Fort Wayne?

_____

4. Use the answer from number 3 to answer this question: If there were 320 families residing in these villages, how many gallons of shelled corn would each have had, had they been divided equally?

_____

5. Using the answer to number 4, let's say each family had 5 persons. How many gallons of corn did each person have a year if it was divided equally? Based in this number, and the fact that this was only the amount of corn left behind, would you say the Native people relied much on their horticultural activities for food?

_____

6. Coo-coo-chee's bark cabin, according to Oliver Spencer's measurements, would have had how much square footage?

_____

7. What is an *aperture*, and why was it needed in the roof of the cabin?

_____

8. What is a *trammel* in the context of this passage?

_____

Miami Village, 1810.

Right: Potawatomi brother and sister in their finest clothing, 1830.

Native American Homes, 1750-1830

By 1800, many Miami, Delaware, and other Native communities were living in homes that resembled more European construction than that of Native origin. Some families kept their traditional, dome-shaped wigwams next to their log cabins because the wigwam could be kept warmer in the wintertime. Native American cultures, like all cultures, change with time. Their villages did too. In 1820, many Miami families lived in log cabins, had European introduced horses and oxen, grew wheat and other foreign crops, and raised hogs and chickens, just like their white-American neighbors. **Can you name two major Native America villages in your state between 1750 and 1830?**

_____

_____

Student Article: Grades 5-12

Native American & Pioneer Technology: A Wigwam Versus a Cabin

The Native American wigwam is generally stereotyped as a small hut that could barely keep its residents comfortable from the harsh weather outside. Nothing could be further from the truth when it came to living in wigwams well insulated for the winter season. In many ways, the Native American wigwam and Euro-American pioneer cabin were very much alike, with one exception: pioneer log cabins were not as heat efficient as wigwams.

Cutaway view of the interior of a wigwam.

A small fire, used for cooking, warmth, and light, was located in the center of the wigwam. The ingenious design and shape of the dome wigwam reflected heat from the fire in the center, and circulated it evenly within the interior living space. In contrast, most Euro-American pioneers built fireplaces on one side of the home, which meant quite a bit of heat produced by the fire was lost to the chimney back wall that was constantly cool from the outside weather – the cool chimney back wall was always draining energy from the fire, making it harder to heat the cabin interior. Keeping the fire in the middle of the home meant all sides around the fire enjoyed its heat, and most heat was kept inside the wigwam and not wasted in heating cold walls. The only drawback to the wigwam's fire was it released more smoke into the interior of the home, making it nearly impossible to breath near the ceiling (one major reason the ceiling couldn't be too low).

The wigwam walls themselves helped to trap heat inside. The reed matting created layers of air spaces that gradually went from cold on the outside to warm on the inside. Our modern conventional homes do this as well, stuffing hollow walls with insulation to create air pockets that keep the home warm. In contrast, pioneer log cabins were built of solid walls. This meant the warmth on the inside was being lost to the cold solid wall that separated inside from outside. A cool wall attracts warmth radiating from the fire, and as it reaches the cool wall surface, the warmth dissipates.

Pioneer cabins also had another problem with walls when it came to keeping a cozy interior – gaps in the walls. The chinking between the logs was notorious for cracking off and exposing openings that let cold air in. Even where cabin roofs met the walls, there were numerous cracks that let the cold in. All these openings caused drafts that pioneer fireplaces couldn't compete with. Contrary to pioneer cabins, wigwams tended to be sealed well when many mats were layered along the walls and ceilings. Indeed, when we think about a home with cold drafts, pioneer log cabins should come to mind over the well-insulated winter wigwam. The wigwam, when built correctly, was a perfect dwelling to cope with the harsh winters of the Northeastern Woodlands.

Project: Make a Sitting Mat

Subjects: Art (Cultural Arts), Social Studies (American History, Cultural Studies)
Grades 1-4

Students will paint their own designs on natural material, woven grass mats.

Materials Needed
-1 grass beach mat per student (dollar beach mats)
-Paint and paint brushes
-Newspapers or drop cloths to protect floor
-Optional: Images of Northeastern Native American mats in museums. One great on-line source is the American Museum of Natural History's Online Ethnographic Collection of North America. Go to *http://anthro.amnh.org/north* and use the following keywords: 'mat' for Search, "MIDWEST" for USA Regions, and "ALL" for Culture.

Procedure
Go over the many decorative designs found on reed mats (optional). Have students design and paint their own 'sitting mats.' Make sure there is enough room to spread out, and that the floor is protected or the painting is done outside. When dried, students can use their mats for usual classroom functions throughout the year, including while sitting outside for special programs.

Woven reed mats were used to line the interior walls for extra insulation, and as ground coverings to create an interior floor. Such interior mats were usually woven with dyed materials that created aesthetically pleasing geometric designs. Photo of the interior of the author's a-frame wigwam exhibit, 2009.

Design Your Own
Woodland Indian Reed Mat

Interior house mats were expertly woven with dyed reeds into geometric patterns. Design your own mat in the blank space above.

Create Your Own Design
On A Natural Fiber Woven Bag

The Native American people made woven bags to store food and clothing.

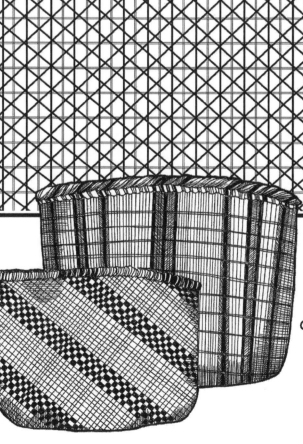

These storage bags were woven of natural fibers from certain plants and tree barks. The designs were created by weaving colorful fibers, colored with dyes obtained from from certain rocks, clays, nuts, and plant roots. The panel above is for you to decorate with a design of your own.

Cut & Fold a Bark Pouch

Directions:
Color the bark pouch and cut it out of the page (keeping tabs connected). Fold along the dotted lines to create the bottom of the pouch. Next tape the tabs under their matching sides (A to A, B to B).

Optional:
When finished, use a hole punch to make 2 holes near the rim on opposite sides. Attach a piece of yarn to both holes to create a handle.

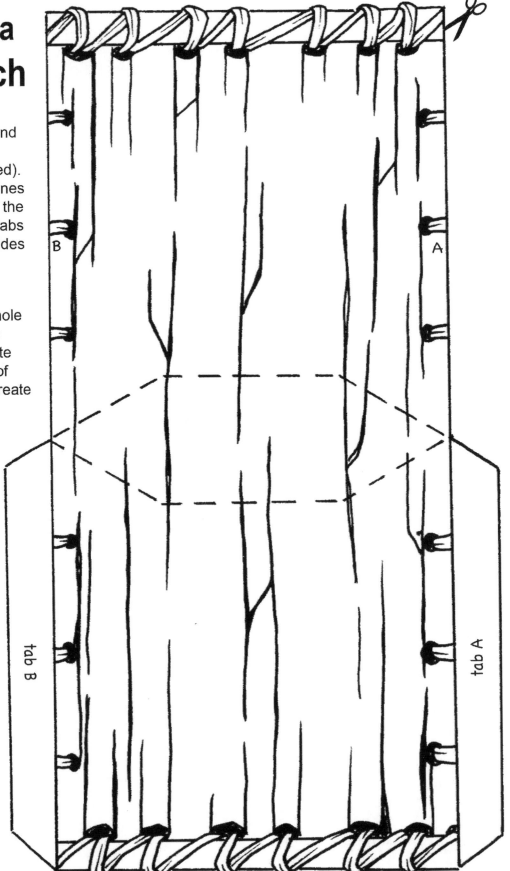

B

A

tab B

tab A

Photo of Poplar bark pouch.

Project: Make a Clay Pot

Subjects: Art (Cultural Arts), Social Studies (American History, Cultural Studies)
Grades 1-5

Students will create replicas of historical Woodland Indian earthenware cooking pots.

Materials Needed
-Air-Hardening Clay
-Incising and Smoothing Tools (toothpicks, smooth stones, natural sponges, etc.)
-Cups or Bowls for Water
-Round Bottom (interior) Cups or Bowls
-Burlap (from a fabric store or use potato sacks)

Preparation
Lay newspaper or tablecloths over exposed tables or floors that need to be protected.

Procedure
With "Woodland Indian Earthenware: Making a Clay Cooking Pot" handout on page 89, have students make these kinds of cooking vessels. The bottom mold can be made of short cups and bowls lined with burlap to simulate the native textiles used on pottery (let the bottom of the pot dry overnight before taking it out of the mold and peeling the burlap away). After pressing the bottom to the mold, build up the pottery walls with coils of clay. Smooth the coils as much as possible. Decorate the pot by incising geometric designs into the clay. Let the pottery dry completely. Do not actually cook in or eat from these pots. These are only meant to be replicas.

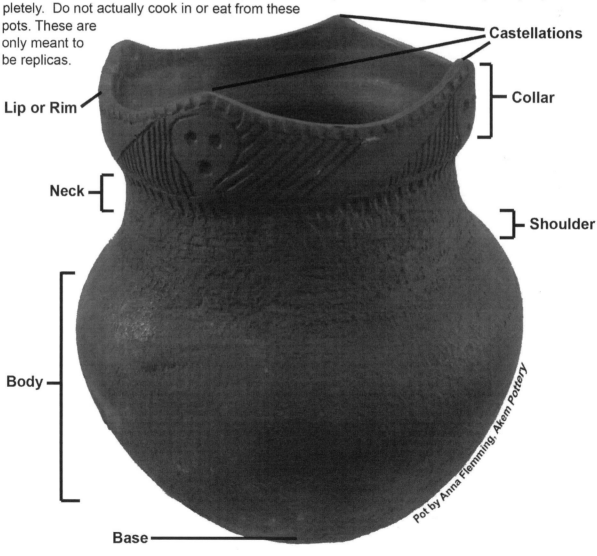

Castellations

Collar

Lip or Rim

Neck

Shoulder

Body

Pot by Anna Flemming, Akem Pottery

Base

Design Your Own Pottery Etching

Instead of painting, most Woodland Indian clay vessels were decorated by etching geometric designs into the clay before it was fully dried. Decorate the large, blank pot below with your own geometric designs.

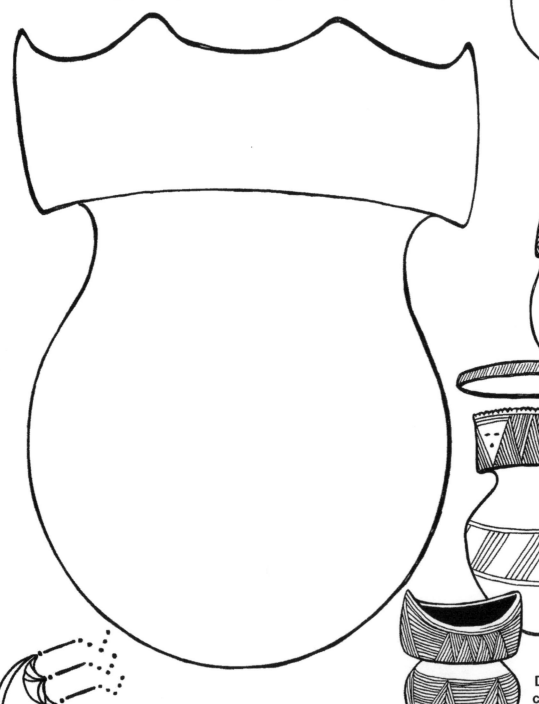

Stone tool used to incise pottery.

Pictured here are four Delaware incised cooking pots and one ceramic disk, which was probably used as a lid or a flat cooking surface.

Northeastern Woodland Indian Earthenware Pottery

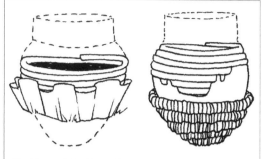

Cooking pots had round or pointed bottoms to help dispurse heat. Uneven heating over a fire could crack pots. This was the first part of the pot to be formed.

Making a Clay Cooking Pot

First, clay was gathered from the source, such as a cache of clay in a lake bed. It was cleaned of contaminants and dried. Then it was pulverized and mixed with water to bring it back to its tacky-clay state. The clay was mixed with ground-up pieces of rock, shell, or broken pottery to temper it.

Tempering the clay made the pot stronger when heated. A ball of this tempered clay was molded in a grass or textile lined hole or basket to create the round bottom of the pottery vessel. The walls were then built up with coils of clay. The coils were pinched together, plastered, and smoothed.

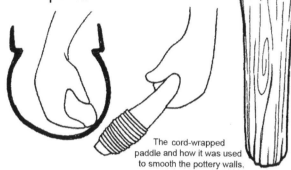

The cord-wrapped paddle and how it was used to smooth the pottery walls.

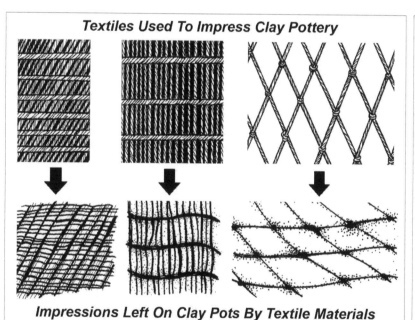

Textiles Used To Impress Clay Pottery

Impressions Left On Clay Pots By Textile Materials

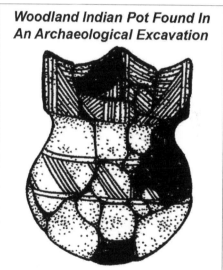

Woodland Indian Pot Found In An Archaeological Excavation

The etching designs on Woodland pottery can help archaeologists put broken pots back together, and date them.

Sometimes a paddle wrapped in natural fiber strings was used to smooth the vessel walls and paddle away any air bubbles that might be trapped in the clay. If the bubbles remained, the pot could break when baking it. The pot was decorated before it was fired. Some Native people used textiles woven from plant fibers to imprint the pottery. Many Woodland Indian vessels were also decorated by incising. The pottery artist would take pointed tools and scratch out designs on the walls of the pot. The pottery was then left to fully dry before it was finally fired. Baking the pottery in a fire made the pot hard and able to hold liquid.

89

Project: Make an 'Imprint on Clay' Chart
Subjects: Art, Social Studies (American History, Cultural Studies)
Grades 3-5

Description
Students will imprint pieces of clay with the same sorts of materials the Woodland Indian people used. Through this exercise, students can gain some understanding of 1. how Native artisans achieved desired pottery textures, and 2. how archaeologists must work backwards from pottery impressions to figure out the materials and textile weaves used to imprint the clay.

Materials
-Air-hardening clay
-1/2" - 3/4" wooden dowel (about a foot in length)
-Role of jute string
-Small decorative fishing net (from craft store)
-Dry corn cobs (you can get corn cobs from squirrel feed corn)
-Yard of burlap (from fabric store or a potato sack)
-2 yards of woven jute rug tape/edging (from fabric store)
-A project board for each student
-A paper plate for each student
-Scissors
-Markers
-Glue

Preparation
Take the jute string and wrap a 4" long section of the dowel with it to create a pottery paddle.

Procedure
First, have each student take a paper plate and write their name on it. Next, have students flatten five pieces of clay (one for each imprint). Imprint each piece of clay, one with the cord-wrapped paddle (by paddling the clay), one with the corn cob (by rolling it over the clay), one with the net (pressed in), one with the burlap (pressed in), and one with the woven rug tape (pressed in). Let the clay pieces dry overnight or longer (until dry) before attaching them to the project board. Have a sample piece of each impression material ready for each student to glue on their boards with the corresponding clay pieces (for the cord-wrapped paddle, just give each student a knot of jute string). Label in marker to complete the chart.

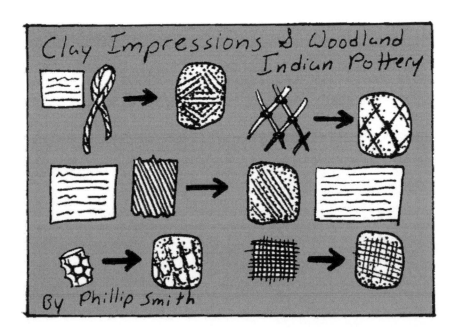

A Native woman cooks food over
a hot fire in her earthenware pot.

Student Article: Grades 7-12

Northeastern Native American Farming

The Importance of Growing Food Among the Native American People

For horticultural-based people like the Miami, Delaware, Wyandot, and Shawnee, farming secured the bulk of the foods they consumed through the year, not hunting. Over half of their diet consisted of crops from the garden, and corn, beans, and squash were highly desired foods, as observed by French trader Nicolas Perrot:

"The kind of food which the [Native people] like the best and which they make the most effort to obtain are the Indian corn, the kidney bean, and the squash. If they are without these, they think they are fasting, no matter what abundance of meat and fish they have in their stores,..." – Nicolas Perrot.

All Corn is Indian Corn

More than just the decorative "Indian corn" we hang on our doors is Native American; all corn is truly Indian corn. All corn in the world today derive their genetics from the many original varieties of Native corn produced in the Americas before European contact. The cornmeal used in corn bread muffins is made from Indian corn, your grits are made from Indian corn, and the sweet corn on the cob you enjoy at barbecues is Indian corn. Native American corn came in many sizes and many colors, however, most Native corn grown historically in our state was white, flesh, and yellow in color, with a couple varieties of blue and red corn.

Can Never Have Too Much Corn

Every day meals were usually corn-based dishes. People like the Miami, Delaware, and Shawnee made hominy, corn puddings, corn soups, and corn breads. Corn bread was made of either dried, ground cornmeal or of mashed green (ripe) corn, or a mixing of both. Corn bread, a staple of Native American diets, was made by cooking it on hot coals or hot rocks, steaming it in green leaves, frying in hot shallow animal fat, boiling in hot water, or baking in the ashes of a hot fire. Cornbread sometimes had other ingredients, including nuts, berries, or pieces of meat. Corn bread has been noted to be sweetened by maple sugar, but, by far, the favorite corn bread consumed by Native people was smeared with animal fat or dipped in meat drippings or broth.

8-Row Historic Northeastern Indian Corn

Like All Good Sisters, They Helped Each Other Grow

Three Sisters gardening was an original practice of the northeastern Native Americans. This gardening technique was defined by complimentary crops – specifically planting a combination of corn, squash, and beans in the same field (as opposed to monoculture where only one crop is planted in a field). Many Native people referred to these crops as the Three Sisters, and like all good sisters, they helped each other grow. Semi-climbing beans found the corn stalks to be sufficient support, while bush beans shaded the base of the corn roots, keeping moisture in the soil where it was needed. Squash did the same as bush beans only over greater distance; the plants vines crawled between the corn mounds, presenting their large, wide leaves to the sun. This not only stopped the hot sun from scorching the earth and stealing moisture, it also discouraged weeds from taking hold. Native farmers only needed to hoe their gardens up to two or three times in the early summer, thanks to the ground coverage of beans and squash. By combining plants, they cultivated more with less work when compared to pioneer farmers. They also didn't need to put themselves in dangerous debt just to farm, as so many European farmers had to do, as the Native people relied on equipment they made themselves at no cost. They needed no loans to purchase metal plows, draft animals, and other equipment. Native farmers didn't need to keep domesticated farm animals for their plow power or manure – a big cost saver. While farming with debt may not seem like such a big deal, keep in mind that if debt wasn't paid in an allotted time, you may be made to forfeit your farm, which wasn't unusual as farms many times failed to produce a sellable surplus. Farming without debt, as the Native people practiced, assured your farm was yours, even if you didn't produce a decent crop. Native farmers need only worry about producing enough crops to feed their families, while the pioneering families worried about both crops to feed their families and their farm animals plus possibly losing the farm farm to debt.

Corn and bean dishes were common in Northeastern Native diets.

Delaware Blue Corn

Corn and Beans: A Beneficial Relationship in the Garden and on the Plate

Sure, the corn stalks provided a structure for bean vines to grow on, but that wasn't the only beneficial result of growing both corn and beans together. Semi-climbing beans also made a latticework between the four to six corn plants sown in each mound. The bean web worked to strengthen the corn against the damaging effects of strong winds and heavy rains that could bend the vulnerable stalks. Corn cannot prosper without human intervention, and part of that intervention may have included methods of supporting weak stalks with beans.

And the codependent nature of beans and corn didn't stop aboveground. Corn needed lots of nitrogen, an element vital to plant cell growth. Beans (legumes) "trapped" nitrogen due to the type of bacteria they host in their roots. When the nitrogen loaded bacteria died, it released its nitrogen into the soil. This is referred to as "nitrogen fixation." Fixation defines the process in which soil bacteria converts atmospheric nitrogen into a stable and biologically usable form. Corn, notorious for draining garden soil of nitrogen, was fed annually a renewing source nitrogen created the by bacteria. Combining corn and bean plants extended the life of Native cornfields by not draining the soil of nutrients with the same intensity as monoculture. By relying on their knowledge of complimentary planting, they didn't need to give extra time to fertilizing their fields with manure like the pioneers did.

Combining corn and beans also continued after the growing season, as corn and bean dishes were very popular. Soft whole beans were baked in corn breads, or the dry beans were ground into a meal that was mixed with cornmeal and made into breads, puddings, and liquid baby food. Combining whole kernel corn and beans made a dish referred to as succotash, a Native plural meaning "cooked whole grains." While the flavor combination was considered complimentary, the combination of such had less superficial benefits on the diet of the Woodland Indian peoples. The nutritional value of corn and beans were boosted when consumed together, as together they formed a "complete protein." A complete protein is a protein that contains all of the essential amino acids. Complete proteins are found naturally in meats and few plant sources, making the combination of corn and beans crucial in the diets of the corn-based peoples of Native America, including many communities in our state.

Squash: A Favored "Ground Fruit" of the Native American Garden

The horticultural Woodland Indian people were noted to love the taste of the squash and pumpkins they cultivated. These plants that were grown across floor of their cornfields (3-Sisters cultivation) were coveted for their refreshing flavor. Its flesh was added to soups, breads, and "samp," a favorite dish similar to cream of corn. Squash and pumpkins were also enjoyed alone, roasted and mashed or just plain raw - the name "squash" is shortened from the Atlantic Coastal Algonquian term "askutasquash" meaning "to be eaten green" or "to eat raw." Whether summer or winter squash, it was consumed with much delight. Delaware cooks were noted to favor steaming the squash in its own juice, which they believe yielded the most pleasant of flavors. To do this, they put only a minimal amount of water with the squash in a pot, then covered it with green leaves and heated it over a fire; the steamed squash was consumed, and the broth left behind was sipped up. To save the squash past winter, they were cut up into rings and hung to dry. Being dehydrated they would save for months, if not years.

Another Cultivated Plant - Neither From Jerusalem nor an Artichoke

Another plant cultivated in Native fields was the sunflower. Sunflowers produced seeds that could be eaten, but many utilized the seeds to make sunflower oil. To do this, they crushed the seeds, and then boiled the seed mash in water to extract the oil. Such oils were used for anything from cooking to skin and hair conditioner. But there was a type of sunflower coveted for its edible tuber – the Jerusalem artichoke. No, the Jerusalem artichoke was neither from Jerusalem nor an artichoke - this name seemed to be a corruption of an Italian term for the edible root. The Jerusalem artichoke is a sunflower plant that originated in America, and because of this mislabeling, many grocery markets that do sell the tuber do so under the name "sunchoke." The Native people are believed to have cultivated this plant, and those who didn't still harvested and ate the sunchokes that volunteered to grow around the corn fields. Sunchokes were boiled, roasted, baked, fried, or just eaten raw.

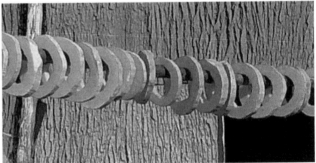
Squash is cut into rings and hung to dehydrate in the sun.

Sources:
-"A Woodland Feast. Native American Foodways of the 17th & 18th Centuries" by Carolyn Raine
-"History, Manners, and Customs of the Indian Nations Who Once Inhabited Pennsylvania and the Neighbouring States" by John Heckewelder
-"How Indians Use Wild Plants for Food, Medicine, & Crafts" by Francis Densmore
-"Indian New England Before the Mayflower" by Howard S. Russell
-"Memoir on the Manners, Customs, and Religion of the Savages of North America" by Nicolas Perrot in "The Indian Tribes of the Upper Mississippi Valley and Region of the Great Lakes."
-"Nitrogen Fixation by Legumes" by W.C. Lindemann, Soil Microbiologist, and C.R. Glover, Extension Agronomist. New Mexico State University, College of Agriculture

A Woodland Indian mother and daughter
harvest corn in their garden, 1600.

Growing Food

People like the Delaware, Miami, Shawnee, Potawatomi and Wyandot relied heavily on their gardens for foods.

Hoes & Dibble Sticks

In these cultures, women were the main farmers, but men also had gardening tasks to perform. Men had to cut down trees and burn back the underbrush to clear the fields. They usually also had a hand in harvesting and burning dead stalks left after the harvests. The women took charge of the planting, hoeing, and weeding. These women were expert farmers: they soaked seeds to start them sooner, they combined certain plants that benefited each other in growing, and these farming women created new and different corn varieties.

A Native woman offers tobacco to the soil before planting. Such an offering can be thought of as a form of prayer.

Taking More Than Farming Away From Native Women

Euro-Americans tried to make the gender roles in Native societies resemble theirs, where men were the farmers. But farming was more than just a task - it was Native women's livelihoods. Through farming and gathering, Native women provided more than half of the food their families consumed, and they used the surplus for trade. Their farming activities were respected and probably reinforced woman's rights to own property. Euro-Americans weren't "freeing up" Native women of their hard work - they were taking away their occupation and whatever rights that were associated with it. Native men and women both understood the ramifications of women losing their livelihoods, as one Native man demonstrated by stating, *"My young men are to...take up the work of the women; they will plow the field and raise the crops; for them I see a future, but my women, they to whom we owe everything, what is there for them to do? I see nothing!... Have pity on my women when everything is taken from them* (Alice Fletcher: 1888)."

Delaware Women Hoeing Their Garden

1500

1700

Bringing Home the Harvest

Large amounts of crops had to be processed in a timely manner.

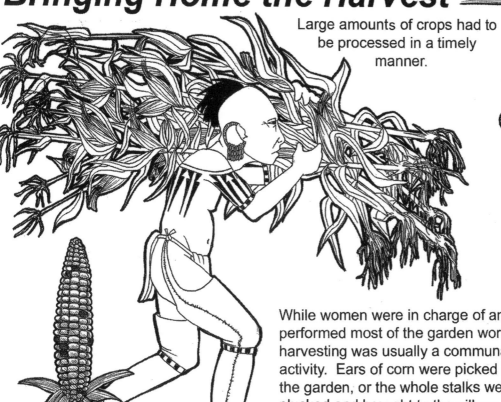

While women were in charge of and performed most of the garden work, harvesting was usually a communal activity. Ears of corn were picked in the garden, or the whole stalks were plucked and brought to the village where people were waiting to husk the corn. Some corn wasn't fully dry at harvest time and so had to be braided and hung to finish drying.

Husking Bees
Many Woodland Indian communities conducted 'husking bees,' where groups of people came together to process corn for drying while enjoying each others' company. Singing and joking was usual, and mothers proudly showed off their unwed sons and daughters. Husking bees were a perfect time to socialize.

97

The Math of Woodland Indian Farming

Directions: Imagining yourself as a historic Native American farmer, answer these questions.

1) On average, an adult eats one ear of corn a day, and a child eats one half an ear of corn a day. In your longhouse there are 8 adults and 6 children. What is the least amount of ears of corn needed to feed your family for a year?

Answer:_____

2) It takes 4 sq. ft. of garden space to grow about 11 ears of corn. How many sq. ft. are needed to grow enough corn to feed your family for one year? Use the answer from question 1 to answer this question.

Answer:_____

3) Not only does your family grow enough corn for themselves, but they also grow extra corn to feed guests, to contribute to feasts and festivals, and to trade to Europeans. This means your family will grow about 350 extra ears of corn. Using the information from question 2, what is the total size of your family's garden including the area needed to grow extra corn for sharing and trading?

Answer:_____

Delaware women and children
drying corn, squash, and beans, 1816.

Name _____   Date _____

Growing Food Among The Native American People

Much of the food Native American people ate was from their gardens. There was a lot of work involved in growing food.

The land had to be cleared of all the trees. Why do you think they had to remove the trees from the garden area?_____

_____

_____

_____

The men would chop down trees with their stone axes.

To make the work easier, they would set fires to the bases of the trees.

The fire would do most of the work by burning through the bottoms of the trees. The men then had less to chop. Then the women took over. Women were in charge of the gardens. They would rake dirt into little hills, and then plant seeds into the hills.

They planted different seeds for different plants. Can you name 3 kinds of crops they grew?_____

_____

While the plants grew, they were taken care of by the mothers and children. They weeded the garden, scared away animals that would eat their crops, and brought the plants water when it had not rained in a long time. When the crops were ready, everyone helped to pick them.

Activity: 3-Sisters Cookout

Subjects: Health (Nutrition), Social Studies (American History, Cultural Studies)
Grades 1-5

Description
Students will enjoy a meal of corn, beans, and squash cooked in historic Native fashion on an open fire. Use this activity as the backdrop for discussions about nutritional values and benefits.

Ingredients
-corn on the cob (still in husk), one for each person
-sugar pumpkins, one for every 5-7 people
-green beans (fresh, not canned or frozen), one pound for every 5-7 people
-sunflower oil
-maple syrup (pint for up to 5 sugar pumpkins)

Materials
-cast iron pot or camp pot (must be able to go over a fire - no rubber handles)
-grill and bricks (to make a flat surface to set pot on over the fire)
-large spoon (to stir and scoop the beans)
-pair of grilling tongs
-oven mitts
-clean plastic bucket or storage bin (to soak corn in)
-paper plates
-plastic spoons
-enough firewood to cook for up to an hour (plus a way to start it and put it out)
-blankets or mats for students to sit on (tip: complete *Activity: Make a Sitting Mat* first, on page 83.

Procedure
First, soak the corn (in its husk) in a bucket of water for at least 2 hours before cooking. Some teachers and/or chaperones should light the fire 45 minutes in advance of the students' arrival. 20 minutes after lighting the fire, place sugar pumpkins next to the fire, and on top of coals as the wood burns down. The sugar pumpkins will take an hour to cook. Keep rotating them to blacken all sides of the pumpkins. When the students arrive at the fire area, put the corn (still in its husk) on the coals. Rotate corn to blacken all sides. Dip back into the water up to 2 times to keep the husk from catching on fire. While the corn and pumpkins are roasting, heat about a half an inch of oil in the metal pot. Throw green beans in (already snapped of their ends) and stir and fry until brown on most sides. Then serve. Once cooled, beans can be eaten with fingers. Corn should be ready when husk is black and burned a bit on all sides. Peel back husk and enjoy. Pumpkins should be black and unable to keep their shapes. Cut into their tops, scoop out the seeds, mash and mix some maple syrup into the pumpkin meat. *Tip: Assign a chaperone to each food being cooked, making sure each item is rotated and cooked well.*

Discussion
Corn, beans, and squash provide much in the way of nutrition. Discuss what vitamins and minerals are present in each food, and how much protein and fiber a serving of corn, beans, or squash provides. What are the benefits of diets high in fiber, and what does protein do for the body? Take the discussion further by referring to *Lesson: A Complete Protein* (p. 103), and discuss why consuming corn and beans together is beneficial. Make sure to address the maple syrup. Why is it that maple sugar/syrup has more vitamins and minerals than processed white cane sugar? Why is sugar necessary in our diets, but too much can be harmful? Refer to *Activity: Tap a Sugar Maple Tree* (pgs. 115-6) for more information on the nutritional content of maple sugar/syrup.

Name _____   Date _____

Directions: Draw a Woodland Indian '3 Sisters' garden in the box below.

My 3 Sisters Garden

Name _____ Date _____

Directions: Draw the animals that might try to eat garden plants in the box below.

Animals In The Garden

Lesson: A Complete Protein

Subjects: Health (Nutrition), Science (Biology), Social Studies (American History, Cultural Studies)
Grades 5-12

Discussion

A complete or whole protein is a protein source that provides all nine essential amino acids, and provides them in the correct proportions that supports biological functioning in the body.

The nine essential amino acids are:
- Tryptophan
- Threonine
- Isoleucine
- Leucine
- Lysine
- Methionine + Cystine
- Phenylalanie + Tyrosine
- Valine
- Histidine

Essential amino acids are amino acids the human body cannot produce but needs to survive. We must be able to obtain these amino acids through our food. Students should understand how protein benefits the human body, and how much we should consume on a daily basis.

Complete proteins can be found in meat, poultry, fish, milk, and eggs, as well as a few plant sources. Grains are particularly known to lack substantial amounts of some of these amino acids.

Corn, the main grain and food staple of the horticultural Northeastern Native Americans, is considered a healthy food with a fair amount of nutritional value, with notable exceptions. One of these exceptions is corn protein failing to provide good amounts of tryptophan and lysine. However, pairing corn with other vegetables, such as beans, raises the nutritional value by creating a "complete protein." Have students look up the essential amino acid levels of corn and beans (kidney or white navy beans), as well as their other nutritional values (fiber, minerals, vitamins, etc.).

Bean and corn dishes were prevalent in Native American cuisine. Succotash was a Native dish of Northeastern Native communities; the word "succotash" comes from Native terminology which translates to "cooked whole grains." It was originally a dish of only corn and beans (with animal fat for flavoring), until American Southern cuisine redefined it to include tomatoes, okra, and/or pork.

Take the lesson further by discussing other popular bean and grain combinations from other world cuisines such as:
- Chickpeas and Couscous
- Hummus and Pita Bread
- Lentils and Rice
- Red Beans and Rice
- Corn Tortilla Chips and Refried Bean Dip
- Bean Burrito with Corn Tortilla
- American Southern Succotash
- Bean Chilli and Corn Bread

Consider throwing a "Complete Protein" feast. Have each student provide a dish that combines grain and bean ingredients as its main components. Such a tasty event might provide a good backdrop to discussions on nutrition and culture.

Lesson: Hominy for Health

Subjects: Health (Nutrition), Science (Biology), Social Studies (American History, Cultural Studies)
Grades 5-12

Background

The word "hominy" comes from the Virginia Native American term "rockahominy," which had probably referred to maize (corn) in some capacity, whether it be general or a certain dish or product. Some believe it specifically referred to parched cornmeal, but the term is now applied to a certain corn dish we know today as hominy which originated among the corn consuming peoples of the Americas.

Hominy is not a variety of the maize species - it is the product of a process called nixtamalization. The general process included using an alkali to remove the hulls and swell the kernels. In the Northeast, the historic Native peoples used ash and water to create the alkali bath that was used to remove or burn off the hulls of the Flint corn, after which, the kernels - now hominy - were rinsed of the alkali solution. Large amounts of ash residue, or lye, was poisonous if consumed, so the hominy had to be rinsed thoroughly.

The finished hominy could be cooked and served right away as whole kernels, mixed with meat, fish, root vegetables, or beans. They also cooked it with maple sugar and/or bear grease for flavor. The hominy could be mashed into a pudding and eaten, or the mashed hominy could be patted into small cakes and shallow fried, baked, or boiled to make dumplings and breads. Or the hominy could be dried and saved for later use, at which point, it could be hydrated and treated as just mentioned above, or the dry hominy could first be ground into a flour and then hydrated and used to make corn breads or pudding (grits).

Besides giving the corn a pleasant texture and taste, and softening the hard Flint corn kernels (the common modern descendent known as decorative Indian corn), nixtamalization also changed the nutritional makeup of the corn kernels. While it decreased the overall nutritional value of the corn (as it destroyed the hull), it actually boosted the absorbency of some vitamins it provided. For example, nixtamalization released niacin in the hull into the kernel where it was freely able to be absorbed by the human body. The human digestive system does not digest corn hulls well, an area of the kernel that contains vitamins and fiber. Without this process, corn-based peoples, such as many Native American societies, could have suffered of pellagra.

It is also worth noting that traditional tortillas were made not from plain cornmeal but from hominy meal. Here in the Northeast, the Native people used ashes to create the alkali needed for the nixtamalization, however in the Southwest and Central America, the Native peoples used lime for their alkali. Tasty and nutritional hominy was produced of either alkali solution.

Discussion

With this information in mind, hold a classroom discussion on how the Native peoples manipulated their foods to meet their nutritional needs. Define nixtamalization. What different ingredients can create an alkali suitable to make hominy? What is the most commercial alkali used today to make the canned hominy sold in our supermarkets? Research pellagra and what it did historically to some poorer communities in the American South. Could they have avoided such a disease if they had turned more of their corn into hominy like the Native Americans? Does pellagra still exist and is it rare? Why does it still exist and where in the world?

Take it Further

Consider making a modern "Native American Foods Stew." Use two 14.5 ounce cans of hominy and cook for a least an hour in its own canning juices and water, then combine with canned diced tomatoes and turkey broth. Add diced sweet peppers, potatoes, leeks and cook for another hour or so. Finish with a can of cooked red kidney beans and diced summer squash, then season to taste. Cook for only 15 more minutes then put into the fridge overnight, and heat and serve in class the next day.

The Native people ate corn almost everyday. They enjoyed corn soup, corn bread, and roasted cob corn. They especially liked to eat corn with beans, a dish called succotash, and they enjoyed corn made into tasty hominy.

The hominy had to be rinsed several times to make sure all the ash residue was gone. Too much ash residue can be poisonous if eaten. The rinsed, clean hominy is very nutritious. Hominy had more niacin than plain corn.

Hominy was made by boiling corn in water with ashes. The ashes removed the outer layer or hull of the corn kernels. It also swelled the kernels making them large, chewy, and very tasty. The hominy was then rinsed.

Activity: Cook Traditional Green Corn Husk Bread

Subjects: Social Studies (American History, Cultural Studies)
Grades 1-7

This particular manner of baking bread was recorded as an Iroquois dish in the early 1900's. While recorded from the Iroquois, it was most likely traditionally made by many Native communities. No "recipes" as in ingredient measurements were recorded historically, so I have given the general measurements I use when making this dish for my own Native foods cooking demos.

Their many cornbread recipes called for two major types of cornmeal batter: the type made from dry cornmeal and the type made from juiced green corn. This recipe combines both batters, as many Native American cornbreads did. Because they didn't use wheat flour, the bread has a very strong, corny taste. And because they used no leavening agents, it is a very dense type of bread. Traditionally made with no European introduced ingredients, such Native bread can be a great food for those on wheat, egg, and/or milk-free diets.

Procedure:

Follow the following recipe and bake traditional green corn husk bread for your students to try.

Ingredients (Enough For 30 Students):
- 24 fresh cobs of sweet corn
- 3 cups of traditional cornmeal or pre-cooked cornmeal (pre-cooked is smother and recommended)
- 2/3 cup of maple syrup, or up to 1/4 cup maple sugar
- ---Optional--- cup of fresh/frozen berries (blueberries, blackberries, and/or raspberries are appropriate for Indiana and Ohio) or crushed nuts (chestnuts, hickories, or walnuts) to add to the batter (Warning: be very aware of your students' allergies before serving certain fruits and nuts in your cornbread)

Instructions:

Along with the ingredients, you will also need a cheese grater, package of cornhusk, a small 2-3 quart pot that can be put into the oven, and a lid (doesn't have to be the same size as the pot). Soak the cornhusk in water 4 hours before baking, or the night before.

Forty minutes before baking, husk the corn, then taking the corncobs, grate them on the cheese grater over or on a dish to catch the mashed kernels and juices. Make sure all sides of each cob are grated, and you have gotten as much juice from the cobs as possible. Be careful not to scrape your skin across the grater; children shouldn't grate the corn. By grating and not cutting the kernels off, more corn juice is extracted and fewer hulls are put into the cornmeal dough (and those hulls that are have already been cut open, releasing the soft interior corn kernel. In case fresh corn is out of season, you can substitute canned cream-of-corn that has been processed through a blender (about 3 standard cans). While this substitution works, it is not recommended as first choice as it does sacrifice the fine taste (a little more sugar may need to be used in this treatment) and freshness is what this bread was traditionally known for.

Preheat the oven to 375-390 degrees. Combine the grated corn kernel mass and juice with a cup of cornmeal and mix together. Then add in and mix together the maple sugar or syrup into the batter. The quantity of sugar depends on your liking - sugar to taste. Take the husks out of the water they have been soaking in, and line the bottom and sides of the pot with them, 2 layers. This is tricky for many, so you may want to practice this before you make the batter. Carefully spoon your batter into the husk-lined pot. If you are adding berries or nuts, it is suggested that they are added while the dough is being spooned into the vessel. After an inch or two of batter is added, add some berries or nuts, and add another layer of batter and repeat. This will help to distribute the berries or nuts throughout the loaf. Cover top with more husk and the pot lid.

Bake for 1 hour and 20 minutes, then check to make sure it is cooked through and through. Prick with a wooden skewer to test the bread interior. If it needs more time, put back in the oven and take out when ready. Cut back the top husks and serve with a spoon.

Tip: Follow up this meal with related nutritional questions like: "Why might it be more beneficial to pop open the kernels than just cut them off the cob?" and "Do the hulls inhibit the human digestive system from absorbing most the nutrients found inside the kernels?"

Uncovered baked green corn husk bread.

Native Technology: The Mortar & Pestle

What is a Mortar and Pestle?

A mortar and pestle is a tool used to grind whole foods into flours, meals, and powders. The mortar provides a concave area to hold the food within it securely while pressure is applied with the pestle to the food. The pestle is the cylindrical tool used to crush the food in the mortar. The pestle is moved up and down, grinding the food in between the walls and floor of the mortar.

Illustration: An older man burns out a new mortar for his niece. The woman grinds corn into meal using a smaller wooden mortar and pestle, about 1600.

Illustration: A Delaware woman grinds meal in her wooden mortar and pestle, about 1800. The mortar and pestle continued to be a viable food processing utensil long after European contact and influence.

The Wooden Corn Mortar and Pestle

Mortars and pestles could be made of stone or wood, and many were small for processing little amounts of foods, medicines, dyes, and more. It was however the larger "corn mortar" and pestle that was used to process daily amounts of foods efficiently. Well known to process corn into meal, these wooden mortars and pestles crushed most of the family meals, including beans, nuts, and dried foods in general. Corn mortars were usually made of an upright log, with a basin made in the top. This was accomplished by using fire to hollow it, and scraping away the ashes as the fire burned to reveal a cavity. Every mortar needed a pestle. The pestles could be up to 3 feet in length, and were heavy too. This was so the weight of dropping the pestle on the foods crushed the foods with ease. Care was taken to shape the end of the pestle to fit snugly to the bottom of the mortar, so the food would be smashed efficiently which would save time and energy. While women generally used the mortars and pestles to process the corn into meal, it was the job of the men to make their female relatives mortars and pestles.

20 Modern Dishes That Resemble or Are Born of Historic Northeastern Native American Dishes

Boston Baked Beans	Hominy
Clam & Fish Chowders	Hushpuppies
Clambakes & Steamers	Johnny Cakes (Pone)
Cornbread & Spoon Bread	Nut Breads & Berry Cakes
Cranberry Sauce	Onion Soup
Cream of Corn	Polenta
Dumplings	Baked Squash
Escalloped Oysters	Succotash
Fried Green Beans	Tamales
Cooked Greens & Salads	Turkey & Goose Roasts

Worksheets: "Turtle Island Eatery" Menu and Q&A Worksheet
Subjects: Social Studies (American History, Cultural Studies)
Grades 4-7

Description
Students will learn about Native American foods and diets of the Ohio and Indiana region in 1750 by reading about it in a 'menu' format. They then can answer the questions posed to them on the following Q&A page.

Procedure
Make copies of the menu (next 4 pages) for each student. Review it as a class. Point out ingredients students are familiar with, like corn and maple sugar, that originated with the Native people. Highlight dishes, like hominy and johnny cakes, that originated with the Native people which we still make and eat today. Take note of what are considered non-Native ingredients, like pork, and non-Native tastes, such as salty (as in directly making the salty flavor by adding salt).

Next, make copies of the menu "Questions & Answers Worksheet" and pass them out to the students. Choose to answer the questions as a class, or, have students complete the worksheets for homework and review the answers as a class.

Answer Key For Questions & Answers Worksheet:

Number 1:
All fresh produce were only available at one time of the year, when they were ripe. However, most dishes on the menu can be made with dehydrated foods. Cornmeal, used in corn bread, is from dried corn which can be stored year-round. Corn on the cob needs green corn, or ripe corn, still in its husk. There are no dried substitutes for corn on the cob. Another example is blackberries in puddings and breads which could be used fresh or dried for these dishes. However they have to be fresh to snack on as a ripe fruit.

Number 2:
Meat was not the main food of Indiana and Ohio's Native people. Large kills like deer were sporadic, and not a controllable food source like that of their gardens. Meat, whether fresh or dried, was not eaten everyday. Most Native people of this area may be described as horticulturists who hunted and gathered (not hunters and gatherers who gardened). Much more food was gained through their farming than their hunting activities. Even those who relied little on farming acquired more foods through gathering, which included fishing.

Number 3:
Corn was the main crop of the Miami, Shawnee, Delaware (Lenape) and neighboring tribes. It was a widely available crop grown in high quantities. It was easy to dry and store for later use. Because it created the largest percentage of a single food eaten by the Native people, it was found in almost every dish and recipe, including foods and formulas made for babies.

Number 4:
The answer is d. more than 60%
Remind students that more than corn came from the Americas. Potatoes, tomatoes, chocolate, vanilla, peanuts, pecans, maple syrup, cranberries, many varieties of peppers, beans, and squash, and much more.

Turtle Island Eatery

*Specializing in Traditional Foods
From All Native Communities of The
Old Northwest Indian Territories*

Established 1750

Menu

Turtle Island Eatery Foods From All Native Communities of The Old Northwest Indian Territories, 1750.

Soups
All Soups Come With Baked, Boiled or Fried Husk Bread

Wild Onion & Garlic Soup
Wild onions and garlic boiled in deer or rabbit broth.

Dry Corn Soup
Few varieties of dried Northern Flint Corn, hydrated, and boiled down with a bit of maple sugar for flavor.

3 Sisters Soup
Corn, beans, and squash soup. Squash blossoms are added to thicken and flavor.

Crawfish Chowder
Crawfish, mussels, Jerusalem artichokes, and corn.

Small Game Stew of the Day

Corn, beans, Jerusalem artichokes and 2-3 different meats and fish. Usual catches are catfish, turtle, duck, turkey, rabbit, beaver, raccoon, and/or squirrel.

Sides
-Mashed Jerusalem Artichoke
-Kettle Fried Green Beans*
-Cooked Greens (Lamb's Quarter)
-Roasted Corn on the Cob*
-Roasted Onions & Garlic*
-Baked, Boiled or Fried Husk Bread
-Boiled Chestnuts
-Wild Rice with Blueberries
(Ojibwa harvested - Imported from the Western Great Lakes)

Puddings

Parched Corn Pudding
Dry roasted corn is crushed into meal and cooked into pudding. Seasoned with Maple sugar and bear grease.

Hickory Nut Pudding
Hickory nuts crushed into a meal and mixed with cornmeal and cooked into pudding.

Corn & Squash Pudding
Squash and cornmeal cooked into pudding. Seasoned with maple sugar.

Extra to add blackberries to pudding.

By The Pot or Scoop

Baked Scraped Green Cornbread*
Green corn scraped off the cob (with its own juice or milk) combined with dry cornmeal is baked in a green leaf lined kettle. Order single servings or a full kettle for your table. A large kettle will feed a party of 14-18.

Baked Squash With Hickory Nuts*
Squash baked in its own shell is mashed with hickory nuts and seasoned with maple sugar. Order a scoop or the full squash. Each squash feeds up to 4 diners.

* Dishes from in-season foods.

111

Specials

Hominy
Delaware Blue Flint Corn, soaked in hardwood ashes and rinsed thoroughly. Choose between traditional (Native-style seasoned with maple sugar and bear grease) or ethnic (European-style seasoned with salt and butter).

Succotash
Baked corn and beans. Choose from traditional (Native-style seasoned with bear grease) or ethnic (with chunks of European salt pork).

Baked Beans
Beans slow baked over a low fire in clay kettle. Seasoned with maple sugar. Served with a baked, boiled or fried husk bread (cornmeal bread cooked in corn husk).

Dumplings
Dumplings made from Miami White Flour Corn. Dumplings are boiled in your choice of fish, turkey, or hickory nut broth with chunks of vegetables and greens.

Deer Dippers*
Roasted and skewered deer meat (venison). Comes with bear grease and maple sugar for dipping. *For the whole table: Order Fondue-Style Deer Dippers. Feeds up to 6 diners.*

Liver & Onions*
Deer liver grilled on a hot rock. Served with roasted wild onions.

Baked Fish
In season fish, cased in clay and baked in an open fire. Served with a baked, boiled or fried husk bread.

Shellfish & Root Medley*
Hot-stone roasted mussels, crawfish, ground nuts, and Jerusalem artichokes.

*Check for the availability of fresh venison dishes. Fresh meat is served every 2 weeks, as it is hunted. Fresh roasted ground nuts, Jerusalem artichokes, and wild onions are seasonal. When out of season, these roots can be served in a soup (made from dried root vegetables). The availability of the other dishes (fresh or dried) are year-round.

Patron _____   Date _____

House Salad

Fresh baby onion tops, lamb's quarters, young milkweed greens, and cattail shoots (young inner sprouts)*

Seasonal Fresh Snacks

-Blueberries*
-Blackberries*
-Raspberries*
-Squash Slices*

Beverages

-Sassafras Tea
-Parched Corn Coffee (Iroquois recipe)
-Corn Broth (water from boiling corn bread)
-Berry Drink (from in-season berries)*
-Maple Sugar Water

* Dishes from in-season foods.

Fresh Take-Home From Our Bakery

Ash Cakes
Dry cornmeal bread baked on hot rocks.

Johnny Cakes
Dry cornmeal bread fried in animal oil.

Green Corn Fritters*
Scraped green corn mixed with dry cornmeal, fried in animal oil.

Acorn & Corn Fritters
Cornmeal and leached acorn nut meal bread, fried in nut oil.

Cattail Root & Corn Biscuits
Cornmeal and cattail root flour bread, baked on hot rocks or in an iron skillet.

Husk Bread
Cornmeal bread wrapped in corn husk, baked, boiled or fried.

Baked Scrapped Green Corn Bread*
Scrapped green corn, in all of its juice/milk, combined with dry cornmeal is baked in a green leaf lined kettle.

Turtle Island Eatery
Foods From All Native Communities of The Old Northwest Indian Territory, 1750.

Menu

Questions & Answers Worksheet

1. Some dishes are only seasonally available, while others are available year-round. For example, most of the corn breads are made and eaten all year long, however, corn on the cob is a seasonal dish. Why is this when both are made of corn?

_____

_____

_____

2. The "Specials" page of the menu states that fresh deer meat is only available once every 2 weeks. Why is fresh deer only available every two weeks or so? What does this say about the Native American diet during this time? According to the whole menu, do they eat more meat or more vegetables?

_____

_____

_____

_____

_____

3. So many of their dishes use corn as an ingredient. Why?

_____

_____

_____

4. **Make an Educated Guess**
What is the estimated percentage of foods we eat today that originated in the Americas? Circle One:

a. less than 30%   b. more than 30%

c. more than 45%   d. more than 60%

5. **Become The Chef**
So many Native dishes, like the corn dishes, are variations of other dishes. Combine 2 or more dishes in this menu to create a new, unique dish. Name the dish, describe it, and draw a picture of it in the space at the right.

Draw Picture of Dish Here:

Name of Dish:

Description of Dish:

_____

_____

_____

Activity: Tap a Sugar Maple Tree
Subjects: Science (Environmental Science), Social Studies (American History, Cultural Studies)
Grades 1-8

What you will need:
-Access to Sugar Maple trees
-Drill (preferably cordless or manual, depending how far the trees are from a power source)
-Taps (metal or plastic - plastic is usually more available and less expensive)
-Drill bit that matches tap size (snug)
-Rubber mallet
-Buckets to catch sap (some hang on trees, others sit on the ground with optional tubing to guide sap)

Procedure:
Read "Nutritional Value and Today's Sugar Culture" on the next page. You will need to look up the start of your 'sap run' season, as this will vary depending on your location, elevation, and the weather (ex. for some, tapping may start in mid-February, others at the end of February, and still others in March - the northern and southern regions of Indiana and Ohio can have a couple weeks difference in the start of the sap run season). If you can not easily find this information, contact a local maple syrup producer who can tell you when they start their tapping and collecting.

Locate mature Sugar Maple trees (no less than 1 foot diameter). With your students, tap a tree (or a few). Only adults should use power drills. You will do this by drilling straight (*not* at an angle) into the tree about 3/4 - 1 inch depending how big the diameter of the tree is. Remember, your tap has to get past ALL bark layers, which on good size trees is usually 1/2 - 3/4 inch thick. The height of the tap can be 2 - 3 feet above the ground. Using the mallet, hammer the tap into the hole so it is snug. Hang or place catching container below tap.

Come back every day to collect the sap.

Take the lesson further:
-As part of an environmental study, you may want the students to take note of the size of the tree and its location, plus temperatures each day (highs and lows) and the measurement of sap they collect daily. Ask students to keep a chart and look for patterns.
-Discuss why the sap is clear, and what minerals it contains (use the next page in your lessons).
-Consider a field trip to a local sugarbush and maple syrup producer. Most offer school programs even if they are not open to the public.

At the end of your season, remove the tap(s). Sometimes a tap will try to heal closed, and you may have to drill the tap again in the middle of the sap season. If this happens, use it as an example of the tree's nature to heal itself.

Top: The author's husband Mark taps trees on his Indiana property. Bottom: The author's Maple grove or sugarbush, with Sugar Maples tapped with plastic spiles, tubing, and buckets.

Activity: Tap a Sugar Maple Tree
Subjects: Science (Environmental Science), Social Studies (American History, Cultural Studies)
Grades 1-8

Maple Syrup/Sugar vs. White Cane Sugar
Maple syrup is a very different kind of sugar in today's world. Unlike cane sugars that are now highly refined and processed to take out all impurities, most maple syrup and sugar only go through minimal processing, leaving behind more key minerals and vitamins than white sugar (and even most brown sugars too). While the calorie content is no different than white sugar, maple syrup/sugar boasts significant amounts of calcium (20mg/Tbsp) and potassium (35mg/Tbsp), along with magnesium, manganese, plus small amounts of iron, phosphorus, zinc, and copper. Some vitamins found in maple syrup and sugar include niacin, riboflavin, and trace amounts of folic acid, as well as higher amounts of amino acids and antioxidants than white sugar. Maple syrup and sugar owes its natural brown coloration to the tree minerals and vitamins still present in the minimally refined product. However, sugar is sugar, and too much is never good, but a little more healthy ingredients straight from the tree is always worth investigating.

Copied But Never Duplicated
Contrary to popular belief, maple sugar is not "like" brown sugar. Some believe because they look close in color, that maple sugar might taste the same as brown sugar, but brown sugar being made of cane lacks the maple flavor. And most brown sugars are still refined, just with added molasses for color and texture. Few are less refined cane sugars, which is a closer product to maple sugar in the sense of limited refinement (not taste), and is becoming more of a trend in America's culinary scene. Other products, like the majority of pancake syrups sold in US supermarkets are maple flavored, but contain no actual maple syrup. These breakfast syrups are usually corn syrups masked in artificial maple flavor additives, and therefore offer none of the nutritional vitamins and minerals found in tree sap. In fact, natural maple syrup and sugar owes its distinctive flavor to its amino acids.

Take it further for your students:
Look up the nutritional value of maple syrup, and the way it is processed (most maple syrup producing states provide this information online). Discuss why so many minerals and vitamins are found in the syrup. Why does maple sap from which the syrup is made have all these minerals and vitamins?

Maple Syrup's Nutritional Value
List those ingredients you wish to discuss with your students

Mineral/Vitamin/Other:	Measurement Per _____:	Daily Value:
_____	_____	_____
_____	_____	_____
_____	_____	_____
_____	_____	_____
_____	_____	_____
_____	_____	_____

About Maple Sugar and Historic Foodways

Origin and Regional Production

Maple syrup and sugar originated among the Native Americans of the New England and Great Lakes regions. The sugar is obtained from evaporating the sap of the Sugar Maple tree, the highest sugar content of any sap in the Maple family (about 2% sugar). The Sugar Maple tree, also known as the Hard Maple tree, is native only to the eastern United States and the adjacent region of Canada. While Canada and Vermont are thought of as the only places maple syrup and sugar is produced, many other states produce substantial quantities of maple products including Michigan, Pennsylvania, New York, Ohio, and Indiana. Some maple syrup and sugar producers are located as far south as Maryland and Tennessee. In 1850, twenty-seven states reported citizens producing maple sugar, more than cane sugar producing states, which totaled only nine in that same year. It was also in the mid-19th century when maple syrup started becoming more popular than maple sugar, and in 1885, an ever increasingly affordable cane sugar began to undercut maple syrup and sugar prices - a trend that continues to date.

Salt Vs. Sugar in Historic Native Cuisine of the Northeastern Cultural Region

For sugar producing Native Peoples, their main seasoning of choice was maple sugar, even on meat and fish. Salt however was not as popular in many communities, if even consumed at all as a condiment in most Northeastern societies before European contact (with exception to Mississippian cultures like the Angel Mounds People who very likely produced salt from local saline springs). A couple accounts speak about some post-contact Native Peoples stopping by saline waters and procuring salt, but the practice seems very limited and possibly encouraged by European newcomers. We should also keep in mind for those many Native Northeastern communities that did not consume pure salt as a condiment aboriginally, that certain cooking methods they practiced added "salty flavor" to foods, such as cooking directly on hot stones. Still, it was shocking for the European newcomers to meet societies that placed little value on salt when compared to themselves. Aboriginal culture didn't value it for food preservation (those noted to procure salt didn't seem to use it in the process of preserving meats). Contrary to popular thought, smoking and drying foods for storage doesn't need salt to assist in the process, and the Native Peoples didn't employ it for such although they were noted to dry almost every type of meat, vegetable, and fruit. Nor did they have a taste for it as much as many Native Peoples of the Northeast had a taste for sugar. One Native scholar pointed out that even as late as the early 20th century, many Iroquois households rarely placed salt out for use during family meals, unless non-Indian visitors were expected. An Ojibwa informant of the same time claimed that his ancestors used sugar in the same quantity that the white people had used salt. It was this culinary difference that caught the attention of early European explorers and traders.

The author demonstrates historic period Native American maple sugaring for event and museum visitors. Left: Wearing an 18th century Native outfit, Jessica stirs kettles of hot sap evaporating over the fire at the National Maple Syrup Festival (2010). Right: Jessica paddles hot sugar while it cools to granulate it (2010).

AD 1500

A DAY IN A NATIVE AMERICAN SUGAR CAMP

FIRST WE HAVE A MEAL. WE WILL NEED LOTS OF ENERGY.

TODAY WE ARE HAVING HOMINY. HOMINY IS A CORN DISH.

NEXT, WE HAVE TO GATHER SOME FIREWOOD.

WE NEED LOTS OF FIREWOOD TO KEEP THE FIRES GOING.

WE NEED TO KEEP THE FIRES HOT ALL DAY AND NIGHT SO WE CAN EVAPORATE THE MAPLE SAP.

NOW WE NEED TO GO AND GET THE MAPLE SAP. I WILL NEED MY AXE FOR THIS JOB TOO.

WE TAP THE TREE BY CUTTING INTO THE BARK. THEN WE PUT THE END OF A FLAT STICK OR BARK PIECE INTO THE GASH. THIS GUIDES THE SAP THAT LEAKS FROM THE CUT AWAY FROM THE TREE.

AND WE PLACE A BARK OR WOOD BUCKET BELOW THE TAP TO CATCH THE SAP.

THE TREE LEAKS LOTS OF SAP WHEN THERE ARE WARM DAYS AND FROZEN NIGHTS.

EVERY DAY, WE GO TO EACH TREE AND COLLECT THE SAP.

GATHERING GALLONS OF SAP CAN BE A HARD JOB...

...BUT WE GET TO DO IT TOGETHER. WE TALK AND LAUGH WHILE WE WORK.

WE BRING ALL THE SAP BACK TO THE CAMP WHERE IT IS DUMPED INTO POTS AND TROUGHS.

CONTINUED ON NEXT PAGE

Name _____   Date _____

THE CLAY POTS ARE FILLED WITH SAP AND PLACED OVER THE FIRE.

STEAM IS CREATED WHEN THE SAP BOILS.

THE WATER FROM THE SAP EVAPORATES LEAVING THE SUGAR BEHIND.

THE SYRUP AND SUGAR LEFT BEHIND TASTES SO GOOD!

BUT OUR DAYS AT THE SUGAR CAMP ARE NOT JUST FILLED WITH WORK.

WE PLAY TOO!

MY BROTHER AND I LIKE TO PLAY GAMES IN THE SNOW.

THE ADULTS HAVE FUN TOO. MY AUNT TELLS FUNNY JOKES WHILE THEY WORK.

GRAMPA TELLS HIS STORIES AT NIGHT.

SOON THE DAY IS OVER AND IT IS TIME TO GO TO SLEEP. MY MOTHER CHECKS IN ON ME TO MAKE SURE I AM RESTING.

I WILL NEED MY REST BECAUSE TOMORROW IS ANOTHER DAY OF MAPLE SUGARING.

THEN & NOW

THAT MAY HAVE BEEN A LONG TIME AGO, BUT REMEMBER, MANY NATIVE AMERICAN PEOPLE STILL TAP TREES AND MAKE MAPLE SUGAR TODAY.

119

Where Maple Syrup Comes From

_____
_____
_____
_____
_____

Delaware boys collect Maple sap, 1775.

Native boy spears fish trapped in a fish weir.

Food From the Water

Many foods that Native Americans ate were from the water. They gathered fish in fish weirs and gill nets, and caught them with harpoons (fishing spears), catching baskets, and hoop nets. Sometimes they fished with hooks made of bone and copper. They also collected fresh water mussels, clams, and crawfish from the rivers. Shellfish were collected in large quantities, and could be gathered throughout most of the year.

Trapping Fish In Weirs

The Native Americans built fish weirs in shallow waterways. Fish weirs are fences in the water used to guide fish into small areas and trap them. The fish weirs were made of sticks strapped together to make fences, or they were made of stones built into walls. The shape of the fish weirs funneled the fish into small areas where it was easier to catch them with spears and nets.

What kinds of fish would the Native American people have caught in your state?

_____

_____

_____

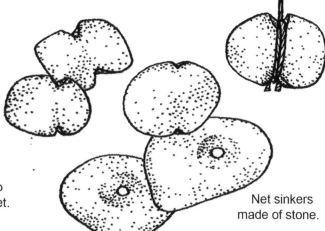
Two bone fish hooks.

Net sinkers made of stone.

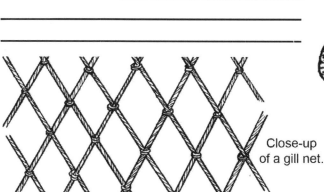
Close-up of a gill net.

The Fish of Indiana

Directions: Find out what kind of fish are native to Indiana's rivers and lakes. Draw these fish in the space below. Don't forget the shellfish.

The Fish of Ohio

Directions: Find out what kind of fish are native to Ohio's rivers and lakes. Draw these fish in the space below. Don't forget the shellfish.

Gathering Animals

The Native people relied on gathering land and water animals (which includes fishing) to provide meat for their diet, bones for tools, and shells for utensils and decorative purposes. Below are some common land and water animal foods they fished and gathered. Use the word key to fill in the name of each game animal below the correct image.

Key Words: Bird Eggs, Crayfish, Fish, Frog, Mussels, Turtle.

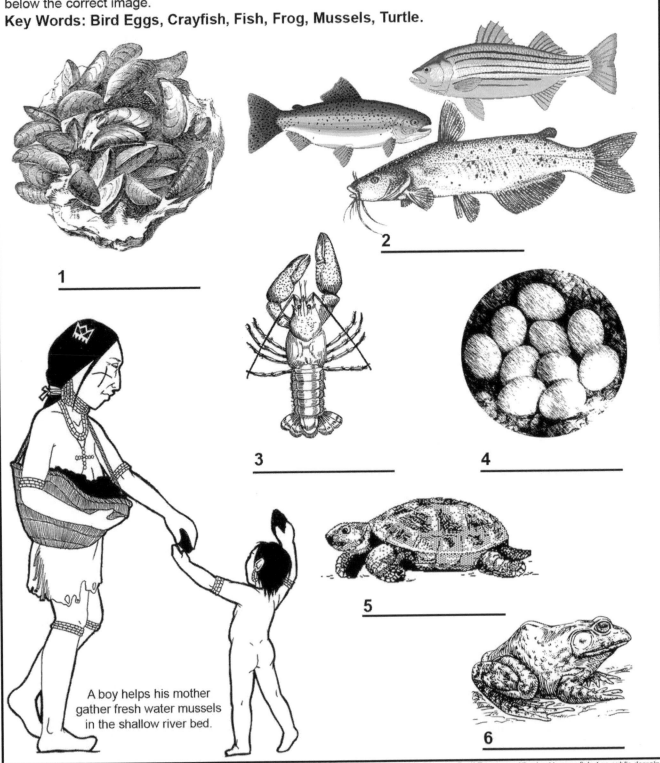

1 _____

2 _____

3 _____

4 _____

5 _____

6 _____

A boy helps his mother gather fresh water mussels in the shallow river bed.

Bass, trout, turtle, and frog from wpclipart.com; mussels by Philip Henry Gosse; eggs by Wilfredor; crayfish and catfish by Pearson Scott Foresman. All animal images listed as public domain.

Name _____ Date _____

Trapping Animals

The Native people relied on trapping (as well as hunting) to provide meat for their diet, hide for clothing, and bones for tools. Below are some common game animals they trapped (and sometimes hunted too). Use the word key to fill in the name of each game animal below the correct image.

Word Key:
Beaver, Fox, Muskrat,
Opossum, Rabbit, Raccoon,
Skunk, Squirrel, Woodchuck.

1 _____

2 _____

3 _____

4 _____

5 _____

6 _____

7 _____

Native American men set a snare to catch an animal. They would also set deadfall and pit traps.

8 _____

9 _____

Hunting Animals

The Native people relied on hunting (as well as trapping) to provide meat for their diet, hide for clothing, and bones for tools. Below are some common game animals they hunted (and sometimes trapped too). Use the word key to fill in the name of each game animal below the correct image.

Word Key: Black Bear, Bison, Bobcat, Cougar, Deer, Duck, Elk, Goose, Pigeon, Turkey, Wolf.

1 _____

2 _____

3 _____

4 _____

5 _____

6 _____

7 _____

8 _____

9 _____

10 _____

11 _____

Native American hunters run after a deer they shot and wounded. Chasing game was a usual practice and it took a lot of energy. Hunting was not easy.

Turkey from an unknown illustrator; cougar and bobcat from wpclipart.com; pigeon appeared in The New Student's Reference Work, vol. 3 in 1914; duck by an unknown illustrator; other animals by Pearson Scott Foresman. All animal images listed as public domain.

Extra Information Relating to the Topic of Hunting

Waste Nothing

So many falsehoods are presented as facts to those learning about Native American cultures. One of the most famous examples would have to be that Native Americans used every part of the animal. They wasted nothing. This is far from the truth. This statement is born of simplifying Native American's cultural values, such as the belief in trying to use what one can, or not killing animals for sport, all to bring respect to an animal's spirit or another deity. The statement also gains strength from the fact that their clothing and tools were many times made of materials from animals. This does not actually mean the Native people used every part of every animal. We know they did throw away enough to leave evidence. After all, why do archaeologists find large amounts of animal bones thrown away into trash pits? They threw animal pieces they didn't want to their dogs (some discarded animal parts were kept away from their dogs, as it was disrespectful towards some animal spirits to let dogs chew upon their bones). With long, far away catches, only what was valued most of the animal was butchered on site and carried home.

But this practice of not wasting was not actually foreign to white pioneers who also made use of hides, ate organ meat, and saved all the fat. This is not a cultural trait that is unique to or defines Native Americans. Yes, the historic Native people, like so many around the world (past and present), wasted little compared to mainstream, modern Americans who believe their foods are more "prime cut" quality and believe themselves to have the security to be picky in their diet. But the truth is that we also don't waste animals either, although many in our society may not know it because they are so shielded from our modern food processing culture. From dog foods to gelatins to blood fertilizers, American farmers follow the tradition not of just the Native American people, but of humans worldwide. We dry blood, grind bones, make leather, process gelatin, and mold scraps of "unsavory" cuts of meat and organs into canned meat products and deli meats. The truth is our own culture wastes even less of the animals we process than historic Native American cultures!

So why is this a big deal. Because we like painting a dreary picture of survival and hardship when we speak of historic Native American life, whether it's correct or not. When we focus on this, we are really trying to make our culture look more "advanced" and secure (not "fighting for survival") by calling attention to a historic Native American practice we deem as evidence of their "primitiveness." Knowing we, as modern Americans, use almost every part of the animals our country butchers commercially, we should rethink our motives to focus on this topic, especially in ways that only serve to separate and "lower" historic Native Americans in our perspectives.

The Bison Mystery

Bison in Indiana and Ohio prehistory as a usual and native animal species is highly controversial. One problem is the lack of bison bones in pre-contact archaeological excavations. "Most of the bison remains in Ohio are associated with later cultures, particularly, the Fort Ancient Culture, which thrived in the region between 1000 AD, and 1650 AD (1)." Theories have been put forth insisting that bison are, in fact, a late introduction to the Ohio River Valley region, coming over more often with the decline of the Mississippian of this region. It is thought that with the reduced human population and man-made open fields they left behind (from burning, farming, and deforestation caused by the need for wood resources), the bison started migrating more and more eastward from the Mississippi River area.

There does however exist another and more recent theory. Because bison were usually butchered on site (given the size of the animal), it is likely these bones have been missed because the butcher sites were outside the village areas (therefore outside the usual archaeological excavation sites). This is a very convincing argument, although some might point out that the lack of bone tools made from bison in any great numbers is still problematic (considering bison bones are desirable for tools), as well as the lack of a bison-centered culture among tribes of the Ohio River Valley.

Extra Information Relating to the Topic of Hunting (continued)

One thing we do know for sure is that bison was not a major food animal or resource for the historic tribes of Indiana and Ohio. Some are noted to head west into Illinois to conduct bison hunts, but the animal just doesn't match up to other game animals more relied on by local tribes, especially deer. Their neighbors to the west who resided on the plains had a buffalo-centered culture; the tribes of Indiana and Ohio did not (not in foodways, not in resources, and not in worldviews). Some (like the Delaware) are even noted be indifferent to hunting bison: "...buffalo they shoot little and rarely, as the hides are too heavy and of little value, and if they shot one of these animals now and again, most of the meat is left lying in the woods, where it is consumed by wolves, or other animals or birds (2)." The Native people of this region didn't place nearly as much importance on bison as the Plains tribes.

Quotes:
(1) Sheryl Hartman from "Bison in the Ohio Valley." http://voices.yahoo.com/bison-ohio-valley-5822440.html?cat=37 - Bison is an addition to the Fort Ancient menu according to Penelope B. Drooker and C. Wesley Cowan in their article: "Transformation of the Fort Ancient Cultures of Central Ohio Valley
(2) Quote by David Zeisberger. Ohio History Central. http://www.ohiohistorycentral.org/entry.php?rec=1125

A Native hunter chases game.

Corralling Deer

Some Native hunters would build fences to corral the deer they were hunting. To trap the deer, people would shout or make loud noises by knocking objects together to scare the deer towards the fenced-in area. Once there, the deer were trapped, and hunters would then use their bows and arrows to shoot the deer. In this manner of hunting, a whole village could work together to secure a large amount of meat for everyone.

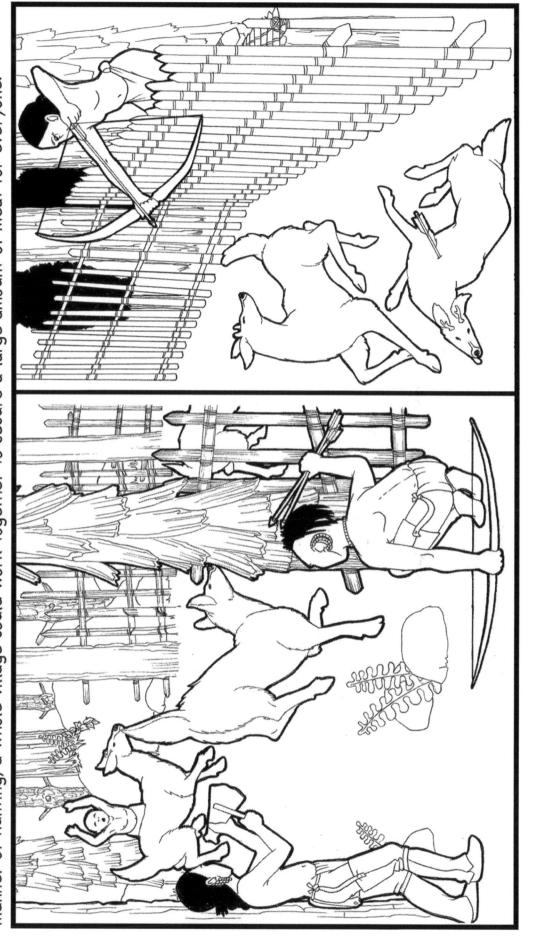

Name _____ Date _____

Directions: Draw the forest animals native to your state in the box.

Animals In The Forest

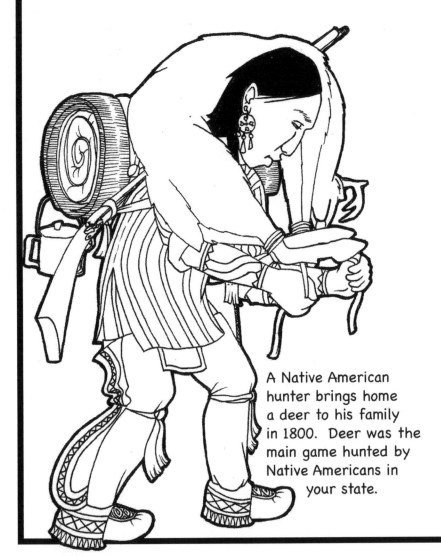

A Native American
hunter brings home
a deer to his family
in 1800. Deer was the
main game hunted by
Native Americans in
your state.

Bringing Home The Game

What Animals Did They Hunt?

By far, deer was the main game sought, however other animals were also hunted or trapped, including bear, fox, raccoon, beaver, otter, rabbit, turkey, and more. Hunting the animal, while extremely exhausting, was only half the work. Once hunted, the animal had to be gutted - removing the guts so it did not spoil the meat in the abdomen.

Preparing for the Journey Home

The game was brought home or to a hunting camp to be fully processed. For some hunters who ventured a few days walk from home or camp, they had to undertake the processing of the meat before heading home so the meat would not spoil. This may take a couple days of drying meat over a smoky fire. It was not unusual for a hunt to last a week or more. Hunting was a serious, physically demanding job, and most hunters felt they should return only when they procured meat, and no sooner.

Tribal Truth

Sometimes men brought the game right to the wigwam door. Other times, hunters would bring it to the outskirts of the village, where they left it (possibly hid it) for their female kin to find and retrieve. Euro-Americans who didn't understand Native American culture came to the conclusion that the men were just "lazy" and wanted the women to finish their job. This however was not the case. In fact, for example, Iroquois women may have actually requested that their male kin leave the animal in a spot they agreed upon away from the home. Why? Because the Native people had a high code of manners and sometimes when a man walked through a village with a kill, he was obligated to offer pieces to the villagers he passed by. However, a woman was only transporting "his" meat and had no authority to give his property away. By retrieving the animal herself, a woman might be able to keep more meat in her household. It was a way to get around reciprocity customs when she desired to keep more meat. When she began to process it, the meat became "her" property, and she was then obligated to give some cooked meat to visitors of her home.

Activity: A Sweet Meat Treat

Subjects: Health (Nutrition) Social Studies (American History, Cultural Studies)
Grades 1-8

Description

A favorite Native dish was venison flavored with bear fat and maple sugar. Students will have the opportunity to try a similar dish.

Ingredients

-venison or buffalo (buffalo can be found at many butcher shops and some supermarkets)
-rendered duck fat (to take the place of bear fat - found at many supermarkets or in French and Asian speciality stores)
-maple syrup

Materials

-stove top
-pot full of water
-knife and cutting board
-skewers
-dipping bowls or cups

Procedure

Dice meat in 1 inch cubes (bite size) and boil in water until done and tender. Take each piece out on its own skewer. Have students dip their skewered meat into the grease and sugar (1 part melted duck fat to 3 parts maple syrup, stirred). Students should only have a couple pieces at most as this is a very rich food.

Discussion

The Native people enjoyed the taste combination of fat and sugar on their meats. What does consuming fat do for the human body? Can you have too much fat in your diet? Too little fat in your diet? What foods do you eat where fat is a condiment applied for flavoring (ex. bread with butter, potatoes with butter, frying eggs in bacon grease, collard greens and bacon grease)? Can you identify a meat you like to eat with sugar for flavoring (ex. honey ham, brown sugar barbecue ribs, sausage or bacon with maple syrup)? Does the combination of sugar and meat seem so different or unusual after identifying some common dishes we eat that include sweet meats?

Photos: Left - Buffalo meat dries over the author's smoky fire (2012). Right - hot maple sugar boils down over an open fire at the Annual Maple Syrup Festival in Salem, Indiana (2010).

Native Technology: The Bow & Arrow

The Arrow

The arrow shaft was made of wood. While the Native people picked the straightest tree shoots they could, no wood ever grew perfectly straight in nature, so the shaft had to be straightened. It was shaved, sanded, steamed and bent, and oiled before attaching the arrowhead and fletching. The arrowhead was made of stone or copper and attached at one end. At the other end feathers were attached to create the fletching. The fletching helped to guide the arrow when shot from the bow.

The Bow

This man carves his bow stave with an adze head made of stone. The man at the right works to bend his bow evenly. Bow making was an art. Manipulating imperfect wood pieces into strong, almost perfect bows required great skill and patience - patience being considered one of the most important attributes for a respectable Native man to demonstrate.

Making quality bows took time. The bow had to be carved, steamed and bent, sanded, and oiled, after the wood had already cured for some time. It was then fitted with a bow string usually made of sinew. A bow could take months to complete.

Name _____   Date _____

Identifying Artifacts

Directions: There are 9 sharp edged tools below that are drawn to actual size. Not all of them are arrowheads. Circle the ones you think are the arrowheads.

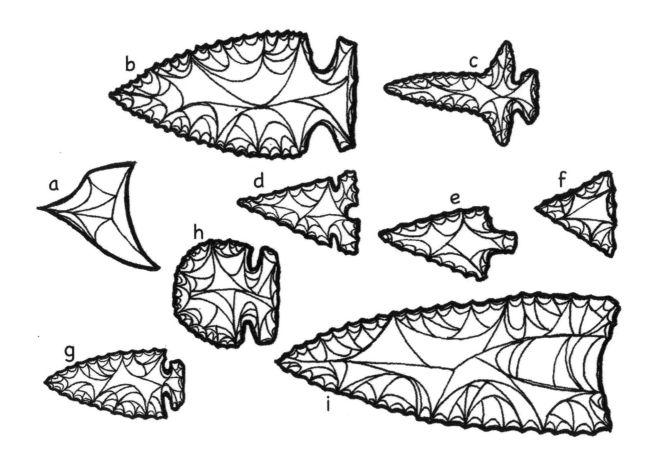

Why do you feel the ones you circled are the arrowheads, and the others are not?

_____

_____

_____

_____

_____

Answers: a is a gouge. b is a knife blade. c is a drill point. d is an arrowhead. e is an arrowhead. f is an arrowhead. g is an arrowhead. h is a scraper. i is a spear point. Remember that arrowheads have to be small enough to work on the arrow. If the arrowhead is as big as b or i, it would be too heavy for the arrow shaft (stick).

Native Technology: Flintknapping

How the Native American People Created Sharp-Edged Tools From Stone

1. Quarry
Large pieces of chert are quarried from chert deposits in the earth.

2. Nodule Flake
The chert stone or nodule is hit with a hammerstone to break off a flake to make, for the purpose of this example, a knife blade.

3. Preform
The flake is 'roughed out' into the general shape of the knife. This roughed out piece is called a preform.

4. Percussion Flaking
A billet, or striking tool, made of antler, stone, bone, or copper is used to remove larger flakes of chert and shape the stone further into a knife blade.

5. Pressure Flaking
After the shape of the knife is finished, the cutting edges are sharpened by pressing an antler end to the edges of the knife to remove little flakes of chert.

6. Edge
The knife can be furthered sharpened by striking the egde in a downward motion. This flakes off little pieces from the other side of the blade. The thinner the chert, the sharper the knife.

7. Hafting
If the knife blade was made to attach to a handle, or hafted, it may be notched. It was then attached to the handle with sinew and glue made from animal products.

Arrowhead

Broken Arrowhead to Awl Point

Broken Arrowhead to Scraper

Recycling

Arrowheads sometimes broke by accident, but that didn't mean they were useless. Archaeologists know Native American flintknappers reworked some old, broken arrowheads into new tools like scrapers and awls. Did you know Native Americans recycled their broken arrowheads? Why might a flintknapper choose to rework a broken arrowhead instead of just starting from scratch?

Woodland Indian Stone Technology

The Native American people made numerous types of tools, utensils, and trinkets from stone. There were two ways to shape stone. Stone axes, hammers, pestles, and pendants were usually made by pecking. Tools could be made from rocks like granite by pecking at it with other stone tools. Arrowheads, scrapers, choppers, and any tool that needed a sharp cutting edge was usually made by a process referred to as flintknapping. Flintknapping shaped smooth grain stone, like chert (flint), into tools by removing flakes of rock to shape the wanted object.

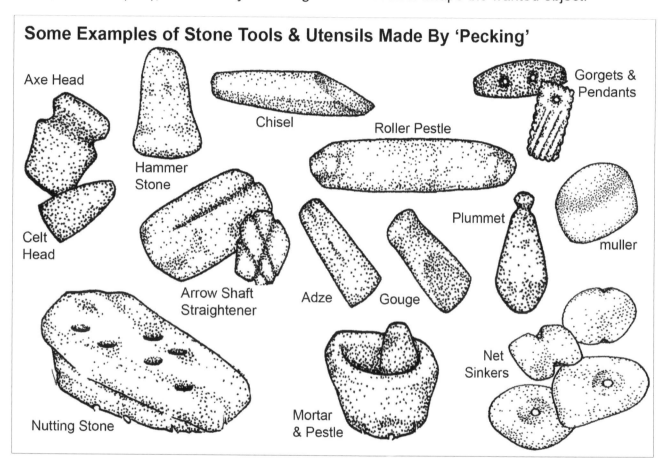

Some Examples of Stone Tools & Utensils Made By 'Pecking'

Axe Head

Chisel

Roller Pestle

Gorgets & Pendants

Hammer Stone

Celt Head

muller

Plummet

Arrow Shaft Straightener

Adze

Gouge

Nutting Stone

Net Sinkers

Mortar & Pestle

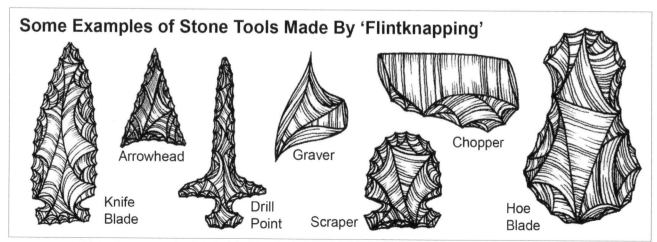

Some Examples of Stone Tools Made By 'Flintknapping'

Arrowhead

Graver

Chopper

Knife Blade

Drill Point

Scraper

Hoe Blade

Pre-Colonial Woodland Indian Copper

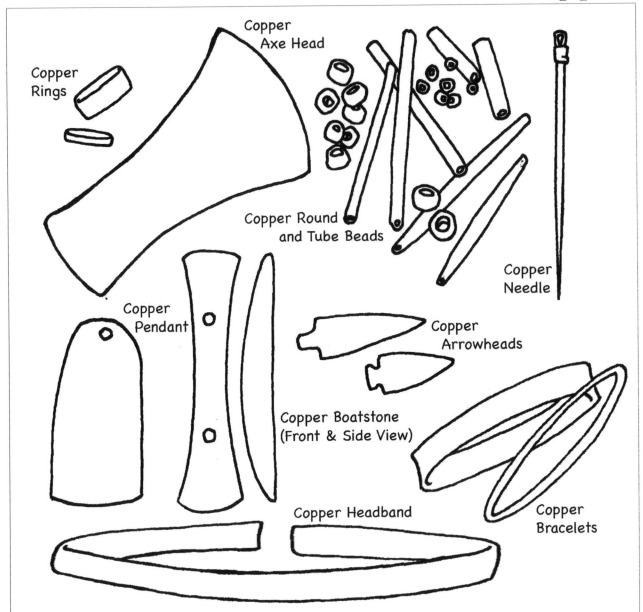

Copper Axe Head

Copper Rings

Copper Round and Tube Beads

Copper Needle

Copper Pendant

Copper Arrowheads

Copper Boatstone (Front & Side View)

Copper Headband

Copper Bracelets

The Woodland Indian people did not just rely on stone to make tools. They also made tools from metal. The metal they used was **copper**. Copper was collected from large copper **quarries**. One such place with large amounts of copper is around Lake Superior. Copper from Lake Superior was traded across North America by the Native people. To shape the copper, the copper was heated by a fire and then hammered into many usable items.

Define the vocabulary from the reading:

Copper – _____

Quarry – _____

Make a Straw Arrow

Not all arrows were tipped with stone points. Many had copper arrowheads. Native American people were making tools and jewelry out of Lake Superior copper for hundreds of years before European contact. Below is a copper arrowhead and feather fletching for you to color, cut-out, and make a straw arrow with.

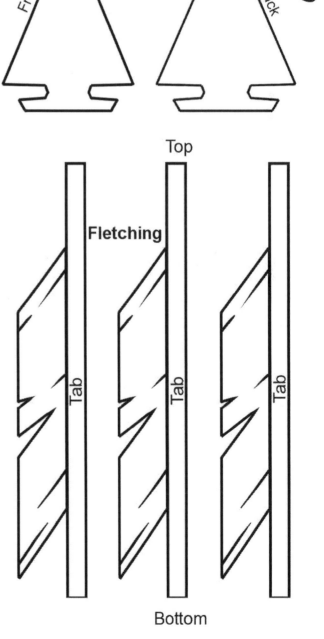

Directions:

You will need a plastic straw, tape, glue scissors, and crayons or markers. Color the back and front of the copper arrowhead and the 3 feather fletchings, then cut them out. On each fletching, fold the tab longways and use its surface to fix onto the straw. Do this by taping the top and bottom of the tabs to the straw. Space each fletching evenly around the straw. Remember the "bottom" of the fletching needs to be facing the end of the straw. Next, take the 2 copper arrowhead faces and attach to the other end of the straw by gluing the straw tip in between the arrowhead pieces (sandwich the straw tip in between the arrowhead pieces).

Class Discussion:

What is fletching and what does it do? The fletching helps to stabilize the arrow which then helps to guide the arrow so it may stay on target. To make the fletching, Native Americans would cut a bird's wing feather in half, trim it, then fix it to the arrow shaft. To attach it they glued it with tacky adhesive made of animal hooves or sap, and then tied it down with sinew. So then, what is sinew? Sinew is string made from animal's tendons.

Student Article: Grades 4-9

More Than Animal Hides
Pre-Colonial Clothing of the Northeastern Native American People

Leather

Most Native American garments were made of tanned (cured) animal hide commonly referred to as leather. Animal hides were processed into leather by skilled craftspeople, most of whom were women. The process of turning animal hides into wearable leather is called hide-tanning. Hide-tanning was more than just a skilled activity, it was a scientific process. Think about it. Taking a biological material (animal skin) that would naturally decompose if left alone and stopping that decaying process by turning the skin into a soft, durable clothing material (leather) with the capability to last for years was an incredible technology. It still is a fascinating process. And while much clothing was made from animal hides, still other clothing materials were utilized.

Textiles

Most would not guess that the Native American peoples of pre-colonial America made garments from a type of cloth they created. Of what material did they make these textiles? Believe it or not, the natural materials used to make fibers still exist to this day in our forests. It grows all around us in the form of certain plants and trees. For example, inner bark layers of certain kinds of cedar trees are fibrous, and can be turned into strings, which then can be woven together to make a 'cloth.' Fibers also come from the stems of plants like nettles, dogbane (Indian hemp), and milkweed. These fibers are fine, and were twisted together to make strong string. These strings could be woven together to make 'cloth' and textiles that were then made into garments. These fibers were many times dyed colors, so that they might be woven into vivid patterns. Many local Native American cultures made some garments, accessories, and even storage bags from textiles made of natural woven fibers.

Pigments

Both leather and textiles were dyed and painted with pleasing colors and patterns. But where did the Native American people find the pigments used to make such colorful dyes? Many believe berries provide such dyes, and for a very few kinds of berries this is true. But most berries did not produce bright colors when they dried. Colorful dyes do come from plants, just outside the berries. Many dyes were made from the roots of plants, including a plant called bloodroot. Bloodroot still grows in our forests today. As the name might suggest, the root of this plant contained a watery red colored juice. When cut, the color is so rich it looks as though the root of this plant is bleeding. However when it dries, the color is more orange-red. If a deeper red was desired, they could mix the bloodroot with crushed red ocher, a type of mineral-rock. Minerals and clays were a great source of color. Pigments existed in many natural sources, all of which the Native American people exploited and processed in an expert manner.

Embellishments

More than just dying or painting clothing, materials were added to enhance garments. In certain areas of the Northeast, quills from the porcupine were flattened, dyed, and woven or sewn into patterns on clothing. We call this quillwork. In other areas of the Northeast, animal fur was dyed and then embroidered into designs on clothing. Even feathers have been sewn onto clothing to create pleasing textures, such as robes of turkey feathers made by many Native communities. Other materials used to decorate clothing included items that may not have been local but traded from far places, such as mica from the Southeast, copper from Lake Superior, or shells and even shark teeth from the East Coast and the Gulf of Mexico.

Name_____   Date_____

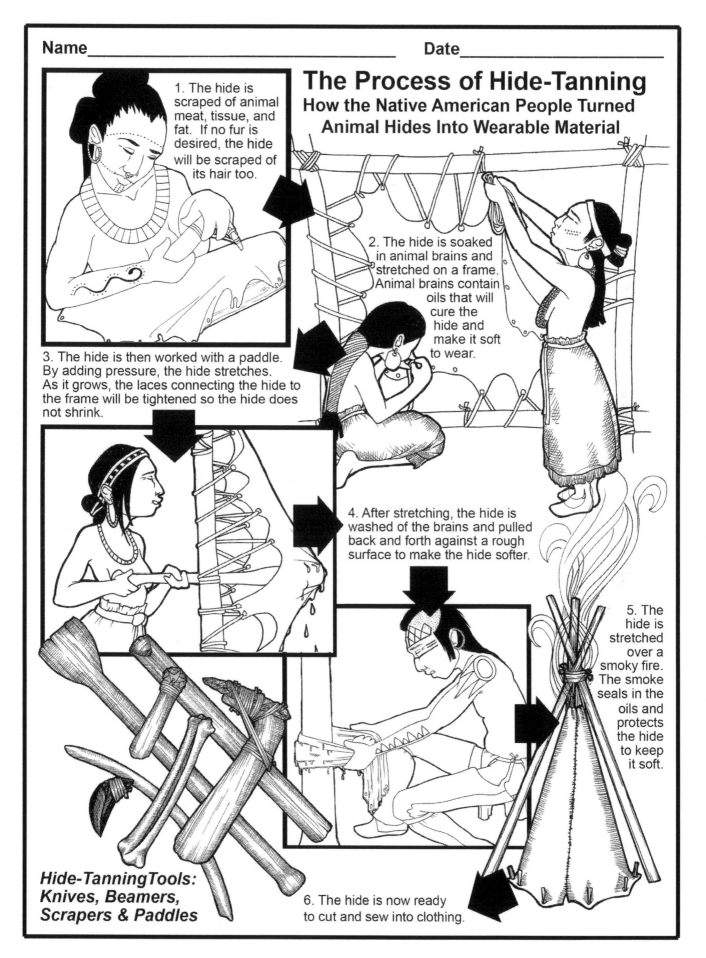

The Process of Hide-Tanning
How the Native American People Turned Animal Hides Into Wearable Material

1. The hide is scraped of animal meat, tissue, and fat. If no fur is desired, the hide will be scraped of its hair too.

2. The hide is soaked in animal brains and stretched on a frame. Animal brains contain oils that will cure the hide and make it soft to wear.

3. The hide is then worked with a paddle. By adding pressure, the hide stretches. As it grows, the laces connecting the hide to the frame will be tightened so the hide does not shrink.

4. After stretching, the hide is washed of the brains and pulled back and forth against a rough surface to make the hide softer.

5. The hide is stretched over a smoky fire. The smoke seals in the oils and protects the hide to keep it soft.

Hide-Tanning Tools: Knives, Beamers, Scrapers & Paddles

6. The hide is now ready to cut and sew into clothing.

Native American Clothing, 1600-1700

1. Native man wearing a turkey feather mantle and wampum headband. The turkey feathers were attached to a fiber woven backing. Not all clothing was made of animal hides - many were made of woven plant fibers. 2. A man carries his disabled nephew to camp wearing a hide coat. The nephew wears a hood on his head in the cold weather. 3. A woman holding a clay pot in her winter clothes, including layers of hide skirts and leggings. 4. An older woman strings squash in summer work clothes that consist of only a hide skirt. 5. Woman (left) and man (right) talk wearing their hide mantles decorated with shell pieces. 6. Man decorated for war wears little else but his breechclout and moccasins. 7. Woman in a fur robe wears snowshoes during winter travel. 8. Girl wears a tube dress with detachable sleeves (known as a strap dress). 9. Mother and child gather mussels. The woman wears jewelry daily. Young children usually wore little to no clothing in the warm part of the year. 10. A man plays a flute for his love on a cold night, bundled in a bear fur. These Native people wear jewelry, facial and body paint, tattoos, and lots of decorative embellishments on their clothing.

Native American Clothing, 1750–1850

1. A man in a European-style wool vest wears a silk turban. 2. A woman gathers firewood in her summers clothes of a wrap skirt and leggings. 3. A woman grinds corn into flour wearing trade silver brooches on her linen jacket. 4. Three women playing a dice game wear their finest during a celebration - their large collar calico shirts are plastered with silver brooches, their wool wrap skirts decorated in silk ribbon appliqué, and one wears a wool hat with a silver hat band. 5. Man in a ruffled cotton shirt carves a trough for his wife. 6. A woman paddling maple sugar also wearing a ruffled shirt - such shirts were worn by both men and women. 7. A girl wears a cool weather outfit complete with a linen bed gown (a European-style outer garment). 8. A man in mourning has stripped himself down to just his breechclout. Individuals mourning the loss of loved ones typically strived to look as sad on the outside as they were on the inside. 9. A hunter brings home a small deer in his striped trade shirt and wool leggings trimmed with silk ribbon decoration. These Native people wear jewelry, facial and body paint, tattoos, and lots of decorative embellishments on their clothing.

Leggings, Sleeves, & Hoods
The Ingenious Design of Native Clothing

The clothing worn by the historic Native peoples of our region was made to fit their lifestyle and environment. A usual clothing pattern shared by all tribes was the use of detachable garments that made basics (like breechclouts, wrap skirts, and tunics) change from fair weather outfits to cool weather outfits. This was especially seen in their use of leggings worn with skirts and breechclouts instead of wearing full pants - the legging was secured below the knee by a garter or attached at the top to a belt around the wearer's waist to keep it in place. They wore separate sleeves with sleeveless upper garments instead of wearing long-sleeve shirts. This was done by suspending the sleeves around the chest or with a strap. But why did they not just attach the leggings and sleeves directly to the garments? Some mistakenly believe it is because the Native peoples didn't know how to make such garments. This is untrue – the Native peoples were (and still are) very intelligent. Their Native American relatives to the Arctic north made use of full body suits for living in their environment. Scholars believe the ancestors of the local Native peoples also made these types of body suits and full coats and pant garments long ago in the Archaic time period (mainly because they lived in a different environment).

The real reason why people like the Miami, Delaware, Shawnee, Potawatomi, Ojibwa, Ottawa, Wyandot, Mingo and others wore their clothes with detachable sleeves and/or leggings was because it worked for their environment and lifestyle. For example, if a Miami person came into his or her very warm wigwam from the bitter cold outside, his or her outfit made it possible to take off minimal articles of clothing to make themselves comfortable. Otherwise, the Miami person might have to change every garment from cool weather clothes to warm weather clothes just because they came inside. You might want to think of Native American detachable sleeves and leggings as outerwear like coats since they functioned very much in the same way. And if a person needed a bare arm while doing a specific task outside in the cold, they could easily take off one sleeve instead of a whole upper garment, which kept the wearer warmer.

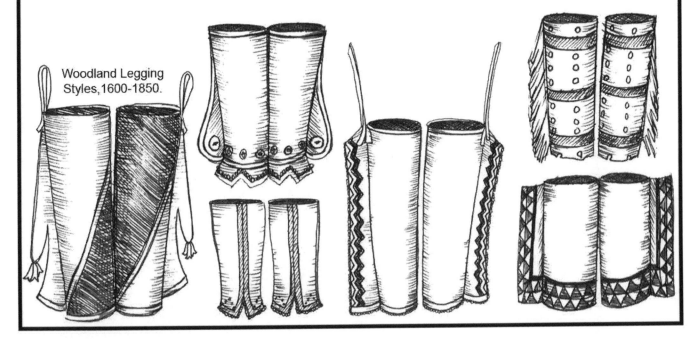

Woodland Legging Styles, 1600-1850.

Leggings, Sleeves, & Hoods Continued

You might at times wear special outer garments not just for warmth but for protection too, like wearing a raincoat, and the Natives peoples did the same thing. Leggings were sometimes worn even on hot days to protect the wearer's legs from underbrush while walking in the forest, or from scorching his or her shins while working near a cooking fire. Some tribes like the Abenaki and Ojibwa (Chippewa) were also known to wear separate hoods not attached to coats. Such hoods could be added to any outfit to make the wearer warmer when he or she was outside. Most hoods tended to be pointy in shape and some were highly decorated. Because of this, these hoods became more than just a hat to keep a person's head warm. In the same way you might wear a hat to complete your outfit, the Native peoples would sometimes wear their hoods for the same reason.

Center-Seam Moccasins

The soft-sole moccasins of the local historic Native peoples were very unique. These shoes, called center-seam moccasins, are known as such because of the predominant seam that runs along the top of the shoe. There is actually only two seams in most center-seam moccasin construction: the one on top of the foot and another short seam in the back of the heel. But what makes these moccasins truly unique is that each shoe uses one piece of leather each. If you are wearing sneakers right now, look down and count how many cut pieces of material were sewn together to make just one of your shoes. More than likely it is made with many pieces of materials, unlike center-seam moccasins.

Native Americans weren't the only people to recognize the benefits of moccasins. Many pioneers also wore Native-style moccasins for a few reasons, including availability and durability. Although moccasins were no more waterproof than Euro-American hard-sole shoes, when they did get wet, they dried quicker. And unlike hard-sole shoes that usually needed a cobbler to make, soft-sole moccasins were easily made by any individuals who could sew and get their hands on a piece of leather. For this reason they were also cheaper. It wasn't unusual for Native American children to have several pairs of moccasins each, but poor Euro-American pioneer children usually only had one pair shoes each, worn primarily for church services and used in winter, otherwise, they went barefoot inside and outside.

Name _____   Date _____

Woodland Indian Quillwork

Top: Porcupine quill.
Bottom: Flattened & cut quill ready to be used.

Quillwork is decoration made from porcupine quills. The quills are flattened, dyed, and sewn into different folds and weaves to create different designs. Quillwork decorated clothes, bags, and shoes.

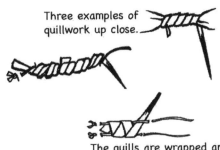

Three examples of quillwork up close.

The quills are wrapped and sewn in different methods and different designs.

Make Your Own Quillworked Moccasins

Directions: Color and cut out the 2 moccasin flaps and center seam patch.

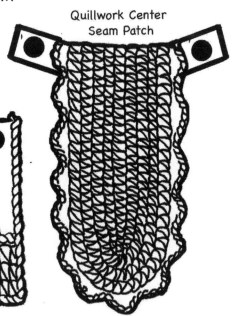

Quillwork Center Seam Patch

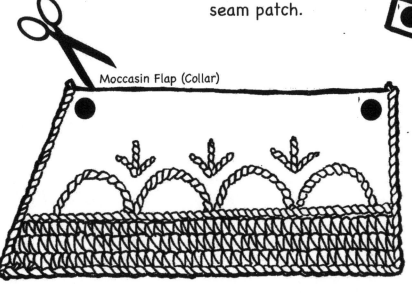

Moccasin Flap (Collar)

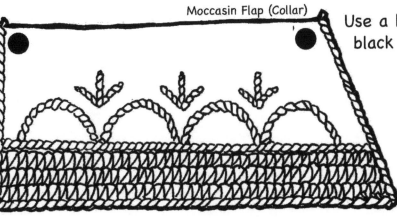

Moccasin Flap (Collar)

Use a hole punch to cut out the black circles and lace together with a piece of yarn.

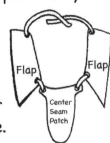

Flap   Flap
Center
Seam
Patch

Wear over your shoe.

More Than Just Designs

Quillwork Bag by
Ralph Heath

While designs and patterns were created just for looks, some designs on garments and bags were more than just decoration. Designs might represent religious beliefs or pay respect to deities. The hunting bag pictured above depicts Double Thunderbirds made from dyed embroidered porcupine quills. While this might seem at first "different," the truth is we also do the same thing today. Clothing decorations (designs, emblems, print) can reflect the wearer's likes, interests, beliefs, and even economic status. Why do you pick the printed or decorated garments you wear? What are you hoping to communicate to others about yourself when they see your clothing's patterns and designs?

_____

_____

_____

_____

Cut & Fold Hunting Pouch: To make this shoulder bag, color and cut out the pouch decorated with a quillworked Thunderbird. Fold it along the two dotted lines to create the front and back of the pouch. Staple or tape the sides together (leaving the top flap free). Color and cut out the cones with deer hair, and tape cone clusters to the bottom of the flap and bag. Attach a string to each side and wear over your shoulder.

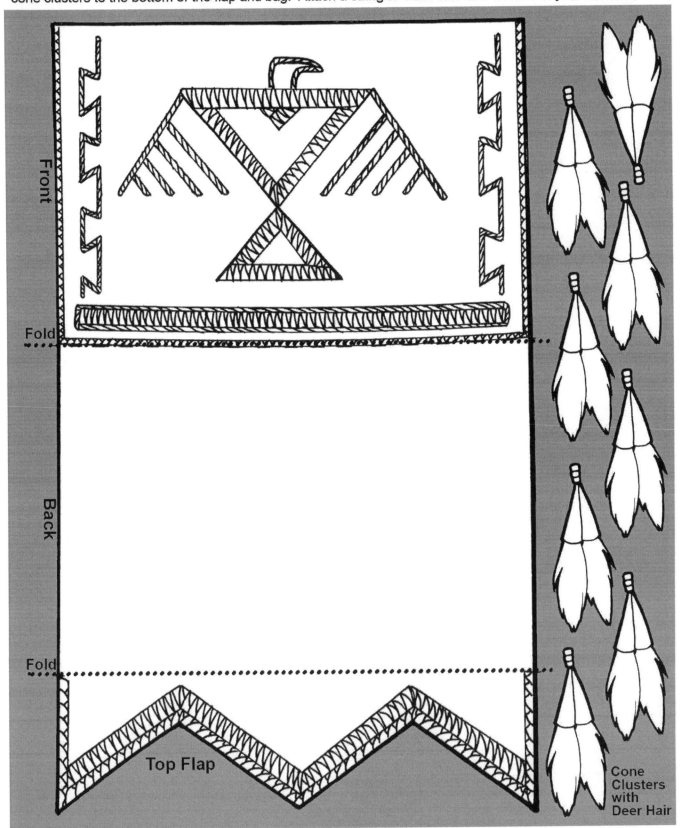

Front

Fold

Back

Fold

Top Flap

Cone Clusters with Deer Hair

Project: Make a Fingerwoven Yarn Strap

Subjects: Art (Cultural Arts, Textiles), Social Studies (American History, Cultural Studies)
Grades 3-5

Background

Fingerweaving (or finger-braiding) was a technique used by both pre-contact and post-contact Native Americans to create belts, straps, sashes, garters, and more with strands of natural plant fibers (pre-contact/post-contact) or wool (post-contact). Fingerweaving is different from most weaving techniques because it doesn't rely on tension (tension loom), and all strands play the role of weft (horizontal) and warp (vertical) strands.

Description

Students will each make a short fingerwoven strap or bracelet using yarn in a simple diagonal weave. This is not unlike finger-braiding friendship bracelets.

Materials

-Thick to normal weight yarn in many colors
-Scissors

Procedure:

Tie 10 18-inch long pieces of yarn together at one end for each student. Divide strands in half, creating 5 in front and 5 in back. Take the left strand in front (J) and draw it in between the front and back strands from left to right, creating a horizontal weft (1). Then switch the front to back strings: A to front, B to back, C to front, D to back and so on (2). Again, take the furthest left strand in front and draw it in between the front and back strands from left to right (3). Take the previous weft strand that passed from left to right (J) and make it a vertical strand again by folding behind new weft (A) on the right side (4).

Some Fingerweaving Online Sources Include: http://www.nativetech.org/finger/beltinstr.html - http://francosfiberadventure.blogspot.com/2010/02/fwdiagtut.html - or plug in the term "diagonal fingerweaving pattern" into a search engine.

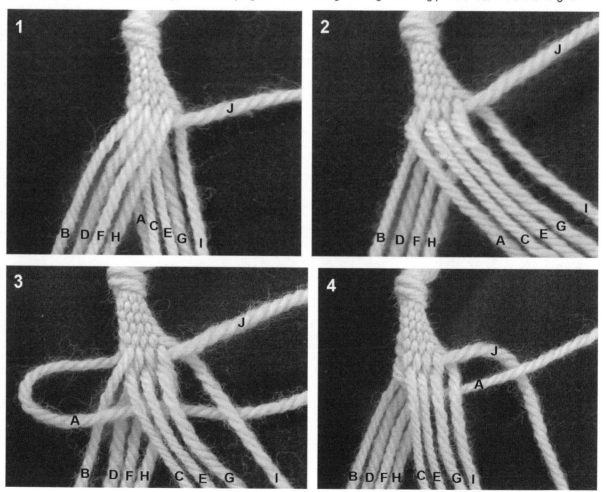

Cut & Fold Finger-Woven Bag

The Native Americans made shoulder bags out of woven trade wool yarn. This was done by a method called finger-weaving or finger-braiding. Such a method resembles friendship bracelet braiding, and the Native Americans made bags, belts, and garters in this manner. This bag below also has glass trade beads woven within, as well as round silver pins called brooches attached for decoration. Color the bag below, fold it along the dotted line and staple or tape the seams up the sides, then attach a string to each side and use as a pouch.

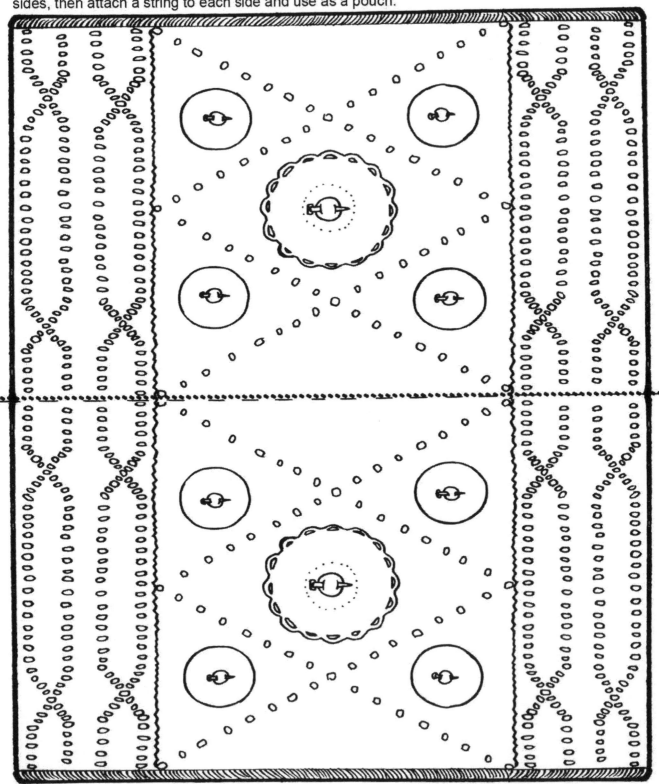

Name _____   Date _____

Woodland Indian
Silk Ribbon Appliqué

Native Americans used trade silk ribbons to decorate their clothes, moccasins, and blankets. In the 1800's, the Miami, Shawnee, Potawatomi, and Delaware people cut, overlapped, and sewed different colored ribbons together to create geometric designs. This art is called 'ribbon appliqué.' Color the ribbon appliqué work on the left side of this page!

Project: Construction Paper Ribbonwork
Subjects: Art, Social Studies (American History, Cultural Studies)
Grades 1-4

Background
Cut-ribbon applique decoration was used to make colorful geometric designs on clothing. It consisted of, in historic times, taking silk trade ribbon, cutting and folding the long edges into the desired shape, and overlapping the ribbons to create the pattern.

Procedure
You can simulate this process and art form in your classroom using colored construction paper. Simply cut out strips of different color construction paper using the templates to the right. Next, take the bands of construction paper and overlap letting each one only show the smallest patterned edge. To achieve the design illustrated to the right, make sure to alternate the two stencils. The stencil will create the pattern seen at the right side of this page when each stencil is alternated (A, B, A, B...), or the page border design to the left can also be created by alternating this stencil every two times (A, A, B, B...). Once students see how one template will make this type of design, students can then create their own pattern, trace it and cut out several strips of construction paper "ribbon applique," and overlap them to create the same type of classic ribbonwork pattern.

Take it further: The geometric designs found in ribbonwork are often symbolic. Find a Native artisan who specializes in ribbonwork or a powwow dancer who wears it, and ask about the meaning of the ribbonwork they create or wear. Share these examples of symbolism with your students and challenge them to assign symbolic meaning to the geometric designs they create in their own ribbonwork.

A

B

Construction Paper Ribbon Applique Template

Construction Paper Ribbon Applique Template

Ribbonwork Design

Design Your Own
Wampum Collar & Bracelet

The term 'wampum' refers to white and purple beads made of east coast seashells, especially clams called quahogs. These beads were traded from coastal tribes to inland tribes. Wampum beads were used for many purposes, including being made into 'strings' to remember speeches and made into belts to solidify treaties. Wampum beads were also used just for decorative reasons. The Wyandot (Huron) mother and daughter to the left wear headbands, belts, collars, and bracelets made of wampum. Wampum was highly valued among many Native American communities.

Color and cut out the bracelet and collar. Attach string to the holes. Use the strings to fasten around neck and wrist.

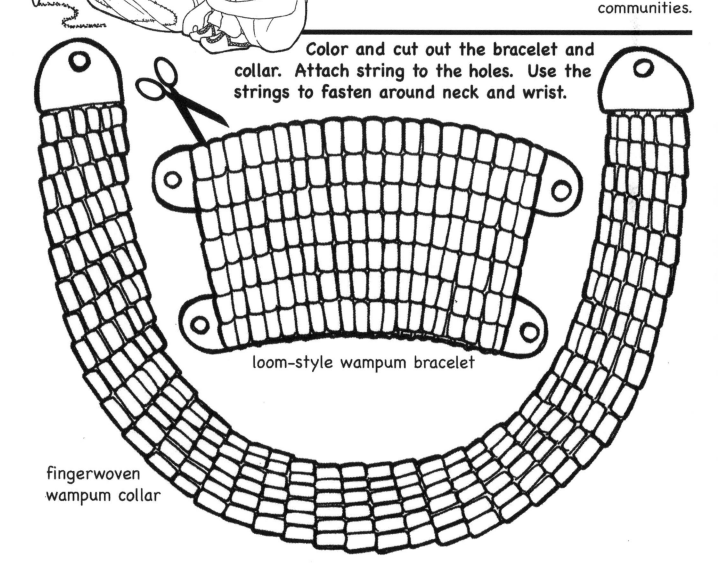

loom-style wampum bracelet

fingerwoven wampum collar

Euro-American Interaction

Including the Neighboring Iroquois's Influences on Euro-Americans and Effects of Native American Foods on the World

Topics Represented in This Section:

The Beaver Wars & Native-French Hybrid Culture; Fur Trade; Native American Perspective of Euro-Americans; Iroquois Influences of Democracy; European & American Encroachment; Westward Migration of the Delaware; Gnadenhütten & Prophetstown; Land Cessions & Boundaries; Little Turtle, Tecumseh & The Shawnee Prophet; Removal of Shawnee From Ohio; The Indian Removal Act; The Potawatomi Trail of Death; The First Capital Punishment Sentencing For Murdering Native People; Native Americans Influence the Fight for Women's Suffrage; Foods of Native America.

Development of a Hybrid French-Native Culture

The Beaver Wars: Why The Miami Were First Met in Wisconsin as Refugees

The Beaver Wars, also known as the Iroquois Wars, refers to a series of conflicts in the Great Lakes region committed by Iroquois war parties against neighboring Iroquoian and Algonquian tribes starting in 1641 and lasting until 1701. The basis for the war was the demand of furs for European trade which resulted in a depletion of beavers and fur-bearing animals in Iroquois territory (New York state and adjacent areas).

Fur traders Trading with Indian People. Date 1777. Source: Library and Archives Canada.

Such a depletion and demand led Iroquois warriors to search for these resources outside their territory. This Iroquois invasion and attacks on neighboring tribes were only encouraged by the Dutch and English who stood to profit from the pelts brought in by the Iroquois from neighboring regions, including in lands "claimed" by the French. The Iroquois invaded Ohio and Indiana among other regions, forcing those who resided in these locations to remove away from the threat. Many, including the Miami, settled near Green Bay, Wisconsin, where they made first contact with Europeans. They returned to their homelands in Indiana and Ohio after the threat of Iroquois attacks had passed. In 1701, the Great Peace of Montreal was signed, and the threat of Iroquois attacks in Indiana and Ohio were over. But there were lasting effects on those cultures who fled their homelands and relocated to refugee centers in Wisconsin – such lasting effects were the result of cultural exchange with the French.

The Beaver Wars Help Create a New French-Native American Culture

We know that many of the tribes who were a part of Indiana and Ohio's frontier history were first met in Wisconsin as refugees from the Beaver Wars, and as refugees with the hardships they experienced, they changed their traditional lifestyles to fit better within the stressed environment they were dealt. Part of that change came not just from influences of neighboring tribes, but influences from the French, who actively participated in sharing cultural traits and becoming a part of a new culture that shared both Native and European values.

Why did the French in the region do this? Well, much of the business the French conducted was in furs sales, and they wanted to encourage these local tribes, like the Miami, Kickapoo, Potawatomi, and so on, to trap many beavers and other fur-bearing animals so they may trade the furs to French companies and exporters. But there was a problem – although the French came to this region with high hopes of obtaining large amounts of fur from the western Great Lakes Native people, what they actually found were tribes displaced, struggling, and more interested in protecting themselves from the threat of Iroquois raids than caring about trapping for French interests. And those who did want to trap and trade found the trek to French posts treacherous and open to Iroquois attacks. To make matters worse, the French-allied tribes were in the middle of social unrest. Some tribes quarreled with each other, some plotted against each other with Iroquois alliances, and many of the French traders antagonized Native hunters resulting in disputes and sometimes even murders. Rumors of French factions encouraging Iroquois attacks were circulated by both Native Americans and some French. Some Native communities, tired of the fighting and in fear of the future of their societies, appealed to French authorities for their help in extinguishing tribe-to-tribe fighting and to keep their French traders in check.

At this point, French authorities realize that if they have any hope of growing their trade business and making money from this region, they must first aid the Native people in rebuilding their own

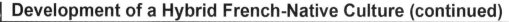

societies so they may then become interested in the fur trade business. And so the French authorities do just that, creating a French-Algonquian alliance in the region. They see themselves as mediators to keep peace among tribes forced to live within close quarters. Father Le Clercq concludes: "If we wish to settle in those countries and make any progress,… it is absolutely necessary to keep all these tribes, as well as others more remote in peace and union against the common enemy – that is the Iroquois." If unity among these tribes weren't encouraged, some may disappear entirely, making all efforts for a thriving business of the French fur trade with numerous Native trappers all but impossible. Govenor Denonville knew and commented that it was "absolutely necessary to reconcile them before thinking of deriving any advantage from them." While European powers were known to derive authority in new regions by conquest, it was actually mediation and aiding the Native societies in gaining their power back that in fact created French dominance in the western Great Lakes.

Although the French gained power in the region among allies by diplomacy, they still warred to take back power their enemies had drained of them. The English- and Dutch-backed Iroquois posed a serious threat in their fur trade profits. The French wanted to keep Dutch-English-Iroquois expansion from growing too far west into the Great Lakes, where they, the French, claimed territory and derived their valuable resources from. They created a mixed-military of French, Algonquian, and Huron to defend against Iroquois attacks (although they did not succeed early on). However, in the 1660's, New France welcomed soldiers from their motherland to help in their defense. They also sponsored feasts for Native warriors traveling east to attack the Iroquois, as well as offered supplies and gifts to the warriors' female kin, and they issued new criteria that allowed New France to conduct the direct sales of arms to allied Native peoples (at times they repaired Native Americans' guns at the king's expense).

The Changing State of Women's Roles & Status After European Contact

With European influence came European values of gendered work, nuclear families, and patriarchy. Much of this influence gained by the Miami, Kickapoo, Potawatomi and other local tribes was from the French-Algonquian alliance in the western Great Lakes. Because refugee communities in distress usually look for new beliefs to explain their situation (religion) and new practices to better their situation (customs, daily lifeways), they are very responsive to outside influences. In this case that outside influence was of a European source.

With the European fur trade comes a stronger practice of male dominance in families. Not only do the French and English recognize men as the authority of Native tribes (far more than women), they bring with them the patrilineal passing of family names and male inheritance, and in their European fashion, call Native men's families by the head men's names, judge a person's influence by their relationship to strong men (even in matrilineal societies), and even more, push a new career for Native men as full-time trappers that will systematically steal away women's role as co-providers. Now so much of the material items a Native family needs are obtained by trading away the men's spoils of trapping, whereas before so many items were obtained through women's work and skill independent of men's duties. Add to this that trapping becomes a dominant practice in so many Native families, so much so, that many of those who practiced a very sedentary farming lifestyle traditionally abandon it for travel and trapping. Ironically, when we think of the Northeastern Native people, we like to think of their traditional culture as a more mobile one, when in fact, most horticultural tribes were more sedentary prior to European meddling (it is interesting to note that later on as settlers filter into the Indiana and Ohio region, they attempt to make Native cultures once again rely more on their farm work [as many had before European contact] so they might confine them to smaller tracts of land – there is a large history of European manipulation, both passively and proactively, of Native American lifestyles to benefit colonizing Europeans).

Development of a Hybrid French-Native Culture (continued)

Where Native women had practiced in the political realm traditionally, such was on the decline after European contact, partly because of rhetoric that chastised Native men for "letting" women do "men's jobs" and because of European officials' reluctance to meet with female leaders. It is interesting to note that the Winnebago, a patrilineal post-contact people, had also a practice of passing their chief titles in the women's side of the family, from uncle to maternal nephew (such as was practiced in matrilineal tribes). Some scholars believe this points to a matrilineal past for the Winnebago before the adaptation of patrilineal clan membership and inheritance, which was probably influenced by European trade culture.

Further Reading:

"Atlas of Great Lakes Indian History" by Helen Hornbeck Tanner.

"Handbook of the North American Indians, Vol. 15: Northeast" edited by William C. Sturtevent and Bruce G. Trigger.

"Iroquois Wars of the 17th Century" by the Wisconsin Historical Society. http://www.wisconsinhistory.org/turningpoints/tp-005/?action=more_essay

"Native American-French Interactions on Eighteenth-Century Southwest Michigan: The View From Fort St. Joseph" by Michael S. Nassaney, William M. Cremin, and Lisamarie Malischke.   In the publication: "Contested Territories: Native Americans and Non-Natives in the Lower Great Lakes, 1700-1850" edited by Charles Beatty-Medina and Melissa Rinehart.

"Native Women's Status Takes a Hit Under Tecumseh and the Prophet's Leadership" by Jessica Diemer-Eaton. http://voices.yahoo.com/native-womens-status-takes-hit-under-tecumseh-and-11963002.html?cat=37

"The Middle Ground: Indians, Empires, and Republics in the Great Lakes Region, 1650-1815" by Richard White.

Notes:

_____
_____
_____
_____
_____
_____
_____
_____
_____
_____
_____
_____
_____
_____
_____

Worksheets: Fur Trade Word Search and Reading

Subjects: Social Studies (American History, Cultural Studies)

Grades 4-7

Description

Students will read about the fur trade economy and its impact on Native cultures. Afterwards, they will complete the "Fur Trade Word Search."

Procedure

Copy and distribute the next 3 pages to your class. Go over the reading (first 2 pages) and assign the word search for classroom work or homework.

Notes:

_____

_____

_____

Left: Trade shirt made of cloth from India. Such prints were popular in 18th century Native American attire. Right: Trade wool garments, fingerwoven wool garters, glass wampum beaded belt, cut-ribbon applique skirt, trade mirror, silver brooches, and Native American dolls made of European manufactured materials.

Some Extra Background:
Common 18th Century Trade Items To Native Americans

- metal awls
- axe heads
- beaver traps
- bone combs
- brass bracelets
- brass kettles
- brass thimbles
- brass wire
- candlesticks
- clasp knives
- copper rings
- cut saws
- door hooks & hinges
- fire steels

- glass beads
- glass wampum
- gunpowder
- gun flints
- iron hoes
- laced hats
- looking glasses
- metal gorgets
- muskets
- musket lead balls
- pipe tomahawks
- pewter plates
- pewter spoons

- razors
- ruffled shirts
- sewing needles
- silk handkerchiefs
- silk ribbon
- silver brooches
- silver ear bobs
- scissors
- tea kettles
- thread
- vermilion (red dye)
- wool blankets
- wool coats & jackets

Trade Items From A Native Perspective

Most trade items offered to the Native people became popular and wanted not because they were something 'new' to the Native culture, but because they were similar to materials or objects already in use. For example, silver was not so 'new' as it was like copper which was already valued for its decorative and spiritual uses.

Directions: Connect the trade item (left) to the Native item it replaced (right).

a. Metal Knife	1. Stone Axe
b. Musket	2. Clay Pot
c. Metal Axe	3. Flint Knife
d. Trade Silver ———————————	4. Copper
e. Wool & Cloth	5. Bow
f. Iron Kettel	6. Hide & Natural Fiber Textiles

Looking at the items you have connected, which one is 'better'? Is it the one made of iron or the one made of stone? Which material lasts longer? A tool may seem better just because it is much more complicated but tools with more parts may be more likely to break down. And remember, muskets are not the rifles we have today. Loading and shooting a musket ball takes up to one minute! An arrow can be drawn back and fired in just seconds.

A Consumer Driven Market

The Native people were sometimes hard to please. In many cases they demanded quality items even when traders attempted to make more money by stocking cheaper and poorly made items and materials. More than quality, traders noted that the Native people had fine taste, and they were not afraid to reject goods that did not meet their standards. Men preferred their new shirts to be very bright in color with floral designs. Women were noted to reject riding hats that did not have gold trimmed edges. Traders, in turn, stocked only the items that would sell to the Native people. Native Americans tastes dictated the fur trade market.

Name_____ Date_____

The Fur Trade Fosters An Unequal Relationship

In the early days of the Fur Trade, both Native and European parties benefited quite equally from the exchanges. Europeans made a new career that could be quite profitable while Native people were able to purchase materials from around the world. As one Native man pointed out, a beaver was just a beaver to them, however, with the Fur Trade the beaver was "magical." It turned into iron pots, or muskets, or axes, or hats, or anything a Native person could wish for. **What did this man mean metaphorically when he said the beaver was magical, that it turned into other things?** _____

_____

How The Fur Trade Helped The US Acquire Native American Lands

The Native people became reliant on trade items. By 1800, most did not use bows and arrows to hunt, they did not make tools from stone anymore, or pottery from clay. The knowledge and skill to make these items were lost with the older generations; there was no need for the younger generations to learn to make these things when Euro-Americans made so many metal pots, knives, axe heads and other items, and traded them so cheaply to the Native Americans. When the United States decided to "buy" lands in present day Indiana and Ohio, tribes like the Miami, Delaware, and Shawnee had no real choice but to comply. The Native people were now reliant on these foreign goods, and the United States took advantage of this situation;

A Native woman makes a clay pot to cook in, 1500.

the United States had the power to stop the flow of trade goods to Native communities. Without Euro-American manufactured goods, the Native people would suffer. The fur trade destroyed the independence of Native American communities by encouraging Native people to become reliant on these non-Native manufactured goods, thus making the "selling" of lands a more compulsive act rather than an equal exchange.

| **Find All 18** **Words In The** **Fur Trade** **Word Search!** (on the next page) ➡ | blankets brass pots cloth glass beads gun powder hats | iron hoe blades iron kettles metal axe heads metal knife blades muskets silk ribbon | silk scarfs silver brooches scissors stockings trade shirts wool |

Fur Trade Word Search

Find the trade merchandise that was demand by Native Americans.

```
s  i  l  v  e  r  b  r  o  o  c  h  e  s  d  f
m  e  t  a  l  k  n  i  f  e  b  l  a  d  e  s
e  i  s  i  l  k  s  c  a  r  f  s  o  g  s  t
t  r  a  d  e  s  h  i  r  t  s  i  c  j  g  o
a  o  g  l  a  s  s  b  e  a  d  s  o  h  u  c
l  n  m  s  c  i  s  s  o  r  s  m  k  o  n  k
a  h  a  t  s  r  m  u  s  k  e  t  s  m  p  i
x  o  m  b  r  o  s  i  l  k  r  i  b  b  o  n
e  e  s  r  d  n  g  c  l  o  t  h  m  e  w  g
h  b  l  a  n  k  e  t  s           a  s  d  s
e  l  w  s  s  e  s  f               w  e  s
a  a  o  s  d  t  w  c                   r  f
d  d  o  p  e  t  a  s
s  e  l  o  i  l  s
f  s  a  t  s  e  i
m  o  y  s  a  s  e
```

Illustration: Delaware mother and daughter pick out items to trade for. The daughter invited her husband to comment on cloth she has picked to sew into a shirt for him.

Name_____ Date_____

A Delaware mother and daughter trade for European tools and trinkets.

Musket

Cloth

Iron Kettle

Wool Blanket

Brass Pot

Tin Cup

Copper Tea Kettle

Scissors

Axe

Silver Jewelry

Glass Beads

Metal Knife

The daughter picks out cloth to make a new shirt for her husband.
She asks if he likes the cloth she has picked, and he agrees with her choice.

More On Native American Culture and The Fur Trade

Foreign Fashion Changes Native Diets, and Lifeways

With the fur trade era, the diets of the Native people were influenced by European economy. Indeed, the demand for small fur bearing animals like beavers changed the importance of trapping in Native communities. Before, trapping was a leisurely way (compared to hunting) to secure meat. Men and women would set traps around the village, farmlands, and woods. Now, men found themselves devoting more time to intensive trapping. This meant a slight shift in diets as more meat from trapping became available. A shift in time devotion also took place. While women, for example, devoted more time to stretching and cleaning animal hides for trade, they gained time for such work by giving up practices such as pottery making. The traders provided iron, brass, and copper kettles to cook in. In a sense, the same time was devoted to obtaining her cooking vessels, only instead of making them directly, her hide-tanning bought the pots. This replacement of material goods, and becoming reliant on outside sources for daily living utensils, materials, and tools is an important point that students studying the fur trade should know. This reliance, born from the abandonment of skills like pottery making and stone tool production during the fur trade era, would come to haunt the Native peoples when the United States looked to acquire Native lands we know today as Ohio and Indiana.

Trade Goods: Less Novel - More Familiar

It is a common misconception that all items of European manufacture were novel and "mystical" materials among the Native Americans. On the contrary, most items traded to Native Americans were valued because they resembled materials already utilized in aboriginal society before the arrival of Europeans. Glass beads replaced shell and stone beads, sharp-edged iron tools replaced stone and copper tools, and wool blankets replaced fur robes. Trade silver ornaments produced for trade to Native Americans were most likely in demand because they resembled traditional aboriginal decorations. European silver gorgets were almost duplicates of aboriginal pendants made from shell, stone, and copper. Likewise, silver brooches, many of which were designed exclusively to the taste of Native Americans, also mimicked Native charms attached to leather and textiles. It is possible that the use of trade silver brooches was just a continuing tradition of attaching ornaments to garments that would protect the wearer from mischievous spirits or sickness. In fact, silver seemed to have been desired more than brass and other metals because the brightness of the silver was favored for either aesthetic qualities or possibly supernatural reasons. Silver hair tubes, manufactured by silversmiths in Philadelphia for trade to Native peoples of the Ohio River Valley region, mimicked tubular shell beads and copper tubes of aboriginal manufacture. Silver headbands and hatbands replaced Native-made copper and shell-beaded headbands. While many introduced materials would have caught the eyes of Native peoples, it was not always because they were thought of as foreign and new - rather, many European materials were thought of as a continuation of Native tastes. Value assigned to each item was based partly on the value of its aboriginal counterpart.

Foolish Traders

Many regard Native trading of furs for "trinkets" as *unsophisticated* or *foolish*, however, we should keep in mind that the historic Native people were puzzled, even amused at the thought of Europeans trading valuable guns, silver, and silk for old, torn, worn to rags beaver furs. Such hideous hides were considered borderline garbage to the Native peoples, yet, from a Native perspective, those "foolish" Europeans fell all over themselves to own such furs, even though they were so abundant in the region. The older and more worn the furs, the more they wanted them. It would be like somebody offering you a new hunting rifle for your old, worn sneakers. Whatever you think of a person who would make such an extreme trade for your old shoes is probably close to what the Native peoples thought of such European traders. Remember, history is a series of past human perspectives, and often the Native perspective fails to make the textbooks, resulting in unbalanced versions of history - we should strive to make sure we don't pass on biased history that tends to "make fun" of events unjustly, and at the expense of Native Americans.

Name _____   Date _____

An 18th Century Delaware Perspective of European Mannerisms
Primary Historical Documentation: From a Native Point-of-View

Sometimes the best way to understand the historic Native Americans we learn about is to pay less attention to what we "think of them," and rely more on their observations of other cultures. Only then can we fairly grasp the workings of Native culture and mannerisms, and the depth of their values. The Delaware (Lenape) point-of-view and feelings regarding Euro-American mannerisms were recorded in the 18th century by Reverend John Heckewelder, who was a Moravian missionary to the Delaware. Heckewelder noted, in quite a humorous account, that the Delaware people were not as impressed by the Euro-American mannerisms as much as we might believe. His following passages give you, the student, the opportunity to think more like an anthropologist – to step outside your own "cultural perspective" and judge Native societies less by your own cultural standards. When we can understand the perspective of historic Native Americans, we can better understand historic Native Americans and their culture and history.

The Treaty of Penn with the Delaware by Benjamin West.

that such loud speaking was saved for delivering speeches and addressing audiences in their own social culture, not conversing one on one. The Delaware also observed white inquisitiveness to be borderline rude when they compared it to their [Delaware] managing of the same feelings and coping with the same curiosities:

"They [the Delaware] believe,...that the white people have weak eyes, or are near-sighted. "For," they say, "when we Indians come among them, they [Euro-Americans] crowd quite close up to us, and almost tread upon our heels to get nearer. We [the Delaware], on the contrary, though, perhaps, not less curious than they [Euro-Americans] are, to see a new people or new object, keep at a reasonable distance, and yet see what we wish to see (190)."

"They [the Delaware] sometimes amuse themselves by passing in review those customs of the white people which may appear to them most striking. They observe, amongst other things, that when the whites meet together, many of them, and sometimes all, speak at the same time, and they wonder how they can thus can hear and understand each other. "Amongst us," they [the Delaware] say "only one person speaks at a time, and the others listen to him until he is done, after which, and not before, another begins to speak (189). They [the Delaware] also remark, that when the white people meet together, they speak very loud, from whence they conclude that they must be hard of hearing (190)."

As some Delaware observed, the way Euro-Americans conversed seemed (to them) boisterous. The Delaware people go on to claim

"...They (the Delaware) are very disgusted with the manner which they say some white people have of asking them questions on questions, without allowing them time to give a proper answer... They (the Delaware), on the contrary, never ask a second question until they have received a full answer to the first. They (the Delaware) say of those who do otherwise, that they seem as if they wish to know a thing, yet cared not whether they knew it correctly or properly (321)."

Indeed the Delaware weren't too far off in their observation as historians today have a hard time piecing together Native history with bias and misinformed historical accounts.

Source: Heckewelder, John. "History, Manners, and Customs of the Indian Nations Who Once Inhabited Pennsylvania and the Neighbouring States." Philadelphia : Historical Society of Pennsylvania, 1876.

1755 Map of the Great Lakes Region

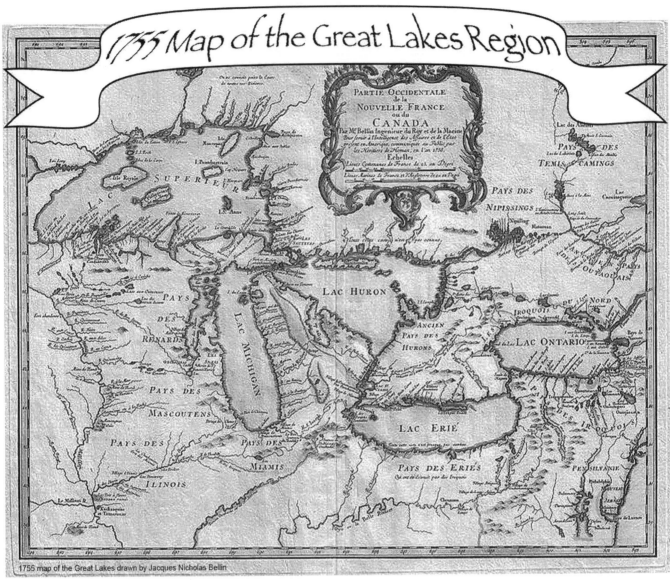

1755 map of the Great Lakes drawn by Jacques Nicholas Bellin

1. What language is this map written in? Why would it be common for maps of this region to be in this language during this time period (around 1755)?

_____

2. What war was just starting when this map was made? What does this war have to do with the Great Lakes region?

_____

3. What treaty cedes this region (including your state) to the British? What year was it signed?

_____

4. Locate and circle where the Miami are according to this map. What body of water are they located near?

_____

5. What does the term "Pays Des" before each tribe's name mean on this map?

_____

Student Article: Grades 5-12

Iroquois Democracy Inspires American Forefathers

How Benjamin Franklin, Thomas Jefferson, Thomas Paine, John Hancock & Other American Forefathers Were Influenced by the Iroquois Confederacy

While Greek ideals and the Roman Republic are credited with influencing the colonists' perspectives of liberty, it was actually the Iroquois and neighboring Native American societies that provided the most tangible examples of working democracies (Johansen, 42).

Benjamin Franklin printed many colonial treaties and minutes from meetings with Native American delegates since 1736. He was hooked on Native ideals of personal freedoms and representation in government, but felt the Iroquois message to unite, specifically Canassatego's speech in 1744 at the Treaty of Lancaster, was exactly what the colonies had to do in the current political environment. Canassatego offered the colonies this piece of advice: "Our wise forefathers established union and amity between the Five Nations" "This has made us formidable. This has given us great weight and authority with our neighboring nations. We are a powerful Confederacy, and by your observing the same methods our wise forefathers have taken, you will acquire much strength and power; therefore, whatever befalls you, do not fall out with one another (41)."

In 1751 Franklin famously wrote to his printing partner "It would be a very strange thing if six nations of ignorant savages should be able to form a scheme for such a union and be able to execute it in such a manner as it has subsisted for ages and appears indissoluble and yet a like union should be impracticable for ten or a dozen English colonies." The reader should understand that Franklin admired the Iroquois for their enlightened government, and by labeling the Iroquois by the false and negative term "ignorant savages," he actually criticized his fellow colonists for not being as "progressive" and "civilized" in their mode of governing as the Native Americans they viewed as "less than" themselves (41)."

BENJAMIN FRANKLIN BY JOSEPH-SIFFRED DUPLESSIS, 1778

In 1754, Franklin spearheaded the Albany Conference; the meeting was to bring delegates together to discuss his plan for creating a union that resembled the Iroquois. At this assembly, a message was addressed to the visiting Iroquois party in response to Canassatego's advice given 30 years previously: "Our business with you,... is to inform you of the advice that was given about thirty years ago, by your wise forefathers, in a great council which was held at Lancaster, in Pennsylvania, when Canassatego spoke to us, the white people, in these very words." They recited Canassatego's speech made at the Treaty of Lancaster, 1744, as Franklin had published it, and continue: "These were the words of Canassatego: Brothers, our forefathers rejoiced to hear Canassatego speak these words. They sank deep into our hearts. The advice was good. It was kind. They said to one another: The Six Nations are a wise people. Let us hearken to them, and take their council, and teach our children to follow it... These provinces have lightened a great council fire at Philadelphia, and sent sixty-five counselors to speak and act in the name of the whole, and to consult for the common good of the people... (Grinde, 29; Johansen, 42)."

Although the Albany Plan was rejected by colonial legislators and the king, as it was far too democratic, it served as a base for a later more successful endeavor: the Articles of Confederation. Introduced in 1776, it was actually a revised draft of Franklin's Albany Plan, the same one that imitated Iroquois democracy (Johansen, 41).

Franklin also used his knowledge of Native American culture to advance his agendas and that of the newly formed United States. When in France, he spoke with influential people about concepts of liberty and Native politics. The French of the period were quite curious of Native Americans, and Franklin (among other Forefathers) used that curiosity to his and the Americans' benefits, especially in their relationship to the French (Grinde, 30).

After the Revolution, Franklin joined the Constitutional Sons of Saint Tammany in Philadelphia, a secret patriotic society that sought to promote liberty and had intense interest in the budding United States government. Interestingly, the society incorporated Iroquois-style ideals into their rhetoric. It is no coincidence that they and other patriotic brotherhoods dressed in Native American style clothing as part of the pageantry (30-31). Keep in mind the Boston Tea Party: the message of the Mohawk-themed costumes was liberty - a concept colonists attributed as a social trait among their Native neighbors absent in their own European backgrounds. Hence the message that the costumes communicated, that the colonists were free "Americans" belonging only to the land and no longer subjected to British rule (Johansen, 41).

Benjamin Franklin was not the only influential patriot to take cues on liberty from the Iroquois and other Native nations. Thomas Jefferson remarked on what he considered to be a better government exemplified by Native peoples than the European monarchial societies of his own heritage. "I am convinced that these societies as the Indians enjoy in their general mass an infinitely greater degree of happiness than those who live under European government (42)." Jefferson was a scholarly man; he complied an extensive work on Native American languages (however it was stolen while moving out of the White House), and his never-ending thirst for gaining knowledge of America's original inhabitants through excavation has led some modern scholars to name him the Father of American Archaeology. The Native peoples of America interested Jefferson so much so that he became the first to propose, in his recommendations to the University of Virginia, an ethnological study of Native American traditions, laws, customs, languages and other cultural traits (Weatherford, 142).

THOMAS JEFFERSON

BY REMBRANDT PEALE, 1800

In 1777, Thomas Paine was appointed to the Committee for Foreign Affairs of the Continental Congress, and was secretary to the Iroquois Treaty at Easton, Pennsylvania. Colonial America used Iroquois imagery as a method of propaganda, as the French were especially fascinated by Iroquois-based ideas. The

Continental Congress published a pamphlet in France also in that same year in which Iroquois concepts of liberty were highlighted. Because of the partly Iroquois influence of democracy on the emerging United States, the pamphlet declares that a victory for the American people is a victory for humanity. While this publication was part propaganda to win the French over, it still admited the Native influences on American liberty. Thomas Paine was reputed to speak a great deal on the Iroquois when in France (Grinde, 31).

During one diplomatic venture in May of 1776, John Hancock welcomed Iroquois chiefs to the Continental Congress in Philadelphia. The party camped outside of Independence Hall during a period of time when Congress was looking towards independence; they were essentially present when the draft of the Articles of Confederation were introduced - they were present on the eve of America's independence. John Hancock, president of the Continental Congress, was, like his infamous peers, well aware of democracy and citizens' rights demonstrated by the Iroquois and other Native nations. John Hancock himself was named "Karanduawn" or "Great Tree" by an Onondaga chief in June of that same year (30). The previous year (1775), his signature appeared on the speech recognizing the Iroquois at Albany for their advice urging the colonies to band together as one nation (29).

John Rutledge, chairman of the Committee of Detail that drafted the first copy of the U.S. Constitution, was also familiar with Iroquois diplomacy. As a young man, he sat down with Sir William Johnson (Indian Agent) and a party of Mohawks while attending the Stamp Act Congress. No doubt Rutledge was briefed in the Iroquois Great Law. Twenty years after the meeting, chairing the Committee of Detail, he was said to have opened the meeting with some passages from the Iroquois Great Law, after which the Constitution was drafted (31). It is also worth noting that earlier drafts of the Constitution contained Iroquois-influenced rhetoric which were later left out of the final version (Burton, 46).

Iroquois and other Native concepts of democracy and liberty greatly influenced our Forefathers and colonists before them. It is important to keep in mind that the Native influence of democracy was not just passively observed by the Forefathers, but also actively explained and taught to them. The Iroquois appointed ambassadors to educate colonial officials of the workings and benefits of the Great Law of the Iroquois (Grinde, 30). New practices of democracy, such as admitting new states, initiating impeachment of unfavorable presidents, the electoral college system, and even the practice of one representative speaking at length with colleagues not interrupting (the "one person speaks at a time" rule) were all introduced concepts courtesy of the Iroquois and other Native American societies (Weatherford, 138-140).

In 1987, a resolution acknowledging the Native influences on the formulation of the Constitution (and the American Forefathers) was introduced:

Senate Concurrent Resolution 76:
To acknowledge the contribution of the Iroquois Confederacy of Nations in the development of the United States Constitution...

Whereas the original framers of the Constitution, including most notably, George Washington and Benjamin Franklin, are known to have greatly admired the concepts, principles and governmental practices of the Six Nations of the Iroquois Confederacy; and

Whereas the confederation of the original Thirteen Colonies into one republic was explicitly modeled upon the Iroquois Confederacy as were many of the democratic principles which were incorporated into the Constitution itself;...

Resolved by the Senate (the House of Representatives concurring), That -

1) the Congress, on the occasion of the two hundredth anniversary of the signing of the United States Constitution, acknowledges the historical debt which the Republic of the United States owes to the Iroquois Confederacy and other Indian nations for their demonstration of enlightened, democratic principles of Government...

"Declaration of Independence" by John Trumbull, 1819.

Extra Credit Question:

The Iroquois were not only a democracy - they were a republic (and still are). What is the relation and differences of a republic government to just a democracy? Is the United States a republic, and if so, are they the oldest republic in North America? If not, what nation is?

_____
_____
_____
_____
_____
_____
_____
_____
_____
_____
_____

Sources for "Iroquois Democracy Inspires American Forefathers"

Note on Senate Concurrent Resolution 76: This was introduced in 1987 and passed in the Senate without amendment in 1988 (source: http://thomas.loc.gov/cgi-bin/bdquery/z?d100:SC00076:@@@L&summ 2=m&). A similar resolution was passed by the Senate and House of Representatives in "1988 acknowledging the contributions of the Iroquois Confederacy of Nations to the development of our Constitution..." "Senator Daniel Inouye (D-Hawaii) introduced S.Con.Res. 76 on September 16, 1987. Representative Morris Udall (D-Arizona) introduced similar legislation in the House of Representatives as H.Con.Res. 331 (quote from http://www.senate.gov/reference/common/faq/Iroquois_Constitution.shtml)."

Sources:

Burton, Bruce. "The Iroquois Had Democracy Before We Did." Indian Roots of Democracy. Northeast Indian Quarterly (1988): 44-48. Print.
Grinde, Donald. "It's Time to Take Away the Veil." Indian Roots of Democracy. Northeast Indian Quarterly (1988): 28-33. Print.
Johansen, Bruce. "Indian Thought Was Often in Their Minds." Indian Roots of Democracy. Northeast Indian Quarterly (1988): 40-43. Print.
Weatherford, Jack. Indian Givers. How the Indians of the Americas Transformed the World. New York: Ballantine Books, 1988. Print.

Lesson: Native American Influences Shape US Democracy

Subjects: Social Studies (American History, Cultural Studies, US Government)
Grades 5-12

From S. Con. Resolution 76:

To acknowledge the contribution of the Iroquois Confederacy of Nations in the development of the United States Constitution...

Whereas the original framers of the Constitution, including most notably, George Washington and Benjamin Franklin, are known to have greatly admired the concepts, principles and governmental practices of the Six Nations of the Iroquois Confederacy; and

Whereas the confederation of the original Thirteen Colonies into one republic was explicitly modeled upon the Iroquois Confederacy as were many of the democratic principles which were incorporated into the Constitution itself;...

Resolved by the Senate (the House of Representatives concurring), That -

1) the Congress, on the occasion of the two hundredth anniversary of the signing of the United States Constitution, acknowledges the historical debt which the Republic of the United States owes to the Iroquois Confederacy and other Indian nations for their demonstration of enlightened, democratic principles of Government...

Introduced 9/16/87 - Passed Without Amendment in the Senate 10/7/88

From H. Con. Resolution 331:

...Acknowledges the contribution made by the Iroquois Confederacy and other Indian Nations to the formulation and development of the United States;...

Introduced 7/11/88 - Passed the House of Representatives 10/4/88, Passed in the Senate 10/21/88

Discuss the history that inspired these resolutions in class, and have students look up how Native American societies exemplified democracy before the United States was born:

Q. At what assembly did the Iroquois leader Canassatego urge the colonies to unite?
A. Treaty of Lancaster in 1744 (Donald Grinde, *Indian Roots of American Democracy*, Northeast Indian Quarterly:1988).

Q. What were Canassatego's words?
A. *"Our wise forefathers established union and amity between the Five Nations" "This has made us formidable. This has given us great weight and authority with our neighboring nations. We are a powerful Confederacy, and by your observing the same methods our wise forefathers have taken, you will acquire much strength and power; therefore, whatever befalls you, do not fall out with one another* (Bruce Johansen, I*ndian Roots of American Democracy*, Northeast Indian Quarterly:1988)."

Q. Who famously published Canassatego's words, and endorsed the concept of unity of colonies from then on in his speeches?
A. Benjamin Franklin. Franklin had been printing Native treaties since 1736 (Bruce Johansen, *Indian Roots of American Democracy*, Northeast Indian Quarterly:1988).

Q. What was the year colonial commissioners gave a speech that officially recognize Canassatego's words for partly inspiring the formulation of the United States, and whose famous signature graced it?
A. 1775, signed by John Hancock (Donald Grinde, *Indian Roots of American Democracy*, Northeast Indian Quarterly:1988).

Lesson: Native American Influences Shape US Democracy

Subjects: Social Studies (American History, Cultural Studies, US Government)
Grades 5-12

Continued

Q. What were the words colonial commissioners said to the Iroquois assembled during this 1775 Contintal Congress meeting?
A. *"Our business with you,... is to inform you of the advice that was given about thirty years ago, by your wise forefathers, in a great council which was held at Lancaster, in Pennsylvania, when Canassatego spoke to us, the white people, in these very words."* They recite Canassatego's speech made at the Treaty of Lancaster, 1744, as Franklin had published them, and continue: *"These were the words of Canassatego: Brothers, our forefathers rejoiced to hear Canassatego speak these words. They sank deep into our hearts. The advice was good. It was kind. They said to one another: The Six Nations are a wise people. Let us hearken to them, and take their council, and teach our children to follow it... These provinces have lightened a great council fire at Philadelphia, and sent sixty-five counsellors to speak and act in the name of the whole, and to consult for the common good of the people...(Papers of the Continental Congress, 1774-89, National Archives)."*

More questions to consider posing to your students:
How did George Washington know of Indian values and diplomacy? Did any of his prior jobs on the frontier place him in contact with Native peoples?

Did the classical training (school) of the American Forefathers become a factor in how much they understood Native American politics?

How did the Iroquois government work? Look up (online) the "Iroquois Five Nations Constitution" to find similarities in ours and their government. What government traits did we [Americans] borrow from the much older American Democracy [Iroquois]?

Notes:

_____
_____
_____
_____
_____
_____
_____
_____
_____
_____
_____

Name

Date

Map of European & American Encroachment of North America, 1750-1816

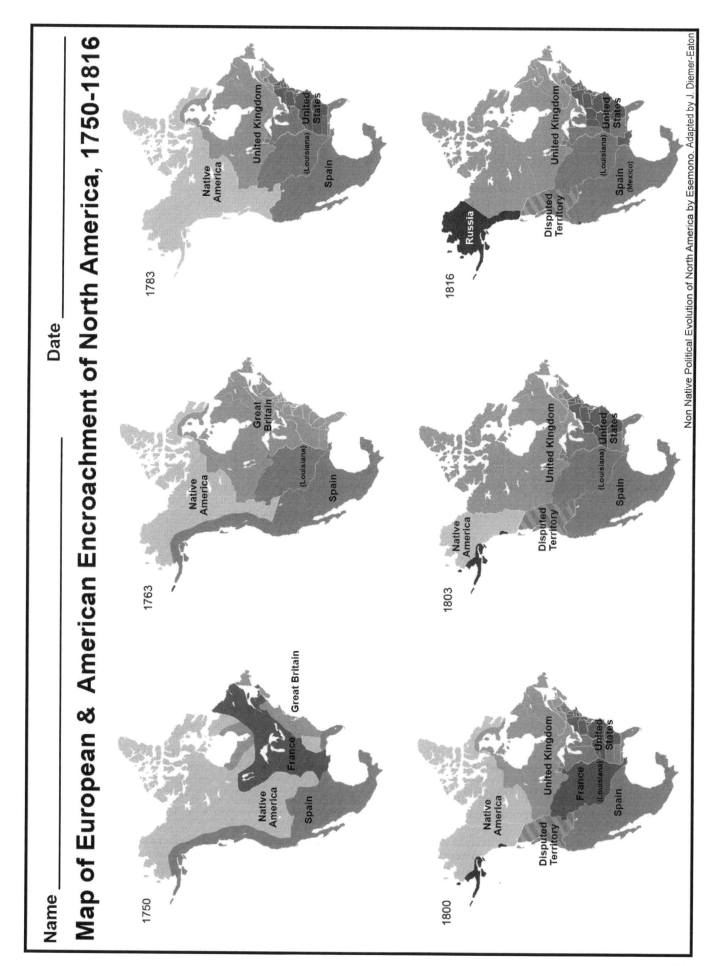

1750

1763

1783

1800

1803

1816

Questions for the Map of European & American Encroachment of North America, 1750-1816

1. Define "colonization." In general, why did European nations seek to colonize lands in North America (not the individual citizens but the European governments)?

_____
_____
_____
_____
_____

2. What European nation claims your state in 1750? Who claimed your state's land first, and still claimed your state in 1750, regardless of European claims?

_____

3. On many maps showing European expansion, lands not claimed by European powers are commonly labeled as "unclaimed lands." Why is this label misleading?

_____
_____
_____

4. What European nation claims your state in 1763? After what war did they acquire the land you reside on now?

_____

5. Louisiana was claimed by which European nation in 1763? Which country claims the same Louisiana territory in 1800?

_____

6. For what reason did this nation want this tract of land under their control, and who was the famous military leader responsible for negotiating Louisiana back from Spanish control?

_____
_____
_____

7. The 1816 map includes the label "Mexico" with Spain. Why would both be included as staking claim to the same piece of land during this time? When did Mexico claim their independence initially, and when did they achieve their independence?

_____
_____

8. One claim to land is fading quickly between 1750 and 1816. Who's territory is quickly disappearing and doesn't even appear on the 1816 map (besides France)?

_____

Delaware (Lenape) Westward Migration Map

Why did the Delaware (Lenape) Indian people move westward away from their homelands?
Do you think they wanted to, or did they have to move even if they didn't want to? Why?

_____

_____

_____

In what years did they reside in your state? _____

Gnadenhütten Crossword

Gnadenhütten was one of a few Christian Indian villages in Ohio constructed for Native converts to the Moravian Church. Established in 1772, many of the residents (Delawares, Mahicans, and white Moravians) had already experienced discrimination from non-Moravians and had been victims of violence in their previous mission towns in Pennsylvania. They removed themselves further west and established towns in Ohio in the hopes of fleeing such percussion. Unfortunately, they also put themselves in between two major opposing posts during the start of the American Revolutionary War: the rebel Americans at Fort Pitt, and the British at Fort Detroit. British-allied Delaware and Wyandot Indian people captured the Moravian Delaware and moved them further north in Ohio where they could be watched while their missionaries were forcefully brought to Detroit to face trial for treason under British law. The captured Moravian-Delaware were soon running out of food, and so about 100 residents were allowed to go to Gnadenhütten to retrieve food stores. During this time, they were surprised by a Pennsylvania raiding party of soldiers. Although the American military leaders warned troops to leave the peaceful and unarmed Moravian-Delawares alone, this Pennsylvania unit did not follow the orders; most of the soldiers accused these residents as being combatants, which they were not. The Pennsylvania unit killed over 90 innocent Delaware men, women, and children in 1782, ten years after the establishment of Gnadenhütten. This became known as the Gnadenhütten Massacre. No charges for these murders were ever brought against the soldiers.

Moravian-Delaware Culture Word Pool

cabbage
carve
chestnuts
corn
earthenware
gender
hominy
horticultural
Lenape
maple sugar
matrilineal
Moravian
mortar and pestle

Munsee
muskets
trade silver
venison
wigwam

Down

1. A traditional grain grown by the Delaware.
3. _____ was made by evaporating sap collected from Maple trees.
5. A Christian religion that believed in conducting missionary work among the Native American people.
7. The Moravians practiced extreme _____ segregation in their everyday life, which was hard for the Delaware to accept who did not practice such.
9. A common word for deer or elk meat.
11. The Delaware people's name for themselves.
13. Small Native home covered with bark and reed mats.
15. The Delaware were _____ people, securing most of their foods from their gardening activities.
17. _____ were used more for hunting than traditional bows (and arrows) by the mid 1700's Delaware.

Across

2. The Delaware were _____, passing their clan membership through the women's side of the family.
4. _____ in the form of brooches, rings, bracelets, and earrings were prized by both Delaware men and women.
6. A _____ was used to crush corn into meal.
8. _____ pottery was used by the Delaware to cook food in before trade metal kettles replaced them in the 1700's.
10. It was the Delaware men, as the traditional woodworkers, who would _____ the wooden bowls, spoons, mortars, etc.
12. The dialect (language) of the northern Delaware people.
14. A dish made of corn treated with an ash-lye solution.
16. A favored nut variety of the Delaware people.
18. _____ and turnips were introduced into the Delaware diet by the Moravian missionaries.

Journey to Prophetstown Maze

Directions: Find your way through the maze and answer the questions below.

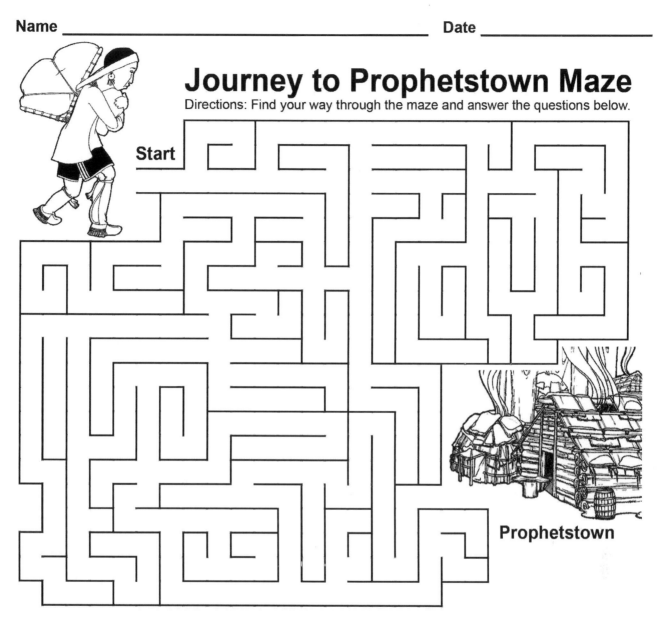

Start

Prophetstown

Why did some Native American people choose to relocate to Prophetstown?
Prophetstown was a place where individuals and families from many tribal backgrounds came to live because they believed in The Prophet's religious guidance and Tecumseh's political campaign. The Prophet claimed that white culture had corrupted their Native way of life. They also agreed with Tecumseh's views, that their own tribal leaders were also corrupt because they made treaties that sold land to the Americans. Many people who believed in The Prophet and Tecumseh's movement packed their belongings and went to live among others with the same views. While The Prophet and Tecumseh had thousands of followers, most Native people in this region did not agree with their movement. Prophetstown was established in 1808, however, it did not last long. The village was mostly abandoned after the Battle of Tippecanoe in 1811. **Why did most of The Prophet's followers abandon Prophetstown?**

_____

_____

Did Tecumseh agree with The Prophet's decision? Did Tecumseh still have followers after the Battle of Tippecanoe? _____

_____

Name _____

Date _____

Land Successions in Indiana

1. Using a marker, place a dot on the map where you live.

2. In what treaty or tract of land do you reside?

3. Research how the land you reside in changed from Native American to Euro-American ownership, and tell the story below:

_____
_____
_____
_____
_____
_____
_____
_____
_____
_____
_____
_____
_____
_____
_____
_____
_____
_____
_____

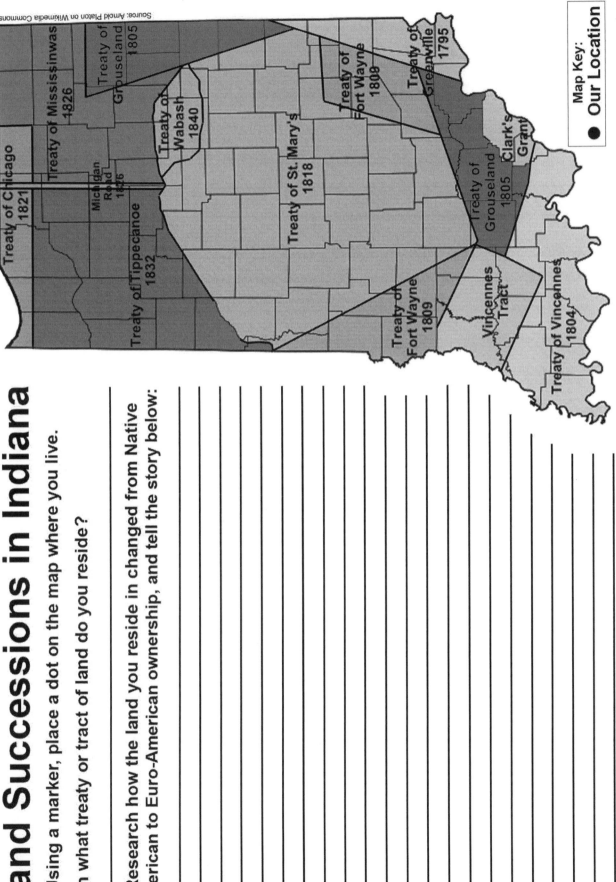

Source: Arnold Platon on Wikimedia Commons.

Treaty of Chicago 1821

Treaty of Mississinwas 1826

Treaty of Grouseland 1805

Michigan Road 1826

Treaty of Wabash 1840

Treaty of Tippecanoe 1832

Treaty of St. Mary's 1818

Treaty of Fort Wayne 1809

Treaty of Greenville 1795

Clark's Grant

Treaty of Grouseland 1805

Vincennes Tract

Treaty of Fort Wayne 1809

Treaty of Vincennes 1804

Map Key:
● Our Location

Contested Territory of Ohio

Describe why Ohio was a contested territory between Native Americans and the United States after
the Revolutionary War.

_____
_____
_____
_____
_____
_____
_____
_____
_____
_____
_____
_____
_____
_____
_____
_____
_____
_____
_____
_____
_____

Credit: Charles C. Royce for Smithsonian Institution

The Treaty of Greenville Solidifies Little Turtle's Authority

Little Turtle's Struggle for Leadership Among the Miamis and Americans, 1795-1809

Little Turtle, Artist Unknown
Image Source: Wikimedia Commons

The 1795 Treaty of Greenville brought a close to the Northwest Indian War, also known as Little Turtle's War. Although Little Turtle helped to defeat Harmar's and St. Clair's armies (an impressive feat), the warriors of various tribal backgrounds later lost the Battle of Fallen Timbers in 1794, and a year later, the Treaty of Greenville dissolved the war. The very loose Native alliance was forced to surrender a large portion of Ohio, much of which was claimed by the Miami.

Little Turtle, a leader of the Miami, made it quite clear when speaking to American delegates and tribal representatives at the Treaty of Greenville, that they, the Miami, were the true owners of a large piece of the mid-west. He outlined the Miami's homelands as extending from Detroit south to the Ohio River, west to the mouth of the Wabash, north to Lake Michigan, and east back to Detroit, claiming half of Ohio and all of Indiana. What's more, it seems as no representatives of the other Old Northwestern tribes objected to his assertion (at least it wasn't noted to be challenged), giving the appearance that the Miami's neighbors, many of whom had established villages inside that perimeter, believed the claim to be correct. As far as Little Turtle was concerned, those tribes were on his People's lands at Miami invitation and they had no real claim to it (although the Miami did see it as each villages' prerogative to be a part of land sales they resided on). Little Turtle was at first angry about the treaty and declared the Miami lands were not to be ceded, but then reluctantly signed his name and declared that he may have been one of the last chiefs to sign it, but he would also be the last one to break it. He kept that promise, and more, Little Turtle realized that Miami lands were their most prized commodity when it came to Miami-American relations.

Little Turtle Signs the Treaty

Little Turtle had already felt, before the treaty discussions, that the Native peoples could no longer hold off an ever-growing sea of Americans, especially without British intervention. His prediction had only become realized by the majority of Native communities after their loss at the Battle of Fallen Timbers (1794). Little Turtle's next move had to be carefully planned. He had to present a strong front during the treaty talks to put as much power back on his side as possible. He displayed anger of the Americans' coveting "his People's land, and so loudly boasted of his role in the Native victory of St. Clair's Defeat (historically the largest defeat of the United States by Native American forces), and after throwing around a little weight, Little Turtle then decided to sign, but did so with the objective of securing annuity payments for any and all sales made on Miami territory. His goal might have been to make the Americans think that pleasing him was key to smooth land negotiations in this defined region, regardless of other non-Miami established villages on the same tracts. If this was his strategy from the start of negotiations, then Little Turtle succeeded, gaining a government-issued annuity for the Miami from the Treaty of Greenville, and becoming a major authority in the eyes of the Americans.

The Greenville Treaty Line
By Peters, William E. (1918)
Image Source: Wikimedia Commons

Little Turtle: Miami Tribal Chief

Little Turtle's role before the Treaty of Greenville was nothing short of complete opposition to Americans, especially on the battlefield, while his role after was one to "keep the peace" between the Miami and a few neighboring tribes with the Americans. Essentially, the treaty solidified his authority to both war captain and civil chief, not only in the Americans' eyes but also on the Miami front. Traditionally, war captains were not eligible for positions of civil chiefs; the two domains were to remain separate. Not only that but war captains did not have any real authority in civil matters, their influence being confined to the battlefield. And while almost any warrior with an excellent track record and the support of his community could climb to the position of war captain, only certain individuals were eligible for the position of civil chief. Eligibility for Miami civil chief was traditionally passed from father to son, or at times, through women. It is interesting to note that in the transition of the chief title, the mothers of the future chiefs become very loud and assertive in public affairs especially while instructing their sons and grooming them to take public office. Her behavior was probably to announce and publicly confirm his coming role.

Indeed, Little Turtle was a war captain, most likely earning his position during the American Revolution. Yet his role as war captain should have also presented an obstacle in gaining authority in civil matters, however in Little Turtle's time, there had been a growing trend among many Midwestern tribes to put more authority in their war captains, blurring the line between war captains and civil chiefs. Little Turtle and his rival Tecumseh were both war captains initially, yet both, taking advantage of European influences that favored single leaders that combined authority of war and civil matters, had capitalized on their war positions to gain authority in all tribal affairs.

What Little Turtle became can be defined in historical terms as an "annuity chief:" a leader whose supporters included both his constituents and the American government; a leader who drew upon his financial resources obtained by American treaties and relations to keep a secured leader position within his tribe. While this explanation might make Little Turtle seem corrupt, it was actually his generosity toward his and allied tribes, his affective management of the Miami's annuities, and his refusal to indulge in riches (debatable) that made him a beloved leader. However, to his rival Tecumseh, any annuity chief was considered to be corrupt.

There is some evidence that Little Turtle's son-in-law, the adopted white-American captive William Wells, may have gained unmerited financial benefits through his relationship to the Miami chief while acting as Indian agent. In fact, William Wells despised Tecumseh and The Prophet long before they were considered threats by Little Turtle. Why? Most likely because the more influence the Shawnee brothers gained, the larger the threat of William Wells not retaining a higher cash flow to the Miami through himself. Such annuities were partly secured by American perceptions of Little Turtle's "control" over a large percentage of Native peoples and lands. The more supporters Tecumseh and The Prophet gained, the less constituents were attributed to Little

Turtle, and that risked a rival chief possibly winning large annuities at the expense of the Miami, and William Wells.

And it wasn't just his son-in-law cited to have had less than the highest ethics, as Little Turtle himself may have given into accepting bribes while making treaties. Little Turtle was granted a personal annuity (bribe) by William Henry Harrison in an 1802 preliminary treaty, and in 1804, with the promise more annuities, Little Turtle signed away lands in the most southern part of Indiana. However, while bribery may have been at play, so was pressure. Corruption seemed to have infected all parties. Potawatomi chiefs had put pressure on the Miami to sell that track for the 1804 treaty, and later had even gone as far as to threatened war on the Miami if they didn't sign the 1809 treaty that ceded yet another track of southern Indiana. The Miami initially didn't want to sell, but the Potawatomi threat was a real one, as they were not only half the Natives present at the treaty grounds, but they also stood to receive the largest share of goods, a "gift" for supporting Harrison during negotiations. Yet, the Potawatomi may have thought they had grounds for such "bullying" as they claimed this reciprocity was long overdue for earlier treaties they signed at the request of the Miami, even if they had been less beneficial for the Potawatomi. It was Little Turtle's endorsement of the 1809 Treaty of Fort Wayne, along with Harrison's denouncement of Little Turtle's chief title, that sealed the fate of his influence.

The Downfall of Little Turtle; The Rise of Tecumseh
Little Turtle, who strongly opposed Tecumseh's anti-American movement, was able up to this point, to keep his Miami citizens happy under his authority. When the 1809 treaty lands were ceded, Tecumseh cited it as evidence for what he believed to be a growing corruption among all the annuity chiefs. Tecumseh's message was essentially that Little Turtle and other annuity chiefs wouldn't stop selling the Indian people's lands until there was no more to sell. The 1809 Treaty of Fort Wayne was the last

straw, and some who had never questioned their annuity chiefs' motives now took a second look at Tecumseh's message. For the first time, Tecumseh was seeing real numbers of local followers. It also marked a serious change in the Shawnee brothers' movement, from the religious to the political. The 1809 treaty catapulted Tecumseh's authority; before the treaty, The Prophet led the movement, and after, Tecumseh led the movement.

As much as Tecumseh was appalled by the 1809 Treaty of Fort Wayne, he was probably aware that it was the lucky break his anti-American establishment was in need of, resulting in attracting large numbers of new followers, including some Miami who were previously supporters of Little Turtle. Little Turtle's authority did suffer a very real setback, but by November of 1811, the Battle of Tippecanoe resulted in the first major blow of The Prophet's and Tecumseh's pan-Indian alliance, and what authority Little Turtle had lost was considerably restored, especially with public respect. Little Turtle died in 1812.

Further Reading:
-"Tecumseh and the Quest for Indian Leadership" by R. David Edmunds.
-"The Miami Indians of Indiana, A Persistent People, 1654-1994" by Stewart Rafert.
-"Thinking and Believing: Nativism and Unity in the Ages of Pontiac and Tecumseh" by Gregory Evans Dowd, in "American Encounters: Natives and Newcomers From European Contact to Indian Removal, 1500-1850" edited by Peter C. Mancall and James H. Merrell.

Notes

_____
_____
_____
_____
_____
_____
_____
_____
_____

Beyond Popular History: The Other Tecumseh and Tenskwatawa

Sometimes respecting Native history means respecting all Native perspectives of that history being discussed. So many times, certain historical figures made into heroes were not always thought of as "heroes" by all Native Americans at that time. In the case of Tecumseh and his brother Tenskwatawa (The Prophet), they were as loved as they were despised among the Native American people of the time, although we tend to only hear of Tecumseh in glowing terms. We owe it to the other half, those who feared the brother's militant and religious movement, to take off our rose-colored glasses and understand why these people, half or more who came in contact with or heard the brothers' message turned away, treating the brothers like a nuisance at best, or like terrorists at worse. This is their history, a short description of why other Native peoples formed a different opinion of Tecumseh and The Prophet, a perspective usually ignored:

Many quote words of unity and peace spoken by Tecumseh, but few know that both Tecumseh and The Prophet lied in many public speeches made in front of Americans. The Prophet was particularly shameless in this aspect, constantly lying and playing a "friend" to con American authorities. Speeches by Tecumseh that make mention of respecting others seem half-hollow given his tendency to do just the opposite to elders who didn't agree with him.

Tecumseh is quoted promoting the virtue of respecting others' religions, yet his brother would not settle but to have all acknowledge him as a prophet, and adapt his new faith with new songs, dances, and medicine bundles – anything else was false and wrong, and a target of his wrath. Tecumseh himself accused white-Christians of murdering their own god (Jesus) (White 384). Their speeches talked of an equal respect and worth, but their actions showed a disgust for both Americans and Native persons that didn't support the Shawnee brothers.

The Prophet seemed to favor a pure Native race, insisting that Natives married to whites must leave their spouses, and mixed-race children of such unions were not welcomed in his village.

The brothers' rhetoric emphasizing masculinity equaling power, and practice of socially dominating the female gender tears away the more traditional equal status of women in Native society – they strip Native women of their traditional political power and reduce them in language as "slaves" and less than men.

The Prophet endorsed witch hunts that did end up in killing some innocent Native men and women. One such 1810 documented case included two Wyandot women and an aged chief being executed for supposed "crimes of witchcraft." In the case of Chief Leatherlips, six of The Prophet's young warriors seized the chief and tomahawked him to death.

Both The Prophet and Tecumseh encouraged assassinations of elderly chiefs who disagreed with the brothers, and even some white-Americans were attempting to stop the witch hunts that terrorized the villages. Tecumseh undermined the authority of civil chiefs by trying to turn young warriors against their elders, and he himself threatened the lives of such Native leaders, and disregarding traditional Native ways, insisted warriors' opinions were to be heeded over the elderly civil chiefs.

Tecumseh himself was not a "chief" in the sense most think, as in inheriting a civil authority position as tribal chiefs (it would be incorrect to define Tecumseh as "chief of the Shawnee"). Tecumseh was a war chief or war captain, gaining his authority through his deeds on the battlefield. In truth, Tecumseh was really a rebel war captain as he refused to heed his own governmental chiefs and councils. Traditionally Northeastern Native war chiefs didn't have much of any influence in civil matters, that is until Europeans unfamiliar with Native government blurred the lines – there was no separation of war and civil duty in Anglo governments, and Tecumseh embraced that concept over following his traditional place under councils of elders and civil chiefs.

Not only that, but after the 1809 treaty, Tecumseh declared himself leader of all Native peoples of the region insisting Americans acknowledge his authority and not the individual civil chiefs, which was an outright lie considering many did not consider him a chief at all.

Half of the Native people (or most) didn't follow the Shawnee brothers, or even like them. Few even fled the area for lands in the west at this time, not because they were too crowded by Americans but because they feared this growing Native militant movement, such as the case of American friendly communities of Wea and Piankeshaw that asked Harrison's permission to remove west into Illinois.

For some Native peoples of this time and place, the brothers were a symbol of hope; for other Native peoples, the brothers were a radical and terrorizing force to be feared. They were both Shawnee leaders and Shawnee exiles; they were both Shawnee heros and Shawnee enemies.

A Note About This Article:
This reading has been included because most educational sources (including textbooks) put Tecumseh (and some other Native leaders) on an unrealistically high podium - a hero who did no wrong (purposely or accidentally) and whose motives were always pure. This leads readers to define such figures as "noble savages" - an offensive concept applied to many Native American figures. Although the "noble" part sounds real positive, this term and concept is anything but. The "noble savage" symbolizes an "uncivilized person" with an innate goodness (natural, instinctual goodness). Problem here is that Native people's responses to their environment and social issues weren't instinctual (like animals) - their responses were guided by reasoning and intelligence. The "noble savage" perpetuates a stereotype that defines historic Native people as simple beings and products of simple cultures. This is not the case. Their actions were based on experience, wisdom, and awareness (the understanding of consequences). Tecumseh was a complex man - he made calculated moves to further his cause, and as any intelligent human in a difficult situation, he had downfalls in his actions and discourse.

Sources:
-Edmunds, R. David. The Shawnee Prophet. University of Nebraska Press, Lincoln: 1983.

-Dowd, Gregory Evans. Thinking and Believing: Nativism and Unity in the Ages of Pontiac and Tecumseh. In American Encounters: Natives and Newcomers from European Contact to Indian Removal, 1500-1850. Edited by Peter C. Mancall and James H. Merrell. Routledge, New York: 2000.

-Tanner, Helen Hornbeck. The Glaize in 1792: A Composite Indian Community. In American Encounters: Natives and Newcomers from European Contact to Indian Removal, 1500-1850. Edited by Peter C. Mancall and James H. Merrell. Routledge, New York: 2000

-White, Richard. The Middle Ground: Indians, Empires, and Republics in the Great Lakes Region, 1650-1815. Cambridge University Press, New York: 1991.

-Willig, Timothy D. Prophetstown on the Wabash: The Native Spiritual Defense of the Old Northwest. Michigan Historical Review, Vol. 23, No. 2 (Fall, 1997), pp. 115-158.

Notes:

_____

_____

_____

_____

_____

Further Insights Into the Article "Beyond Popular History"

Tenskwatawa's insisting on a "pure Native race" was in direct competition with traditional Native values. Many, including the Shawnee, viewed close relationships as being more than just "sharing the same blood." For example, Euro-American and African-American captives adopted into Native families were usually thought of as no less than blood relatives; they were given all the same rights and responsibilities as those of blood relation and the Native ethnicity. It was Euro-Americans that introduced the idea of separating "races," race intolerance, and blood relationships as superior to adoptive relationships.

In Tecumseh and Tenskwatawa's anti-American religious movement, Native women's status comes under fire. As Native people adapt white perspectives of gender inequality, and in understanding such perspectives, they then liken their relationship to Americans through descriptions of male-female power dynamics of European origin. Tenskwatawa and his followers had bought into "domination over women" as the place of men. Tenskwatawa's behavior was nothing new; this is not an unusual phenomenon, and in fact, social issues that include subjugation of a particular race, nationality, or group of people (such as a gender/sex) have many times been born out of unsavory behavior in the oppressed culture too. Many times, this included the "oppressed" oppressing another group of people they felt "over," such as, in this case, the women of their own society. Such behavior psychologically "boosted" men of an oppressed group as they felt some sort of power they perceived was taken from them, and to show force - that they were able to and did get respect, the same as those men who subjugated them. Tecumseh and Tenskwatawa's movement becomes yet another textbook example of partly oppressing the women of their group in response to being treated themselves as second-class citizens (read more about this in the article "Native Women's Status Takes a Hit Under Tecumseh and the Prophet's Leadership" at **http://voices.yahoo.com/native-womens-status-takes-hit-under-tecumseh-and-11963002.html?cat=37**).

Although a belief in "witches," or those who practiced negative manipulation of the supernatural, might seem to be a Euro-American influence, scholars have reason to assume such beliefs (or similar beliefs) were also aboriginal. However, "witch hunts" with the sentencing of capital punishment of offenders was probably somewhat influenced by Euro-Americans.

Why would William Henry Harrison and other American officials care to stop the Native witch hunts? Because such a hysteria in Native country would also affect the safety of surrounding American settlers. Such social discontent and violence could easily find a new outlet among the frontier settlements, and so a relative peace within the Native communities was, at this time and place, beneficial to Americans (indeed there were many times Euro-Americans exploited Native disputes between communities and tribes in order to benefit Euro-American colonization and American expansion, including creating and encouraging the "scalp trade." To learn more about how European influences changed Native war culture, read "Selling Honor: The New Warrior Culture in the Era of Tecumseh" at **http://voices.yahoo.com/selling-honor-warrior-culture-10348703.html?cat=37**).

Notes:

_____

_____

_____

_____

_____

_____

Reading: Newspaper Highlights Tecumseh & The Prophet in Headlines

Subjects: Social Studies (American History, Cultural Studies)
Grades 5-10

Description:

The following seven pages highlight Native American events as if they made the headlines of *The Old Northwest Times* - a pretend historic newspaper serving Native Americans of Indiana and Ohio. Each front page announces major news regarding Tecumseh and The Prophet's movement from the years 1805-1811, plus more general news and announcements to illustrate Native culture of the time. Through reading and discussing in class these series of newspaper front pages (in order), students should gather that:

-Native American politics were complicated just like our modern American politics.
-The anti-American movement was more religious under The Prophet's authority and more militant under Tecumseh's authority.
-The Prophet headed the movement before his brother Tecumseh eclipsed him.
-The Prophet was not the only prophet at this time - there were others.
-The Prophet is controversial in Native communities - many accuse him to be a fraud.
-The Prophet wants Native people to stop being dependant on Euro-American goods by living like their ancestors who didn't rely on such.
-The Prophet conducts witch-hunts which later fosters resentment of his religion by former believers, such as the Delaware.
-The Prophet is blamed for the defeat at the Battle of Tippecanoe, but he has his own excuses as to why they lost.
-Prophetstown in Indiana is established after residing near Greenville, Ohio.
-The Treaty of Fort Wayne influences more Native people to follow the Shawnee brothers.
-The Treaty of Fort Wayne propels Tecumseh's leadership and authority.
-Treaties were usually unfairly pressured upon the Native societies of this time and place.
-The Native people were intelligent and understood American society and its motives, and they knew their history in great detail.
-Tecumseh is not a civil leader by traditional standards - like Little Turtle, he was a war chief (former or practicing) who takes the role of a civil chief, a title usually reserved for another individual who qualified. Duel government (civil and war chiefs respectively) were on the decline due to Euro-American influences.
-Native women's authority in government declines with Euro-American influences.
-Adopting male-dominated farming practices was detrimental to Native women whose cultural roles included farming.
-The Native people were also responsible for the over-hunting of animals, although the reasoning was to supply the demand of Euro-American fashion.
-The Native people of this time wear limited leather garments when compared to their fabric clothing obtained through Euro-American traders.
-Material culture changed, and trends in clothing were a part of Native culture.
-Muskets weren't exactly a better technology than bows - both had their advantages and drawbacks.
-Both Native men and women enjoyed sports and games.

Notes:

_____
_____
_____
_____
_____

THE OLD NORTHWEST TIMES

Native American News of the Indiana & Ohio Territories

Breaking Tradition: The Current Trend of Tribal Leadership

Fort Wayne, IN: Fifteen years ago Capt. Hendrick, delegate of Mahican background, circulated a message of peace among the Old Northwestern tribes, when, upon visiting the Shawnee he observed the obviously "superior" position war leaders took, sitting in front of civil leaders. Capt. Hendrick criticized this new governmental system as foreign to Algonquian practices of restricting war captains' authority to the battlefield. Today many share Capt. Hendrick's alarm over abandoning traditional protocol. Current leaders like Little Turtle, although popularly endorsed as civil chief among his Miami constituents, aren't eligible for the position under traditional guidelines. In the past, civil chiefs were never war chiefs – part of the balance so integral to Native government. Some fear we have let Euro-American culture influence our politics far too much, making war captains into tribal chiefs **(continued A2)**.

Shawnee Man Claims Power of Prophecy

Greenville, OH: Earlier in the year, a Shawnee man was said to have been found slouched over and unresponsive in his wigwam near Anderson, Indiana. The witnesses, his wife and neighbors, all agreed the man was dead, but to their amazement the man seemingly came back to life. The man, Tenskwatawa (formally Lalawethika), claimed to have died for just a short time, during which he visited the afterworld. Upon regaining consciousness, Tenskwatawa told of his vision and a revelation – he claims now to be a prophet selected by the Creator.

Villagers say he continued to have subsequent visions that revealed how the Native people were to live their lives, according to the Creator. Many seem to be taken with his new faith, especially members of his Shawnee band and some Delaware neighbors. Still, this new Shawnee prophet has much competition. The Delaware already have a female prophet, and others claim prophecy in neighboring tribes as well. Some who don't believed in Tenskwatawa's visions have come forth and accused the prophet of hoaxing the public to obtain a higher status. These individuals claim Tenskwatawa had previously attempted to follow in the footsteps of Penagashea, a highly respected prophet and medicine man that passed away the previous year. But Tenskwatawa failed to heal many inflicted with a wave of illness over the last winter, and those skeptics suspect he faked visions to gain the confidence of his community back. If this is true, then his ploy is working. He has been steadily gaining popularity, taking believers away from other prophets and traditionalists. Many are flocking to his new village, currently near Greenville, Ohio, to hear him recount his visions **(continued on B1)**.

Tradition Under Attack

The Shawnee Prophet urges followers to abandon old medicine bundles and dances... says these are no longer relevant, and claims to have new dances and customs. Read about it on **B2**.

Upcoming Naming Ceremony

The Seneca at Sandusky would like to announce their upcoming Midwinter Rites Celebration, as always, to take place 5 days after the Pleiades are directly overhead. All are invited to participate in the Naming Ceremony to welcome all the new babies of last year.

In Style

Potawatomi Seamstress Guild invites all young seamstresses out to the council house at Five Medals Village to learn the technique of cut-ribbon appliqué this Friday evening. **D2**

THE OLD NORTHWEST TIMES

Native American News of Indiana & Ohio Territories

Miami Reaction to Shawnee Prophet - Is Wells Worrying Too Much?

Fort Wayne, IN: Little Turtle seems to be little concerned with Tenskwatawa's newfound popularity. The recent eclipse has done little to convince the Miami that Tenskwatawa is any sort of messenger for the Creator. But not all in Fort Wayne are unthreatened by the recent Shawnee prophet. William Wells, Indian agent and adopted son of Little Turtle, has been warning Native chiefs and American authorities alike that Tenskwatawa is a dangerous influence in the Old Northwest. Wells claims he has seen warriors of several nations pass through Fort Wayne on their way to the Greenville village, and he believes their presence at the Shawnee prophet's village is an ominous warning of the powerful influence of Tenskwatawa. If this prophet is no friend of neighboring tribal chiefs or the Americans, Wells warns that Tenskwatawa might become a powerful rival **(continued on A2)**.

Eclipse Makes Believers Out of Skeptics, But Not All

Greenville, OH: The eclipse witnessed by thousands all over the Old Northwest on June 16th was claimed by the Shawnee prophet, Tenskwatawa, to be a show of his prophecy. At his Greenville village, Tenskwatawa spent the morning in his lodge while hundreds assembled to see the miracle this prophet promised. Among the crowd were his Shawnee followers and enthusiastic delegates from the Kickapoo, Wyandot, Ottawa, and Winnebago. A few Miami and Delaware had also assembled, however, most of these locals refused to entertain the Shawnee prophet's claims. The audience would not be disappointed. As the sun faded, and the "black sun"

6/16/1806

appeared, Tenskwatawa emerged in front of the assembly and shouted, "Did I not speak the truth? See the sun is dark." Having proved his place as a messenger of the Creator, he then restored the sun back to its former brightness (or so he claimed to be the one to do such). Many who doubted Tenskwatawa before now declared their faith in him after the eclipse, but there were still skeptics. A few assembled were disappointed in their fellow citizens for believing Tenskwatawa had anything to do with the eclipse. They accused him as a phony, declaring that he had not changed from the selfish man he had been just months earlier, and insisted his claim to prophecy was nothing more than a ploy to obtain an honored position he didn't deserve. Skeptics pointed out that Anglo scientists had already predicted this very eclipse, and that Tenskwatawa knew of that prediction and claimed the natural phenomena as his own. Tenskwatawa denies such accusations, and insists he preformed the eclipse in direct response to William Henry Harrison's challenge **(continued on A3)**.

Sports

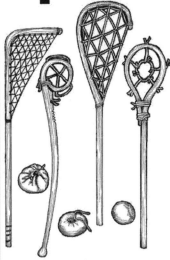

A Changing Game

New lacrosse traditions come to the Old Northwest. **C1**

STOP SELLING!

Last Round of Treaties Breeds Resentment Among Native Villagers
Anti-American Native leaders question the motive of annuity chiefs who signed the Treaty of Grouseland. Chiefs struggle to keep constituents happy in spite of last year's land successions. Learn more on page **A2.**

THE OLD NORTHWEST TIMES

Native American News of the Indiana & Ohio Territories

Shawnee Prophet Struggles to Recruit Followers in Eastern Ohio

Sandusky, OH: The Shawnee prophet struggles to attract easterners due to rival prophet Handsome Lake. A Seneca prophet, Handsome Lake is very much like the Shawnee prophet – both claim visions, condemn alcohol, and conduct witch-hunts with deadly consequences. One would think being of almost the same mind they might team up, but critics of their new religions say there's little chance of that. They claim that both are zealous self-serving individuals that care too much about their own popularity to work together. (continued on A1).

Disillusioned by Others' Religions, The Delaware Revive Their Own

Indianapolis: Most still remember the massacre at Gnadenhütten, Ohio of a couple decades ago. The town, established by Moravian missionaries was the site of the horrific massacre of over 90 innocent Christian Delaware men, women, and children by Christian American soldiers. Ex-Christian Delaware left Ohio disillusioned by their former faith that targeted fellow Christians for their race; they entered Indiana where they were soon met with a new faith. The Shawnee prophet preached early on in Delaware villages, where the spiritually-thirsty residents were in need of hopeful messages. Soon The Prophet's message of hope turned into witch-hunts that claimed the lives of innocent Delawares, and so they turned away from The Prophet's new faith. Such unfortunate circumstances led the Delaware to return to a religion of Delaware origin. The Big House Ceremony was born and is now rising in popularity. Rumored to have been revived by the female prophet known as Beade, the new format of this annual celebration combines elements of Delaware ceremonies formally practiced and fits them into a 12 day long celebration (continued C1).

Women & Politics

Native women facing more and more discrimination in the political realm - Critics say American influences are to blame. **A1**

Midewiwin Seasonal Gathering

Announcing The Ottawa Midewiwin Grand Medicine Society Seasonal Gathering

Where: Toledo Village

When: February 7

What to Expect This Maple Sugar Season

Delaware sugarmakers are ready to tap along the White River. What do they predict for the 1807 maple sugar season? **D1**

Flintknapping Workshop Sponsored by Shawnee Prophet

Flintknapping workshop at the Shawnee Prophet's village council house. Come and learn this traditional skill of your grandfathers. Let's revive stone tool technology!

When: Feb. 8

Where: Prophet's Village near Greenville, OH

THE OLD NORTHWEST TIMES

Native American News of the Indiana & Ohio Territories

Black Hoof's Success in Male-Dominated Farming Criticized

Black Hoof's Village, OH: Quaker demonstration farms have been set up among many Native communities, but no other has taken so well to it than Black Hoof's village. Native proponents of Anglo-style agriculture claim farming is the future for Native men. They point out that with new restrictions to territory placed upon them by Americans, they need to adapt to food-securing activities that don't rely on large tracts of land. This is why Americans are pushing for the domestication of food animals. But animal domestication is not the concern for Natives as is the practice of male-dominated cultivation. Customarily Native women are in charge of farming, own the products of their farming activities, and usually own the farmlands. Some critics speculate that with the loss of women-dominated cultivation, there will be a loss of opportunity for women to be providers and thus more independent **(continued on B2)**.

New Village on the Wabash Causes a Stir

Prophetstown, IN: Earlier in the spring, the Shawnee prophet relocated his intertribal village of believers from Greenville, Ohio to Indiana on the Wabash at the mouth of the Tippecanoe River. William Henry Harrison refers to the new village as Prophetstown, and isn't happy with the move of what he fears will be a group of people hostile to the Americans. Harrison isn't the only one disturbed by the move; some Natives aren't thrilled either with The Prophet's new village site. Little Turtle, who has been increasingly suspicious of the Shaw-nee prophet's motives, took a bold stance and personally warned the moving villagers en route. Meeting them at the headwaters of the Mississinewa River, Little Turtle and fellow delegates strongly suggested they should turn back to Ohio. The Miami official stance on the move is that they gave the Shawnee prophet no invitation to settle upon Miami lands in Indiana. The Prophet insists that he needs no permission to settle upon such lands as he believes he and his Native followers are no less welcomed on all the lands the Creator has made for all Native people to live upon. And, the Shawnee prophet points out, he did have an invitation to settle at the mouth of the Tippecanoe, extended by ally Chief Main Poc of the Potawatomi. When interviewed by the The Old Northwest Times, Little Turtle responded to the so-called invitation of the Potawatomi chief as void, and insisted his offer meant nothing as he too (and those Potawatomi) were residing on Miami home-lands – they had no authority to invite a Miami adversary to reside upon their homelands. The Prophet's followers ignored Little Turtle and his delagates, who were outnumbered and unable to block the moving villagers **(continued A1)**.

Straight-Talk on Treaties & Annuities

Native citizens feel the squeeze of America on their lands. There seems to be more buying of lands that already have American squatters in an attempt to partly cover up illegal occupation. Critics claim that for starters, America should be paying penalties of illegal occupation even before discussing land transactions. The Americans are already in the wrong, yet they are getting the upper hand in all recent negotiations **(continued on A2)**.

Sports

Ojibwa-Ottawa Women's Doubleball Legue is holding tryouts for their 1808 season.
Where: Prophetstown
When: May 20-25

Farmers' Outlook

Wea farming women discuss this year's challenges in planting, the status of Miami White Flour corn, and what farmers can expect this 1808 growing season in the Wabash Valley area. **B1**

THE OLD NORTHWEST TIMES

Native American News of the Indiana & Ohio Territories

Tecumseh Says "I Told You So"

Prophetstown, IN: They are calling the Treaty of Fort Wayne a game changer for Tecumseh. Why? Because as Tecumseh stated, it proved his predictions of "crooked" chiefs continuing to sell lands to no end. Now, those who resisted Tecumseh's message are taking a second look and considering joining his anti-American militant movement. Even some Miami who were satisfied with Little Turtle's leadership are now questioning his motives. Little Turtle denies selling the land for selfish reasons, insisting he tried to resist signing but was pressured by some Potawatomi who threatened violence if he didn't sell (the Potawatomi have yet to comment on these accusations). In any case, the signing of the treaty is driving new recruits to Prophetstown. Some Americans are blaming those who pushed for the treaty before encouraging a better rapport with the Native people for strengthening Tecumseh's influence **(continued on A1).**

The Religious Movement Turns Militant

Warclub with carved head by Red Crow & Sons

Vincennes, IN: Concerns over the Shawnee Prophet's proclaimed peaceful movement are growing. Both American authorities and opponent Native communities fear the religious group has become more militant in nature, especially since the rise of Tecumseh to leadership alongside his brother. Tecumseh is currently putting more emphasis on the movement as a political resistance and combative force. It's obvious to see why Americans are upset; the Americans have been particularly the target of the Shawnee brothers' hatred. And why not? The Americans have recently acquired thousands of miles of Native lands, usually with tactics of coercion and bribery of American-friendly chiefs. But some fellow Native citizens are also on edge about Tecumseh's hostilities; they suggest the Shawnee brothers have a "with us or against us" attitude (continued A2).

Red Crow & Sons
~
Custom Carved Warclubs
Kickapoo Village at Prophetstown

The Big Harvest
1809

With the harvest of green corn over, the start of harvesting dry corn and beans, and mature squashes is now here. With most villages reporting good yields, it seems this harvest is going to be one for the records. Story on **D1.**

Traditional Bag Twining Workshop
Where:
South Bend Potawatomi Village
When:
December 2nd

Concerns in Declining Population of Game Animals Grows

Terra Haute, IN: It's no secret that hunters have been finding it harder and harder to bag game animals ever since the mid 1700's, but lately some hunters claim they can be in the woods for five days without spotting even one deer. So what caused this food shortage to take place? Experts blame the extreme commercialization of furs by French and British traders. Tribal historians cite Native lifestyles just before European settlers as being more dependent on farming for food (speaking of horticultural tribes). Indeed, the French had a definite hand in encouraging tribes to devote more time to trapping pursuits at the expense of their horticultural activities, all to provide French traders with business. Through the fur trade, Anglo trappers and Native trappers over-hunted species that provided furs in demand in European fashion **(continued D2).**

Name_____   September 18, 1810

THE OLD NORTHWEST TIMES

Native American News of the Indiana & Ohio Territories

Prophetstown

Prophetstown, IN: The anti-American stronghold known as Prophetstown, situated at the mouth of the Tippecanoe River on the Wabash, is called home by an estimated 2,000-3,000 persons. Included are Winnebago, Kickapoo, Shawnee, Potawatomi, Wyandot and other residents of varying tribal backgrounds. Little is known of the intertribal village's specifics by outsiders, partly because residents are wary of spies that will bring information back to the Americans. We can say with confidence that the town includes satellite villages, and together they span about three miles along the Wabash River. Their farms are located on the natural prairie at a short distance from the river. Residents have erected a palisade around some buildings, extending down to the river. Like most villages, it includes a council house and residential buildings (mostly wigwams and log cabins). Other public buildings include a communal store house, a medicine lodge, and a building named "House of the Stranger." This is said to be a residence hall for housing new arrivals. They have a race track and ball field **(continued B2).**

Tecumseh Makes Powerful Speech That Reminds Americans of Their Crimes

Vincennes, IN: This past August, Tecumseh, William Henry Harrison and delegates on both sides held a meeting in Vincennes to discuss the current state of Native to American relations. Onlookers witnessed Tecumseh give Americans a bit of a history lesson, just in case the Americans forgot why it is hard to trust them (or they assumed we Native people forgot). The following is an except from his speech: "Brother, I wish you to give me close attention, because I think you do not clearly understand. I want to speak to you about promises that the Americans have made. You recall the time when the Jesus Indians of the Delawares lived near the Americans, and had confidence in their promises of friendship, and thought they were secure, yet the Americans murdered all the men, women, and children, even as they prayed to Jesus? The same promises were given to the Shawnee one time. It was at Fort Finney, where some of my people were forced to make a treaty. Flags were given to my people, and they were told they were now the children of the Americans. We were told, if any white people mean to harm you, hold up these flags and you will then be safe from all danger. We did this in good faith. But what happened? Our beloved chief Moluntha stood with the American flag in front of him and that very peace treaty in his hand, but" he was murdered "by an American officer, and that American Officer was never punished" **(continued on A1).**

Movement is Bringing Back Buckskin

Terra Haute, IN: Wool skirts, cotton shirts, linen jackets are all common garments. Such imported fabrics have been a mainstay of our Native fashion since a century ago. With the affordability of European fabric and the demand to export animal furs, most leather garments fell out of style decades ago. So you can imagine my disbelief to see a group of men wearing full leather outfits. And who were these men? None other than Tecumseh and a small party of his delegates. The men's outfits, consisting of fringed leather shirts over leather leggings, matched like uniforms. The leather outfits symbolized their want for Native people to utilize only Native-made items, and the solidarity of the Shawnee brothers' anti-American movement **(continued C1).**

THE OLD NORTHWEST TIMES

Native American News of the Indiana & Ohio Territories

Tribes Divided Over Impending War

Fort Wayne, IN: An impending war between the Americans and the British has caused Native Americans throughout the Old Northwest to choose sides. The British have long kept some villages in Ohio and Indiana as allies. Now tensions are turning into actions, and clear areas of pro-British and pro-American villages are emerging. One larger cluster of pro-American Native villages are identified in northwestern Ohio, and includes a few Delaware, Shawnee, Wyandot and Seneca populations. In west-central Indiana, pro-British Native communities have gathered around the site of Prophetstown, including Winnebago, Kickapoo, Potawatomi, Wyandot, and Shawnee. Although Prophetstown itself is abandoned at the moment (after being burned by Harrison's troops after the Battle of Tippecanoe), Tecumseh has plans to reestablish the village at the same site this coming spring **(continued on A2).**

Shawnee Prophet Takes Heat Over The Battle of Tippecanoe

Prophetstown, IN: After the defeat of the Battle of Tippecanoe, surviving warriors turned on the Shawnee prophet, blaming him for their defeat. Why do they claim The Prophet is responsible? According to warriors, The Prophet had assured them they would be invulnerable and victorious in their attack on the camp. Responding to such accusations, The Prophet insists he warned them that if they failed to get William Henry Harrison, the Americans would never be defeated. The Prophet points out that their defeat was of their own doing, and had they been successful in taking Harrison, they would have won. When questioned about the promise of invulnerability, The Prophet claimed his wife was not fit to assist him in his rituals that sought to the safety of the warriors. Because of her, the power of his medicine failed. Critics aren't buying it, and believe this is just a cowardly excuse from a false prophet. Angered, warriors captured The Prophet and waited for Tecumseh's arrival from campaigning in the southeast. Upon arrival, Tecumseh was reported to have been angry and furiously questioned his brother as to why he engaged in war after being instructed not to. The Prophet blamed the warriors for wanting to attack and claims he couldn't control them. The warriors have yet to comment on the accusation **(continued on A1).**

Custom Bows

By John Iron Bow

No flintlock can replace the stealthiness of the traditional Native bow...

-Shoot without alarming game

-Hunt with confidence in damp weather

-No expensive repairs

-Reload quicker

Still in Business near Prophetstown

New Study: Cradling Future Generations

Little Turtle's Village, IN: Cradleboard traditionalists tell parents who aren't planning to raise their infants in cradleboards to think twice. Proponents say there are many good reasons our ancestors used cradleboards, and most continue using cradleboards today for those very benefits, such as safety and behavior. Yes, behavior – the cradleboard's snug and safe-feeling shell can sooth even the fussiest of babies. For the few who have abandoned cradleboard use, reading this study that follows cradleboard-raised babies might just change some minds **(continued on C1).**

26th Annual Snow-Snakes Competition at Greentown

The Delaware of the Greentown Village in Ohio invite all to come out January 2-5 for their Annual Snow-Snakes Competition. Teams sign-up info on page **C2.**

Student Article: Grades 9-12

The 1826-1828 Removal of Shawnee From Ohio to Kansas

How US Government Mismanagement Led to Native American Hardship During the Removal Process

On September 30, 1826, over 250 Shawnees and Senecas set forth from Wapakoneta, Ohio, destined to travel to their new homes west of the Mississippi River in Kansas. Much thought and pressure went into the decision to remove prior to this date. Although this community had wanted to stay in their Ohio homes, they came to the conclusion that an offer by the United States to pick up and move west may be for the best. They had already witnessed the Americans' relentless thirst for more lands, and felt the pressure of Anglo settlers crowding their borders and illegally establishing themselves on Native lands. So many Shawnee just wanted to live in general peace within their own villages, but the growing sea of settlers had made such a wish a virtual impossibility within Ohio's borders.

Lewis Cass, Governor of the Michigan Territory, spent some of his career working to remove local tribes from the region, including Black Hoof's Shawnee nation. In order to convince this group to remove, he employed Tenskwatawa, the former Shawnee prophet and surviving brother of the deceased Tecumseh, to help convince his tribe that removal would benefit them. The old prophet, in complying, gained his freedom on US soil (as he had an arrest warrant out for him in the United States), a fine amount of gifts, and a chance to win back some of the influence he lost among his Shawnee community during the War of 1812.

Tenskwatawa, along with traders and government agents, began to preach the benefits of removal to the Native peoples. Black Hoof and many of his followers still resisted removal at this time, but others listened and were somewhat open to the idea. They listed to all the reasons removal was in the best interest of the Native people, including putting distance between themselves and encroaching American settlers, and receiving fertile lands with start-up funds to rebuild their villages at their future locations west of the Mississippi. The Shawnee contemplating removal were also promised complete financial funding for the move, including furnishing guides that would take them to their destination, as well as compensation for the lands they left and the improvements they made on their lands (like their cabins and farms). Those who felt there was no chance of making a life in their home villages of Ohio, and hearing of the "support" the US was offering those Native communities that volunteered to leave, made the unfavorable decision to remove. Keep in mind the decision was partly based on the financial support and well-planned removal route the US government promised the Native peoples. Unfortunately for those Shawnee and Seneca who took the US up on their offer, they would soon come to regret placing their faith in the Americans.

In September of 1826, the few hundred Shawnee and Seneca, including well-known leaders such as Tenskwatawa and Cornstalk, set out following their guides. The removal went wrong from the beginning when the group, led by guides Joseph Park and William Broderick, used a southwest route through Indiana rather than sticking to the flat lands of the northern half of the state. Southern Indiana was a land of hills and ravines, rocky limestone terrain and caves, all covered in thick forests and soggy swamps. This region only slowed the Shawnee's travels, so much so that they didn't reach Vincennes on the western border of Indiana until two months after departing Ohio. Following their crossing into Illinois, the group's horses began to suffer of undernourishment due to the US failing to provide enough funds to purchase the necessary grain for their animals.

The 1826-1828 Removal of Shawnee From Ohio to Kansas (continued)

The US also failed to provide enough funds for the guides to finish the journey, and after the two guides realized their contracted fees had expired, they deserted the Shawnee party in Illinois, hundreds of miles short of their destination.

The group was now without guides and funds, and started to sell whatever they could to purchase the food they needed. They reached Kaskaskia where they expected to be ferried across the Mississippi, but arriving too late, they were met with a river choked with ice and the ferry unable to operate. The local Indian agent, Pierre Menard, was surprised by the traveling Shawnee party, not having been informed that the US government had recently negotiated removal with this Native group that planned to cross through his area. He gave any rations of food he had to spare to the party, and ordered blacksmiths to repair Shawnee guns so they could hunt. He even purchased blankets and distributed them among the more needy of the group (many had been forced to sell their clothing to purchase food). And he wasn't the only one seemingly in the dark about such removals already underway. William Clark, of the Lewis and Clark Expedition, who was then the Superintendent of Indian Affairs, was also not informed of any such traveling group nor given any extra provisions to provide them upon their arrival in his jurisdiction.

The Shawnee were poor, hungry, and according to Indian agent Richard Graham, in miserable condition and in serious need of government aid. Clark heeded Graham's recommendations and appealed to officials at Washington to furnish the funds needed to continue the Shawnee party's westward journey, but to Clark's shock, both the War Department and Congress were unaware that such a negotiation had taken place for this Native group's Ohio lands and that the government was contracted to fund the ongoing removal. Washington had failed to plan for the smooth removal process the Shawnee were promised. Because Congress had passed no special appropriation to assist the Shawnee (although it was already a contracted condition agreed upon by both parties), there were no funds available for Clark to appropriate to the traveling group. The Secretary of War himself, James Barbour, had no idea which Shawnee were contracted to "remove" nor had he any idea of the destination they were appointed (the reader should keep in mind this was before the Indian Removal Act was signed into law).

A breakdown in communication between government officials and government agencies had resulted in a major glitch that only hurt the traveling Native group, robing them of their possessions, savings, livestock, health, and even some lives. The group was able to resume their travel later and did finally arrive in Kansas on May 14, 1828, almost a two year long journey to travel only about 650 miles (the equivalent of about a 12 to 14 hour drive today).

This Native community suffered starvation and sickness which was the direct result of the US government's mismanagement of their removal process, and such mismanagement wasn't unique of this group's experience; many Native groups pressured or forced to remove also dealt with such bureaucratic dysfunction which led to loss of property, and too often, the loss of lives. The criticism of removal is a twofold subject: first, the pressuring and forcing of Native homes and lands to be ceded to America, and second, not fulfilling contracts and promises during the actual removal process. Most history lessons tend to focus on just the first part – the unlawful coercing of land sales or military-forced removals, but most students of history never learn of the logistical nightmare that such removals created, and how the government failed to, in many cases, follow through on their guarantees, which created inhuman conditions for the Native people being removed. Such horrid removal events deserve to be remembered in American history as crimes against humanity, particularly crimes against the original Americans.

Further Reading: "Removal" chapter in "The Shawnee Prophet" by R. David Edmunds. Sources include: Clark to Barbour, April 23, 1827; Graham to Clark, April 4, 1827; Johnston to Cass, October 7, 1826; Menard to Graham, January 17, 1827; Speech by the Prophet, April 2, 1827.

Student Article: Grades 7-12

Indian Removal in Indiana and the "Trail of Death"

By David A. Lottes

The Indian removal act was signed into law by President Andrew Jackson in 1830. Jackson was an honored veteran of the War of 1812 and had personally led campaigns against the "Red Stick Creek" in Tennessee. Despite cooperation with other natives during his campaigns, he didn't believed natives and white settlers could co-exist peacefully over the long term. He believed separating the races was the only road to peace.

Although the removal act was targeted at what were known as the Five Civilized Tribes of the southern United States, the act applied to all indigenous people living east of the Mississippi within the boundaries of the U.S. In many states like New York, Wisconsin and Michigan the act was never fully implemented and it received a lukewarm reception in Indiana. The official policy towards dealings with native peoples in Indiana had long been centered on the acquisition of their lands but there was also an industry built up around providing for their needs through a series of trading posts scattered throughout Indian lands.

In 1830 Indiana was still home to thousands of natives and there had been no open hostility with white settlers in Indiana since the summer of 1813. When the war of 1812 ended in 1815 the British were no longer able to provide Indiana natives with goods so a network of American trading posts was established. By 1830 the fur trade that had long provided natives with the income needed for trade was coming to an end. It had been years since they had been able to provide for all their needs strictly by trading hides for goods as their ancestors had. In the preceding decades leading up to 1830 most tribes had begun to rely heavily on annual annuity payments they received from the United States in exchange for lands they ceded control over in a series of treaties.

The first of these treaties dates back to the 1790s and for the most part they all read the same with the exception of the boundaries which continued to squeeze the native peoples into smaller tracts of land. Each treaty would guarantee that on a given date each year the communities represented by those signing the documents would receive a payment of a specified amount and that the U. S. would prevent any encroachment by white settlement on lands not specified in the treaty. Likewise the native people would agree to cease hunting and dwelling on the lands now designated as reserved for white settlement.

The trading posts that supplied the natives with goods would generally extend lines of credit, allowing the villagers to take whatever they desired throughout the year and then collect the debt annually when the annuity payments were made to the various communities. Often the debt was so high the annuities weren't enough to pay the total owed so the balance due would be added to the account for the coming year, with interest of course. One can imagine how the owners of the trading posts reacted when they learned that the Indian Removal Act had been signed into law and that sooner or later their customers would be leaving for the west.

It wasn't just the natives and owners of the trading posts who were disappointed by the Removal Act. It was also all the suppliers of the goods that flowed through them. Local merchants and manufacturers provided the trading posts with whiskey, cloth, gun powder, beads, wax candles, iron kettles and many other goods in what essentially amounted to guaranteed government contracts worth fortunes.

Nonetheless many of the native peoples and their associates resigned themselves to the inevitability of the new law and made preparations for adapting to a new way of life. The Wea

Student Article: Grades 7-12

Indian Removal in Indiana and the "Trail of Death"(continued)

By David A. Lottes

tribe living near Terre Haute sent a large scouting party to survey lands in the west and brought back their first impressions. Before saddling up they ran an announcement in the newspaper explaining their plans so that they wouldn't be mistaken for a band of hostiles on the warpath.

The Kickapoo, Delaware and many other communities of natives met with government envoys, negotiated payments, and signed over the last of their remaining lands in exchange for land in the west. Part of the Kickapoo got to Kansas, decided they didn't like it, and kept going west into Texas where the Spanish allowed them to live autonomously. To this day a group of their descendants still live along the Mexican side of the Texas border, speaking their traditional language and worshiping in their ancient way.

Some Miami of the Upper-Wabash were fortunate in that their leader, Jean Baptiste Richardville, was by all accounts the wealthiest man living in Indiana when the removal act was signed into law. Jean was the half French son of Tucumwah, sister of Little Turtle, and owner of the most lucrative trading post in Indiana. Jean was well educated, could read and write both English and French, and could speak a variety of native languages. He fought the removal act in the courts until his death in 1841 and managed to prevent the removal of a large number of his people. Basically he purchased land for them to live on and ceased the practice of annuity payments. They gave up their tribal status and became regular citizens of the United States. But Jean could not make arrangements for all the Miami. Several hundred were loaded onto flat boats and sent west via the Saint Mary's, Great Miami, Ohio, and Mississippi Rivers to Missouri.

In the 1830s, on the Yellow River in what is now Marshall County Indiana, a large concentration of Potawatomi began to congregate around the home of a man named Menominee. In 1832 Menominee, along with several other headmen, participated in a series of treaties known collectively as "The Whiskey Treaties" because the natives were often given copious amounts of liquor prior to negotiations. By 1835 all of the land controlled by the Potawatomi in Indiana had been ceded to the U.S., but Menominee refused to participate in the final treaty and by the spring of 1838, his village, now numbering nearly a thousand souls, had still not removed themselves.

Menominee was a spiritual leader among his people; he combined elements of Christianity and native teachings in an effort to help his people adjust to life surrounded by white settlements. Beginning with a Baptist mission and then later a Catholic chapel, Menominee encouraged the new religion in his village. Unfortunately these efforts at assimilation weren't enough to convince the Governor to allow him to remain in Indiana.

In 1838 Governor David Wallace opened the land along the Yellow River for settlement and conflict soon broke out between Menominee's villagers and the white settlers. Natives and settlers began burning one another's cabins and Governor Wallace sent Colonel John Tipton with a group of 100 volunteer militiamen to resolve the situation.

Tipton, like Jackson, was an old "Indian fighter" and did not believe that native people could successfully assimilate into white culture. He called for Menominee and his other headmen to meet with him at a trading post located on the Tippecanoe River near present day Rochester Indiana.

Student Article: Grades 7-12

Indian Removal in Indiana and the "Trail of Death"(continued)

By David A. Lottes

When Menominee's group arrived they were arrested. Over the next few days as many of Menominee's villagers as possible were rounded up at gun point and brought to the trading post where they could see Menominee and their other leaders confined to a large cage loaded in the bed of a wagon.

Tipton and his volunteers burned the homes and crops of the Potawatomie so that they would have nothing to return to. The Artist, George Winter was invited to observe the Potawatomi and sketch the removal. These sketches were to become the only first-hand visual records of the Indian removal. Today some of these portraits are in the collection of the Tippecanoe County Historical Association. On September 4th, 1838, 859 Potawatomi began their march to Kansas. Two months later they arrived in Kansas. Nearly fifty had died on the journey and another fifty or so had escaped. Those who avoided captured or escaped from the march rallied around another Potawatomi leader known as Pokagon in Southwestern Michigan. Like Richardville, Pokagon successfully negotiated arrangements for nearly 300 of his people to remain in their homeland in Michigan.

Father Benjamin Marie Petit arrived in Menominee's village just days after the round up to hear confessions, and perform baptism and communion ceremonies in the chapel. He spoke with villagers who had avoided the round up and learned that his parishioners had been taken to Logansport.

Father Petit caught up to the march in Danville Illinois, by this time Menominee and his followers had resolved themselves to their fate and were no longer attempting to return to their village. Father Petit stayed with the group and wrote letters to the Bishop in Vincennes describing the conditions and daily events of the journey. These letters along with the chalice that Father Petit used for communion ceremonies are now part of the collection of the library at Saint Francis Xavier Basilica in Vincennes Indiana. Father Petit died on the return trip from illness contracted on his journey west with the Pottawatomi from Indiana.

On their march the Potawatomi traveled through Marshall, Fulton, Cass, Carroll, Tippecanoe, and Warren Counties in Indiana before entering Illinois. Just west of Catlin, in Vermilion County Illinois, Colonel Tipton and all but a handful of his Indiana militia soldiers left the group and returned to Indiana placing the Potawatomi under the leadership of William Polke and Father Petit.

Today the descendants of Potawatomi, Miami, Kickapoo, Wea and other native peoples of Indiana live around the world and contrary to what some believed they have managed to assimilate quite well into a variety of cultures. Reservations in the west are still home to these tribes and there are efforts to gain federal recognition of tribal status for some in Indiana.

In 1988 a group of historians and Potawatomi with ancestors who were removed got the "Trail of Death" declared a Regional Historic Trail and placed historical markers at each campsite along the trail throughout Indiana, Illinois, Missouri, and Kansas. Additionally each fall in Fulton County Indiana an annual event is sponsored by the Fulton County Historical Society to commemorate the "Trail of Courage" and recreate what life was like during the days before removal.

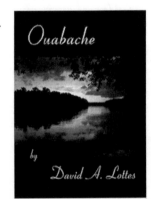

Article courtesy of David A. Lottes, author of "Ouabache." For more information, visit http://www.ouabache.info/

Worksheets: The Indian Removal Act

Subjects: Social Studies (American History)
Grades 5-12

Directions:

Make copies of the worksheet that corresponds to your state. Distribute and have students answer the questions in class or for homework. It is recommended that these worksheets are used as a review to a lesson or textbook section that already discussed the Indian Removal Act and your state's history of Native American removal.

Worksheet Answer Key:

<u>Questions 1-6 on Both Worksheets:</u> 1. The Indian Removal Act was a law that passed making it legal for the United States to persuade (which led to forceful "persuasion") Native American Nations east of the Mississippi River to remove west of the Mississippi to designated lands (ie Indian Territory). It authorized the United States to compensate eastern Native landowners for their territory and improvements, and give them financial aid to relocate and reestablish, however it also acted as the fuel for local government officials to harass Native peoples until they agreed to remove (or were forced to do so by American troops). - 2. President Andrew Jackson - 3. 1830 - 4. Examples include Davy Crockett, Tennessee Congressman; Abraham Lincoln; Future President; Theodore Frelinghuysen, New Jersey Senator; Jeremiah Evarts, Christian Missionary to the Native peoples. - 5. The Trail of Death - 6. 1838

<u>Indiana Worksheet Questions 7-10:</u> 7. Rochester, Logansport, Battle Ground, Lafayette, Williamsport. – 8. In an 1840 treaty the Miami ceded their Indiana lands, although they did not want to leave. – 9. In 1846 the Miami were forcefully removed, destined for land set aside for them in Kansas. – 10. Some Miami were "granted" the right to stay in Indiana during this forced removal (those families exempt included families with strong European-American ties). Many of their descendants remain in Indiana today, and identify as "Indiana Miami" (whereas "Oklahoma Miami" are descendants of the Miami removed from Indiana to the Indian territory).

<u>Ohio Worksheet Questions 7-10:</u> 7. Some examples of the tribal communities and their reserve location in early 19th century Ohio: Delaware – near Morral; Ottawa – Maumee, Ottawa, near Paulding, Toledo; Seneca – Triffin; Shawnee – Wapakoneta; Wyandot – Upper Sandusky. - 8. The Wyandot were "persuaded" to give up their reserve at Upper Sandusky in 1842. - 9. The Ottawa, Seneca (and Mingo), Shawnee, and Wyandot still resided as tribal communities in Ohio before their removals spanning 1831-1842. - 10. Examples of tribal communities expelled before the Indian Removal Act was signed into law include the Miami - most Miami already in Indiana by the early 1800's however an 1818 treaty formally took all their land claims in Ohio and they were restricted to land reserves in Indiana (most were then forcefully removed to Kansas by American troops in 1846); the Shawnee, where some complied with removal to Kansas from Ohio in 1826; most Delaware had left Ohio for Indiana by 1800, with exception to a Delaware reserve up until 1828 in Ohio – during the 1820's, the Delaware remove west to Kansas.

Extra Resources Online:

The Indian Removal Act: http://www.loc.gov/rr/program/bib/ourdocs/Indian.html - http://www.civicsonline.org/library/formatted/texts/indian_act.html - Those Opposed to The Indian Removal Act: http://www.osv.org/school/lesson_plans/ShowLessons.php?PageID=P&LessonID=40&DocID=149&UnitIDD= - http://politics.laws.com/indian-removal-act - http://ngeorgia.com/history/nghisttt.html - The Trail of Death: http://www.potawatomi-tda.org/ - Miami Removal: http://www.units.muohio.edu/mcguffeymuseum/student_exhibits/site/miami%20indians/Bergseth%20website/public.www_corrected/route.htm - Miami - Treaty of 1818: http://www.ohiohistorycentral.org/entry.php?rec=2069 -- http://www.units.muohio.edu/mcguffeymuseum/student_exhibits/site/miami%20indians/Bergseth%20website/public.www_corrected/treaty1818.htm - The Miami in Ohio: http://www.ohiohistorycentral.org/entry.php?rec=606&nm=Miami-Indians - The Mingo in Ohio: http://www.ohiohistorycentral.org/entry.php?rec=608&nm=Mingo-Indians - The Ottawa in Ohio: http://www.ohiohistorycentral.org/entry.php?rec=614&nm=Ottawa-Indians -The Seneca in Ohio: http://www.ohiohistorycentral.org/entry.php?rec=629&nm=Seneca-Indians - The Wyandot in Ohio: http://www.ohiohistorycentral.org/entry.php?rec=646

Indiana Native Americans & The Indian Removal Act

1. What was the Indian Removal Act?

_____

_____

_____

2. What President signed into law the Indian Removal Act?

_____

3. What year was the Indian Removal Act signed into law?

_____

4. This act, although thought to have been voluntary for the Native people in theory, was instead a legal way for the American government to pressure Native peoples off Native lands east of the Mississippi River. Because of this, the Indian Removal Act was very controversial. Name one government official of that time that opposed the act (could be a congressman, senator, later president, etc.). You may have to research this online to find an answer.

_____

5. The Indian Removal Act initiated the famous removal of Cherokee and neighboring tribes from the southeast to destinations west of the Mississippi River, however, these were not the only tribes affected by the Indian Removal Act nor was it the only removal event remembered starting with "The Trail of..." in its title. What is the name of the removal of the Potawatomi from Indiana to west of the Mississippi River?

_____

6. What year did this Potawatomi Removal take place?

_____

7. What places in Indiana did the Potawatomi removal party pass through on their way out west?

_____

_____

8. In what year were the Miami told they had to remove? Did the Miami want to leave?

_____

9. In what year were the Miami forced to remove? Where did the removed Miami end up?

_____

10. Were any Miami allowed by the United States to remain behind in their Indiana homelands, and if so, are their descendants still in Indiana today?

_____

Ohio Native Americans & The Indian Removal Act

1. What was the Indian Removal Act?

_____

_____

_____

2. What President signed into law the Indian Removal Act?

_____

3. What year was the Indian Removal Act signed into law?

_____

4. This act, although thought to have been voluntary for the Native people in theory, was instead a legal way for the American government to pressure Native peoples off Native lands east of the Mississippi River. Because of this, the Indian Removal Act was very controversial. Name one government official of that time that opposed the act (could be a congressman, senator, later president, etc.). You may have to research this online to find an answer.

_____

5. The Indian Removal Act initiated the famous removal of Cherokee and neighboring tribes from the southeast to destinations west of the Mississippi River, however, these were not the only tribes affected by the Indian Removal Act nor was it the only removal event remembered starting with "The Trail of…" in its title. What is the name of the removal of the Potawatomi from Indiana to west of the Mississippi River?

_____

6. What year did this Potawatomi Removal take place?

_____

7. Ohio was known for its Native American "reserves" – land that was reserved for Native communities after treaties claimed all other land. Name one Native tribe that had a reserve in Ohio. Where was one of these reserves located?

_____

_____

8. The Wyandot were the last Native community officially removed from Ohio. In what year did this removal start?

_____

9. What tribal communities were still residing in Ohio in the 1830's, just before they were removed?

_____

10. Even before the Indian Removal Act was signed into law, Ohio had begun to expel its Native populations. Name a Native tribal community that was pressured to leave and were led to destinations west of the Mississippi River during this time.

_____

Worksheets: Trail of Death: Potawatomi Removal from Indiana

Subjects: Social Studies (American History, Cultural Studies)
Grades 6-12

These worksheets are designed to be used as a review to a lesson or textbook section that already discusses the Trail of Death and Indian Removal Act.

Directions:

Make copies of the next three worksheets and distribute and have students answer the questions in class or for homework.

Worksheet Answer Key:

1. The Treaty of Tippecanoe.
2. Chiefs that Sighed the 1832 Treay of Tippecanoe: Louison, Che-ehaw-eose, Banack, Man-o-quett, Kin-kosh, Pee-shee-Nvaw-no, Min-o-min-ee, Mis-sah-kaw-way, Kee-waw-nay, Sen-bo-go, Che-quaw-ma-eaw-co, Muak-kose, Ah-you-way, Po-kah-kause, So-po tie, Che-man, No-taw-kah, Nas-waw-kee, Pec-pin-a-paw, Ma-ehe-saw, O-kitch-ehee, Pee-pish-kah, Conl-mo-yo, Chiek-kose, Mis-qua buck, Mo-tie-ah, Muck-ka-tah-mo-tvay, Mah-qusw-shee, O-sheh-weh, Mah-zick, Queh-kah-pah, Quash-quaw, Louisor Perish, Pam-bo-go, Bee-yaw-yo, Pah-ciss, Mauck-eo-pavv-waw, Mis-sah-qua, Kawk, Miee-kiss, Shaw-bo, Aub-be-naub-bee, Mau-maut-wah, O-ka-mause, Pash-ee-po, We-wiss-lai, Ash-kom, Waw-zee-o-nes.
3. On the Yellow River.
4. This passage promises that the US will financially back Potawatomi movement; really referring to removal to "open" lands west of the Mississippi River (not stated but implied).
5. To acquire the last Potawatomi lands in the state of Indiana.
6. The Potawatomi at Twin Lakes, and their chief Menominee.
7. 859.
8. The US troops burned them to discourage the Potawatomi from trying to go back home.
9. Septemeber 4, 1838 from Twin Lakes (formally), now known as Myers Lake and Cook Lake near Plymouth.
10. Wagons.
11. Chief Menominee, Chief Black Wolf (Makkahtahmoway), or Chief Pepinawa.
12. a. Rochester, b. Logansport, c. Battle Ground, d. Lafayette, and e. Williamsport.
13. Just over 40 perished.
14. November 4, 1838
15. The general reason to force removal of the Potawatomi was for the state of Indiana to claim (and sell) the last of Indian lands in its borders. Although the reserves were not very large tracts of land, it was still the greed of the state to want them open for Euro-American settlers (meaning land sales). In doing this, the state also sought to remove what they felt to be a "complication" of Native cultures surrounded by white settlement (as in future disputes between both populations including those sparked by racism... many Euro-Americans didn't want Native Americans for neighbors, no matter how Christian or assimilated they might be, which would also inhibit surrounding land sales).
16. The Indian Removal Act.
17. Refugee; yes the Potawatomi were refugees as they were forced to leave the lands they regarded as their homelands.
18. According to the Merriam-Webster Dictionary, diaspora means "the movement, migration, or scattering of a people away from an established or ancestral homeland." It is often applied to Jewish exiles, however, the term is applicable to all exiled societies, including removed Native Americans.
19. Citizen Potawatomi Nation, in Oklahoma.
20. Pokagon Band of Potawatomi, in Michigan and Indiana.

Name _____ Date_____

Trail of Death: Potawatomi Removal from Indiana
Answer the following 20 questions about the Potawatomi Trail of Death

1. What treaty did the Potawatomi sign in 1832 that ceded most of their land in northwestern Indiana?

_____

2. Name at least 3 Native Americans who signed the treaty.

_____

3. This treaty created a "reserve" for the Potawatomi to live on (with a new mill). On what river in Indiana was this reserve located?

_____

4. Article V of the treaty reads: "The United States agree to provide for the [Potawatomi], if they shall at any time hereafter wish to change their residence, an amount, either in goods, farming utensils, and such other articles as shall be required and necessary, in good faith, and to an extent equal to what has been furnished any other Indian tribe or tribes emigrating, and in just proportion to their numbers." What does this have to do with impending removal to Kansas, and what is it guaranteeing?

_____

_____

_____

5. In 1836, the Treaty of Yellow River was signed. What was the main goal of the United States in negotiating this treaty?

_____

6. Many Potawatomi agreed to relinquish their Indiana lands for compensation and new lands in Kansas. Some moved west without contest. What group of Potawatomi refused to acknowledge the treaty and remove west of the Mississippi River? What was the name of the chief who represented this village?

_____

7. On August 30, 1838, American soldiers were disbursed to round up the Potawatomi that refused to remove west voluntarily. About how many Potawatomi people did they forcibly gather to remove (an event known as the "Trail of Death)?

_____

8. What did the military do to the Potawatomi's homes and crops? Why did they do this?

_____

_____

9. On what day did these Potawatomi people start their journey to Kansas? Where did they set out from?

_____

Name _____ Date_____

10. What did the US provide the Potawatomi to help transport their belongings?

_____

11. A few chiefs were forced into jail wagons. Name one of these chiefs.

_____

12. Name the present day towns they marched through in Indiana before crossing the Illinois border?

a _____ b _____ c _____

d _____ e _____

13. Of all the Potawatomi marching, the children suffered more than any other group. Father Benjamin Petit who joined the Potawatomi en route commented that the Potawatomi children were especially sick and weak from the heat. Most of the fatalities while traveling were children. About how many in all died on the "Trail of Death?"

_____

14. On what date did the Potawatomi reach their destination of Osawatomie, Kansas? 756 Potawatomi reached Kansas, but less than 103 were recorded as passing away on the march (although the number of fatalities may be under-reported). What happened to the Potawatomi who didn't pass away en route but who also didn't arrive in Kansas?

_____

_____

15. The "Trail of Death" was a government forced exile of the Potawatomi. Why did the United States want to remove the Potawatomi and other Native nations east of the Mississippi?

_____

_____

_____

16. What Act was passed in 1830 that enabled government agencies and officials to plan removals of local Native communities east of the Mississippi River to west of the Mississippi River?

_____

17. What is a term starting with the letter "r" that is often applied to people displaced from their homelands? Were the removed Potawatomi r_ _ _ _ _ _? Why?

_____

_____

18. What does the term "diaspora" mean, and how does it relate to the removal of the Potawatomi?

_____

_____

_____

19. Name a Potawatomi Band in Oklahoma or Kansas whose ancestors were removed from Indiana.

_____

20. What local Potawatomi Band resides in Indiana and Michigan today?

_____

Extra Credit

Describe the Miami removal of 1846: their journey from their Indiana homelands to west of the Mississippi River.

_____

_____

_____

_____

_____

_____

_____

_____

_____

_____

_____

_____

Name _____   Date _____

Student Article: Grades 8-12
Primary Historical Documentation: Selected Passages from Benjamin Marie Petit's Letters, 1837-1838

Benjamin Marie Petit's Account of the Trail of Death

Fighting to Stay On Their Own Land:
"The Indians, Monseigneur, are preparing to leave for Washington to protest against the unworthy manner with which they are treated. The treaty is indeed a thing as illegal as possible and in no wise applicable to our people, who have sold nothing."

The Harshness of the Journey:
"We learned the Indians on the way, bayonets prodding their backs, had a large number of sick in their ranks – that several, crammed into baggage wagons, had already died of heat and thirst. These pieces of news were like so many swords piercing my heart."

"Our trip is a harsh experience; we have much sickness; two of the Indians were buried today. Monseigneur, please pray God to sustain us and to bless the Christian resignation of these good Indians deprived by force of their fatherland…"

"It was Sunday, September 16. I had just arrived when a colonel, seeking a favorable place to camp, appeared. Soon afterward, I saw my poor Christians, under a burning noonday sun, amidst clouds of dust, marching in a line, surrounded by soldiers who were hurrying their steps. Next came the baggage wagons, in which numerous invalids, children, and women, too weak to walk, were crammed."

"I found the camp just as you saw it, Monseigneur, at Logansport – a scene of desolation, with sick and dying people on all sides. Nearly all the children, weakened by the heat, had fallen into a state of complete languor and depression."

"The order of the march was as it follows: the United States flag, carried by a dragoon; then one of the principle officers, next the staff baggage carts, then the carriage, which during the whole trip was kept for the use of the Indian chiefs; then one or two chiefs on horseback led a line of 250 or 300 horses ridden by men, women, children in single file… On the flanks of the line at equal distance from each other were the dragoons and volunteers, hastening the stragglers, often with severe gestures and bitter words. After this cavalry came a file of forty baggage wagons filled with luggage and Indians. The sick were lying in them, rudely jointed, under a canvas which, far from protecting them from the dust and heat, only deprived them of air, for they were as if buried under this burning canopy – several died thus."

"We soon found ourselves on the grand prairies of Illinois, under a burning sun and without shade from one camp to another… Not a drop of water can be found there – it was a veritable torture for our poor sick, some of whom died each day from the weakness and fatigue."

Concerning The Potawatomi's Converted Religion:
"Often throughout the entire night, around a blazing fire, before a tent which a solitary candle burned, fifteen or twenty Indians would sing hymns and tell their beads."

Woman on Horseback. Department of the Interior. Bureau of Indian Affairs. Potawatomi Agency.

Name _____ Date _____

Student Article: Grades 8-12
Primary Historical Documentation: Selected Passages from Benjamin Marie Petit's Letters, 1837-1838

Benjamin Marie Petit's Account of the Trail of Death (continued)

"When the Indians arrived at Quency, the inhabitants, who compared this emigration with previous ones, could not help expressing their surprise at the modesty of our Christians, their calmness, and their gentle demeanor." A catholic lady, accompanied by a Protestant friend, made the sign of the cross, symbolizing religious fraternity. Immediately the Indian woman came up to shake their hands cordially; the [Indians] never fail to do this when they encounter Catholics. The Protestant lady wanted to do as much and tried the sign of the cross, but, betrayed by her lack of practice, she could not succeed. At once an Indian, who knew some English, went up to her and said, "You nothing."

"One day Judge Polke, our principle officer, introduced one of his friends, a Baptist minister. I was in my tent surrounded as usual by Indians. He wanted to shake hands with the Indians, and I told them to approach – that he called himself their friend. Then,… this minister, with that commanding enthusiasm in which his kind are never lacking, cried: "Ah, they are bone of my bone, flesh of my flesh! I truly feel here (putting his hand on his heart) that I love humankind…" When he had gone, I told my Indians that he was a Protestant minister. At this all who had shaken hands with him replied with a grimace."

"The majority of the Protestants in the country had resolved to exterminate or at least expel certain sectarians called Mormons…"

"…The next day we heard artillery and rifle shots. We saw armed troops coming to formation from every direction, and about sixty mules – booty taken the day before from the Mormons. We passed quietly through this theater of fanatic battles, although at our arrival a message had come asking that the Indians join the troops who were attacking the Mormons. The request was wisely rejected."

Timeline and Casualties of the Trail of Death:

"Having left on September 4, we arrived on November 4. The number of Indians at our departure was about 800. Some escaped, and about 30 died – I do not think their number exceeded 650 at their arrival."

Photo: Pisehedwin, a Potawatomi, and others in front of his Kansas farm home, 1877. US National Archives and Records Administration.

Questions For "Benjamin Marie Petit's Account of the Trail of Death"

1. When Petit wrote: "These pieces of news were like so many swords piercing my heart," why did he feel such a way? What was his relationship to this Native community?

_____

_____

2. What religion did this group of Potawatomi identify as? What religious paraphilia do "beads" refer to?

_____

_____

3. When Petit speaks about a Native person calling a Protestant woman "you nothing" and his Native company grimacing at the thought of shaking hands with a Baptist, what does this say about the state of Catholicism and Protestant religions in America? Do you think these Potawatomis' intolerance for another Christian religion reflected the general historic attitudes of different religions sharing space on the American frontier?

_____

_____

_____

_____

4. When traveling through Missouri, the Potawatomi journeyed right through a battle zone between Mormon and non-Mormon locals. What is the name of these skirmishes?

_____

5. When Petit wrote: "The treaty is indeed a thing as illegal as possible and in no wise applicable to our people, who have sold nothing," what Potawatomi group was he specifically referring to?

_____

6. Chief Menominee refused to sign the Treaty of Tippecanoe that would have ceded their reserve in Indiana. These Native people appealed to Washington looking for justice. The Native people felt if they had not ceded their lands, then they shouldn't be pressured to move. Why did the United States choose not to investigate on behalf of this Potawatomi group? What did the US stand to gain by removing the Potawatomi?

_____

_____

_____

7. What does "invalids" refer to? What is the meaning of this term?

_____

_____

Questions For "Benjamin Marie Petit's Account of the Trail of Death" (continued)

8. Why did so many become ill from fatigue, and what issue with the weather made it worse?

_____

_____

9. Petit's numbers of how many Potawatomi left Indiana, how many perished, and how many arrived in Kansas are different from most scholarly sources today. What are the other number figures that have been suggested?

_____

10. It seems as though dozens of Potawatomi have gone unaccounted for, neither perishing en route nor arriving. What happened to these people?

_____

Extra Credit

Here is your chance for extra credit! You will need to do some extra research to answer these four extra credit questions: History and the story of all Americans is the story of different trails that cross at specific times and places. Probably no better example exists of this than the "Trail of Death" in Missouri. When traveling through Missouri, the Potawatomi journeyed right through a battle zone between Mormon and non-Mormon locals. Why were the Mormon and non-Mormons in this area of Missouri fighting? When did this war start and what was the outcome for the Mormons? What was the Missouri Executive Order 44 also known as, and what did it stipulate? The Potawatomi being exiled were asked to join the fight on the side of the non-Mormons; why is this ironic?

_____
_____
_____
_____
_____
_____
_____
_____
_____
_____
_____
_____
_____
_____
_____
_____

The Historical Significance of the Fall Creek Massacre Sentencing

On March 22, 1824, a group of Native peoples camped near the falls of Fall Creek in Madison County, Indiana were ambushed by a group of men. Nine Native persons were brutally murdered: 2 men, 3 women, and 4 children. One victim, Chief Logan, was identified as Wyandott (Wedat) in one historic publication however there has been controversy over his and the group's tribal identity: most likely they were Seneca/Shawnee mixes (Mingo), or possibly part Delaware and/or Miami. No matter the victims' tribal identity, these Native people were murdered, and the surrounding white-American community was generally outraged at the unjust ending of this friendly Native group. With fear of retaliation from the local Native peoples in the region, they rounded up five of the six killers to put to trial. The sixth murderer was Thomas Harper who managed to flee prosecution. Harper was thought to be the instigator of the attack upon Logan and his fellow campers. One of the five brought to justice, Andrew Jones, was only a teenager who accompanied the murdering party and wasn't sentenced. The other four men were tried, convicted and sentenced to death by hanging, but only three were executed (Andrew Sawyer, John T. Bridge, Sr., and James Hudson); one murderer, John Bridge, Jr. was said to have been a young man highly influenced in his actions by his father and uncle in the murdering party, and was pardoned at the last minute.

What is the historical significance of this event? This was the first documented case in which white-Americans were convicted by the judicial system and sentenced to capital punishment for the murder of Native American individuals. The murders and executions were an unfortunate part of Indiana history, however, it was also a triumph for Native Americans who were routinely considered less "human" by white-Americans and therefore not worthy of equal protection by the United States. This wasn't white men who murdered white victims - this was white men who murdered Native Americans, believing themselves to be entitled to do so based on their perceived "superior race." This was an important event for the recognition of Native American civil rights in the US judicial system, and it happened first in the state of Indiana.

Sources:
-Conner Prairie Interactive History Park online: http://www.connerprairie.org/Learn-And-Do/Indiana-History/Original-
   Documents/Fall-Creek-Massacre.aspx
-Indiana Historical Society. "Indiana & The Old Northwest: An Exhibition" Indianapolis, 1980.

Part of Hudson's sentencing statement by Judge William W. Wick, from the Western Censor, Indianapolis, Tuesday, October 19, 1824:

"But Logan was an Indian: he was an hereditary enemy of white men."

"Stop, Sir! If any pretended friends have led you to this precipice, permit me to extend a friendly hand... Logan, although an Indian, is a son of Adam, our common father. Then surely he was not the natural enemy of white men. He as bone of your bone & flesh of your flesh. Besides, by what authority do we vauntingly boast of our being white? What principle of philosophy or of religion establishes the doctrine that a white skin is preferable in nature or in the sight of God to a red or black one. Who has ordained that men of the white skin shall be at liberty to shoot and hunt down men of the red skin, or exercise rule and dominion over those of the black? The Indians of America have been more "sinned against than sinning". Our fore fathers came across the broad Atlantic, and taking advantage... obtained a resting place among the Indians, then the 'lords of the soil,' and since that time by a series of aggressions, have taken from them their homes and firesides - have pressed them westwardly until they are nearly extinct. We have introduced among them diseases and vice; we have done to them wrongs which cry to Heaven for vengeance, and which have, in many instances, brought down upon us a severe retribution."

Student Article: Grades 7-12

How Native Americans Influenced The Women's Suffrage Movement

Living in the land of equality and freedom was far from a reality for early American women. Married women were especially not afforded the same equal standing as men, such as being able to speak or represent themselves at certain government hearings, own land or property separate from their husbands and male kin, or even vote for the next president [1]. Early American women were, in a sense, not full citizens able to fully control their destinies while the white-American men in their midst enjoyed full personal freedoms afforded to American citizens.

SAVAGERY TO "CIVILIZATION"

THE INDIAN WOMEN: We whom you pity as drudges reached centuries ago the goal that you are now nearing

Savagery to "Civilization" drawn by Joseph Keppler, 1914. Source: Library of Congress Prints and Photographs Division. Illustration shows Iroquois women on a rock overlooking women marching with banner labeled "Woman Suffrage." Caption reads "The Indian Women: We whom you pity as drudges reached centuries ago the goal that you are now nearing."

Although early American women exercised fewer rights than men, not every society practiced such gender inequality at that time in history. Many of their Native American neighbors encouraged more equal participation of women in their Native governments. One aspect of this equal participation was women's rights to cast votes and have representation during discussions and policy making. Like any man, such discussions and policy making affected Native women too, whether it be their property, family, or livelihoods. It was these rights that inspired many suffragists to write and speak about Native American women's rights in the hopes of encouraging a young United States to adopt such practices of female equality.

Key persons in the American Women's Suffrage Movement like Alice Fletcher, Matilda Joslyn Gage, and Francis Wright wrote on Native American women's rights. Francis Wright edited a pro-Native American paper in the 1820's; it carried the Cherokee alphabet, an interview with Seneca leader Red Jacket,

and even pointed out the flaws in white-American society when compared to Native American society. Matilda Joslyn Gage, President of the National Women's Suffrage Association, published articles featuring Iroquois culture prominently in the New York Evening Post; many of such articles were reprinted in several other papers as well. It was their hope that by exposing the more equal status Native women enjoyed in many eastern Native American communities, Americans would begin to question why American women were denied the right to vote in the United States government. One focal point was that of Native women's right to own land, animals, homes, household items, and food stores.

One particular story that illustrated the difference in women owning property in early America and Native American societies was recounted by Alice Fletcher at a meeting of the International Council of Women in 1888, where noted suffragists Elizabeth Cady Stanton and Susan B. Anthony were in attendance:

Alice was witness to a Native American woman who decided to give away a horse one day. Alice had heard no previous discussion between the woman and her husband about the horse, and so asked her Native informant, "Will your husband like to have you give the horse away?" The Native woman did not understand what her husband had to do with her choice to give away the horse, as the horse belonged to the woman and not the husband. The informant began to laugh at such a question, and hastened to tell the other Native women gathered in the tent what Alice had just asked. These women too felt the question a ridiculous one. In their society, a Native woman is her own person, and her property is hers to do with as she pleases; a Native husband had no business interfering with her property transactions, nor should it concern him. Alice tried to explain to the Native women why an American woman would have to discuss and more than likely, ask permission of her husband to give, sell, or trade an item of her own away, "but laughter and contempt met" her "explanation of the white man's hold upon his wife's property." The early American woman, unlike the Native American woman, had no real authority to transfer property that, by American standards, was always in the control of her husband, father, and sometimes even her brother or son. She herself was not considered fit to own property as a man, and those American women who did successfully forge themselves a true freedom to own and dispose property like any white-American man were not common or considered usual (Wagner, 225).

Source: Library of Congress Prints and Photographs Division

And it wasn't just suffragists and Native American women who took notice of non-Native women's unequal rights; Native men also noticed, many times in disgust, of how non-Native women were treated as second class citizens by the men of their own society. Alice Fletcher recorded Native men's responses to American oppression of women: "Your laws show how little your men care for their women. The wife is nothing of herself. She is worth little but to help a man to have one hundred and sixty acres (Wagner, 225)."

Even more, Native American men understood the ramifications of the dominant white-American culture pressing assimilation on their own cultures, including the very real adoption of Americans' unequal gender perspectives. Fletcher recounts such an awareness when she met an old chief who was concerned that adopting male farming like white-Americans would only take away the livelihoods and social status of traditional Native farming women: "My young men are… to take up the work of the women; they will plow the field and raise the crops; for them I see a future, but my women, they to whom we owe everything, what is there for them to do? I see nothing! You are a woman; have pity on my women when everything is taken from them (Wagner, 225)." While white-America tried to sell the idea of male-dominated farming as a positive for Native women, the Native people understood the real consequences – for one thing, Native American farming women usually owned the lands they cultivated, and switching to male-dominated farming would only encourage male ownership of lands, not female ownership of farmlands [2].

Elizabeth Cady Stanton was also noted to reflect upon her experience as a long-time missionary among the Seneca. She was especially known to have advocated for the right of women to initiate divorce in disagreeable marriages, a right her Seneca female informants already possessed and practiced (Wagner). Such Native American influences of female equality left an impression on many suffragists and their activism work.

Source: Library of Congress Prints and Photographs Division

In particular, it was the Iroquois who captured the attention of suffragists when it came to voting rights. Among the Iroquois, women had councils that represented them in major decision making roles, and the position of a village chief could not be assigned without the vote of clan matrons (women who were head of their families). It was Iroquois matrons who exercised the authority to start the impeachment process when they felt such a chief was unfit for his office. The chief himself held no authority to put himself in office or keep himself in office; his office depended much on the endorsement of his clan matron (Bonvillian, Parker). And while Thomas Jefferson, Benjamin Franklin, and other Forefathers emulated Iroquois democracy in our American constitution [3], they did not take the Iroquois cue of female voting rights and representation in government, a mistake suffragists sought to ratify in their own times.

Using Native American examples of gender equality, suffragists were able to use a current working example of a society that encouraged female personal freedoms. This first showed such a practice is practical and beneficial to a society, and second, shamed early Americans for not being as "enlightened" as the Native Americans they conveniently and falsely labeled as "less civilized" (notably, the same strategy Benjamin Franklin used to sell Iroquois democracy to become the basis of the emerging United States [4]).

Notes:
[1] "Under European-inspired laws that were adopted by each state after the revolution, a single woman might be economically independent, owning property and earning her living but upon her uttering the marriage vows, she lost control of her property and her earnings. She also gave away all rights to the children she would bear... With the words "I do," a woman literally gave away her legal identity... A married woman could not make any contracts, sue or be sued; she was dead in the eyes of the law (Spittal, 224)." **[2]** "Missionaries insisted that a woman's proper sphere was the home and that Indian men should take up farming. ...this change would not only take away women's economic independence leaving them as dependant as white women;... Indian land, of which women had been the keepers for the nation, was often divided up among Indian men as "heads of the family" (Spittal, 221). **[3]** Iroquois chief/spokesman Canassatego offered the colonies this piece of advice in 1744: "Our wise forefathers established union and amity between the Five Nations" "This has made us formidable. This has given us great weight and authority with our neighboring nations. We are a powerful Confederacy, and by your observing the same methods our wise forefathers have taken, you will acquire much strength and power; therefore, whatever befalls you, do not fall out with one another." An official response is given during the New Albany conference of 1754, where colony delegates address visiting Iroquois counselors, first reciting Canassatego's speech in 1744 followed by the following statement: "These were the words of Canassatego: Brothers, our forefathers rejoiced to hear Canassatego speak these words. They sank deep into our hearts. The advice was good. It was kind. They said to one another: The Six Nations are a wise people. Let us hearken to them, and take their council, and teach our children to follow it... These provinces have lightened a great council fire at Philadelphia, and sent sixty-five counselors to speak and act in the name of the whole, and to consult for the common good of the people..." Predominant men like Ben Franklin, Thomas Jefferson, John Hancock, Thomas Paine and others have written and/or spoken of the attributes of the Iroquois government in which they look for the emerging United States to emulate (Burton, Grinde, Johansen). **[4]** Benjamin Franklin writes "It would be a very strange thing if six nations of ignorant savages should be able to form a scheme for such a union and be able to execute it in such a manner as it has subsided for ages and appears indissoluble and yet a like union should be impractical for ten or a dozen English colonies." The "six nations of ignorant savages" are referring to the Iroquois, and while he uses the unfortunate and false description "ignorant savages," he does so to point out that Euro-Americans who believed themselves to be "more advanced and civilized" than Native Americans (which is the reason for such derogatory language). Franklin admires the Iroquois for their enlightened form of government, and by using such harsh language against the Iroquois, he is actually ridiculing his own society (Johanson).

Sources:
Bonvillian, Nancy. "Iroquoian Women." Studies on Iroquoian Culture. Occasional Publications in Northeastern Anthropology, No. 6 (1980): 47-58. Print.

Burton, Bruce. "The Iroquois Had Democracy Before We Did." Indian Roots of Democracy. Northeast Indian Quarterly (1988): 44-48. Print.

Grinde, Donald. "It's Time to Take Away the Veil." Indian Roots of Democracy. Northeast Indian Quarterly (1988): 28-33. Print.

Johansen, Bruce. "Indian Thought Was Often in Their Minds." Indian Roots of Democracy. Northeast Indian Quarterly (1988): 40-43. Print.

Parker, Arthur C. "The Constitution of the Five Nations." Parker on the Iroquois. Syracuse University Press (1968): 39-44. Print.

Wagner, Sally Roesch. "The Root of Oppression is the Loss of Memory: The Iroquois and the Early Feminist Vision." Iroquois Women, An Anthology. Iroquois Reprints (1990): 223-228. Print.

The Foods We Consume That Originated in the Americas

You may be surprised at how many vegetables, fruits, grains, seasonings, food thickeners and additives were a gift from the Americas - in fact, it has been estimated that over 60% of the foods we consume trace their origins to the New World. To understand the impact of Native American foods, we should first look at some ethnic cuisines outside of the Americas.

Jumping right into our world food tour, let's start with the cuisine of northern Europe. You may be surprised to know that the Irish potato is actually South American in origin. All potatoes came from the New World, all varieties having roots in the Americas, and most cultivated potatoes came from the fields of Native farmers. Potatoes brought northern Europe a crop that could be grown in cooler and damper climates, and a source of vitamin C that boosted their health, but it didn't stop there as potatoes even improved European dental health. Grains encouraged dental caries, but for reasons very obscure, the potato did not produce such high dental caries as grains. The Irish and English adoption of the starchy root was so intense, that it is hard to find national dishes that lack the potato. Where would shepherd's pie be without the filling layer of mashed potatoes, and fish 'n' chips without the chips. Potatoes trumped previous European root vegetables, like turnips, and took its place of importance right next to the cabbage.

To the south, another New World import began to take root. Where would Italian cuisine be without the tomato? Yes, tomatoes were indeed a New World introduction, but as versatile as this fruit was, it didn't take hold right away. It was the book of Genesis that made many Westerners scared to try the tomato, as many thought it might have been the long lost fruit Eve had infamously offered Adam. It would however be poor soil conditions that would convince Italian farmers to cultivate the crop. The tomato grew successfully in soil conditions other crops did not tolerate, and from that point on, Italians had a love affair with the tomato. They pushed aside their traditional cheese and cream sauces, oil-herb dressings, and meat gravies to make room for a whole new condiment for pasta known as marinara. The red sauce's popularity took off, and it's hard to find any person who could define Italian cuisine without the red sauce.

Marinara also became the perfect carrier of New World pepper spices, which only enhanced the red sauce, a job milk-based sauces fell short on. Their neighbors in France did not make much room around their beloved butter and cream-based condiments which, milk coating the taste buds, inherently killed the bold and intense flavor of New World peppers. Italians adopted more than just peppers and tomatoes, as they also fell in love with zucchini - a New World squash, and American green beans and kidney beans. Kidney beans now serve as an integral ingredient of traditional minestrone, considered by many to be the unofficial national soup of Italy.

Peppers, whether it be chili, banana, bell, or others of the Capsicum genus, were adopted around the world for there bold, sweet, and sometimes spicy flavor. Probably not often thought to be a place of pepper culture, the Hungarian and Yugoslavian peoples adopted sweet peppers as spice for stews. Goulash would not be what it is today without paprika - finely ground American sweet red peppers. Paprika not only flavored and colored the stew, but also thickened it. It can be considered the heart of the soup. New World potatoes also found their way into many goulash recipes.

However, peppers may have had a larger impact in Indian and eastern Asian cuisine. Indian curry owes its red spice to New World peppers. Cayenne and hot peppers served as the base of curry, replacing Old World black pepper previously used in curry. Chilies were adopted into local Szechuan and Hunanese sauces, while the Chinese in general mixed chilies with oil that created a condiment that would preserve for use at any time of the year. One of the most popular hot sauces in the culinary world today is sriracha - a chili sauce manufactured especially to compliment Asian cuisine. Similar sauces were created with American originated peppers in Thailand. Bali cuisine boasts a chili sauce, mixed with ground shrimp and lime juice. Balinese dishes also included American peanuts, passion fruit, and avocados, although peanuts may be more well known to Westerners in East-Asian dishes.

Corn, the most well known of New World foods, has been adopted into European, Asian, and African cuisines. Its ability to grow in hotter climates than other grains has made it more than just a pleasant tasting food, but a life-sustaining crop among cultures outside the Americas. Certainly its importance among some African communities cannot be underestimated. It is, however, the extensive use of corn in North American and Latin American cuisine that pays homage to the crop's traditional importance among the Natives peoples of the same lands. Probably in no other cuisine does corn reign supreme than in Central America. Corn is well known in tortillas and tamale meal, but the grain goes further than flour making. Corn kernels converted with lime into hominy is a traditional vegetable added to many pork and chicken soups, and in particular menudo, a Mexican comfort soup featuring tripe (cow stomach lining). Mexico City residents and visitors enjoy the popular street vendor finger food of corn on the cob coated with mayonnaise, and sprinkled with cheese and chili powder.

Four heritage varieties of northeastern corn grown by the Native peoples upon European contact. The second one from the left is 8-Row Miami White Flour corn, said to have been grown traditionally by the Miami in Ohio and Indiana.

Not to be underestimated is corn cuisine just north of Latin America in the United States. No Fourth of July barbecue would be complete without roasted corn on the cob, nor would a New England clambake be considered fitting without cob corn steamed with the clams and lobsters. What's more is both cooking methods - barbecue and clambake - are Native American cooking techniques (the term barbecue is accredited to Caribbean Natives). Bread made of cornmeal is considered by many to be the only bread worthy of being consumed with chili. Pone as loaf bread, muffins, Johnnycakes, hushpuppies, and spoon bread are some regional cornbread favorites, all of which have their roots to Native American recipes. Jalapeño cornbread has gained recent popularity, but mixing vegetables and fruits into cornmeal batter is age old, having been practiced by Native Americans for centuries. Cornbread stuffing is considered by some to be more traditional to have with the Thanksgiving bird, while cornstarch is used to thicken the meat drippings into gravy. Many prefer their fried vegetables and meats with a crunchy cornmeal coating. Succotash and hominy, considered to be American Southern dishes, were first Native American dishes, their names even taken from Native terms. Corn chowder is also based on Native American cuisine. Corn syrup is enjoyed on breakfast dishes, and high fructose corn syrup is replacing cane sugar in many prepared dishes and beverages, most notably soda. It is hard not to find corn syrup as an ingredient in many mass-manufactured prepared foods on American store shelves. With its versatile nature to be a single ingredient or the whole dish, and its flavor profile, it's not hard to conclude that corn has truly penetrated every part of American cuisine.

Wild rice, a grass-grain of North America, has long been boxed and sold as a blend with Asian rice, but it is also gaining popularity on its own due to both its nutritional value and its nutty favor.

Jerusalem artichoke, the root of a variety of an American sunflower, was taken back to the Old World and distributed across Europe by Rome's Farnese Garden in the early seventeenth century. It has only gained popularity in the US fairly recently, popping up in few supermarkets under its common name, sunchokes. Sunchokes are popular on the fine dinning front, and are of particular interest with the medical and nutritional world as the potato-like root posses less of a "starchy threat" to diabetic diets (note: not to be taken as professional nutritional advice).

Tapioca, a well known ingredient in puddings and baby foods, is made from the American cassava plant. Many North American supermarkets carry the root of this plant, where it is known as "yuca," not to be confused with ornamental yucca plant, as the early Spaniards did, which is why the cassava root and the yucca shrub have the same name to date. While it is a very well known in Latin cuisine, it is used in other parts of the world too such as Indonesia, where the root is fried.

European chocolate owes its primary ingredient to American cocoa, only made European by the addition of milk. And while most may think the pairing of milk with cocoa to be only natural, it has been a growing trend among candy producers to offer chili infused chocolate, a combination harkening back to cocoa's Native American roots. French vanilla ice cream and coffee flavorings also owe their vanilla flavor to the American orchid. Vanilla was unknown to the Old World until Spanish contact, and is now one of the most expensive seasonings. Maple syrup, a tasty sugar condiment well known in North America to be poured over pancakes and waffles, or mixed with oatmeal and cream of wheat, is an original flavoring and sugar produced by eastern Woodland Native Americans. It is also utilized in baked beans, barbecue sauces, meat glazes, mashed squash, even in dressings and some beers.

Where would the American Thanksgiving feast be without cranberry sauce or pumpkin pie? Other popular pies that owe their prime flavoring to New World foods include blueberry, persimmon, and pecan. The crocodile egg, or avocado, serves as the basis of many Latin relishes, and many cultures of the world enjoy other American fruits including pineapples, passion fruit, papayas, and New World varieties of strawberries.

Sources: "Beloved Tomato - The Scandalous Fruit" http://www.epicureantable.com/articles/atomatohis.htm ; "Indian Givers: How the Indians of Americas Transformed the World" by Jack Weatherford ; "Jerusalem Artichoke Nutrition Facts." http://www.nutrition-and-you.com/jerusalem-artichoke.html

Are Your Students Aware?

So many of children's favorite foods have ingredients that originated in the Americas. Here are a few examples that students should be made aware of:

potato chips	soda (made with high frutose corn syrup)
french fries	pastas with marinara sauces
chilli dogs	waffles or pancakes with maple syrup
corn dogs	corn chips and salsa
hushpuppies	vanilla ice cream
popcorn	hot chocolate
pizza	peanut butter and chocolate candies
tacos	peanut butter sandwiches
buffalo wings	strawberry shortcake
hot sauce	tapioca pudding
barbecue sauce	pecan pies
ketchup	pumpkin pies

More examples of common foods your students consume that contain ingredients that originated in the Americas:

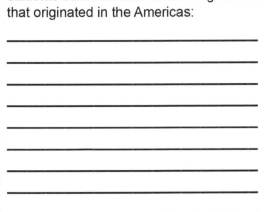

Part of the author's Historical Northeastern Native Foods display.

Some New World Foods

Avocados	Pecans
Banana Peppers	Persimmons
Bell Peppers	Pineapples
Blueberries	Pinto Beans
Chili Peppers	Potatoes
Chocolate	Pumpkins
Corn	Strawberries
Cranberries	String Beans
Jerusalem Artichokes	Summer Squash
Kidney Beans	Sunflower Seeds
Maple Syrup	Tapioca
Papayas	Tomatoes
Passion Fruit	Vanilla
Pawpaws	Wild Rice
Peanuts	Zucchini

It has been estimated that over 60% of the world's foods originated in the Americas.

Directions: List 12 foods you eat that have ingredients that originated in the Americas.

12 Foods I Eat With Native American Ingredients

1. _____

2. _____

3. _____

4. _____

5. _____

6. _____

7. _____

8. _____

9. _____

10. _____

11. _____

12. _____

A Native American child enjoys eating Maple sugar.

Appendix A

Themed Project Cover Pages and Blank Pages for Notes, Essays, Definitions, and Question and Answer Exercises

Name _____ Date _____

The Woodland Indian People
Of Indiana

Grade_____

Teacher_____ School_____

Name _____ Date _____

The Woodland Indian People
Of Ohio

Grade_____

Teacher_____ School_____

The Native American People
Of Indiana

Miami Mother &
Daughter, 1837

Delaware Village, 1800

Culture & History

Grade _____ Subject _____
Teacher _____
School _____

Name _____ **Date** _____

The Native American People
Of Ohio

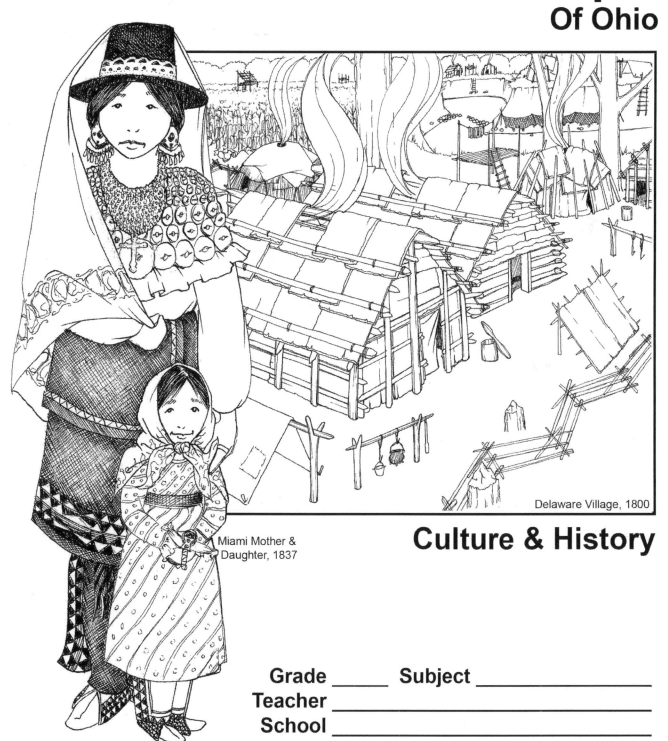

Miami Mother &
Daughter, 1837

Delaware Village, 1800

Culture & History

Grade _____ **Subject** _____

Teacher _____

School _____

Name _____ Date _____

What I Learned About The Native American People

_____
_____
_____
_____
_____
_____
_____
_____
_____
_____
_____
_____
_____
_____
_____
_____
_____
_____
_____
_____
_____
_____
_____

Miami girl holds
her baby brother
in a cradleboard,
about 1810.

Tribe: _____

Language Family:

_____

Homelands:

_____
_____

Homes:

_____
_____
_____
_____

Food-Getting Activities:

_____
_____
_____
_____
_____
_____
_____

More About This Native American Community:

_____
_____
_____
_____
_____
_____
_____
_____
_____
_____
_____
_____

Woodland Indian
Girl, 1775

Date _____

_____

_____

_____

_____

_____

_____

_____

_____

_____

_____

_____

_____

_____

_____

_____

_____

_____

By _____

Quillwork Border of a Native American Shoulder Bag

Name_____ **Date**_____

Definitions

1. _____ :

_____

_____

_____

2. _____ :

_____

_____

_____

3. _____ :

_____

_____

_____

4. _____ :

_____

_____

_____

5. _____ :

_____

_____

_____

A young man plays the flute for his sweetheart.

Name _____ Date _____

Teacher _____ Subject _____

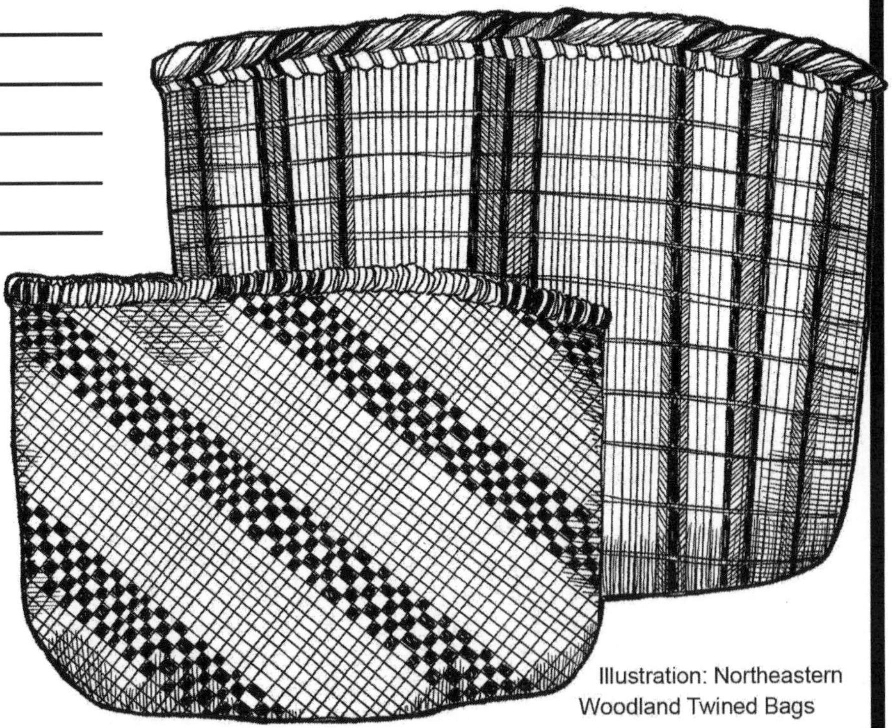

_____

_____

_____

_____

_____

_____

_____

_____

_____

_____

_____

_____

_____

_____

_____

_____

_____

_____

_____

_____

_____

_____

_____

_____

_____

_____

_____

_____

Illustration: Northeastern
Woodland Twined Bags

Name _____   Date _____

Teacher_____   Subject_____

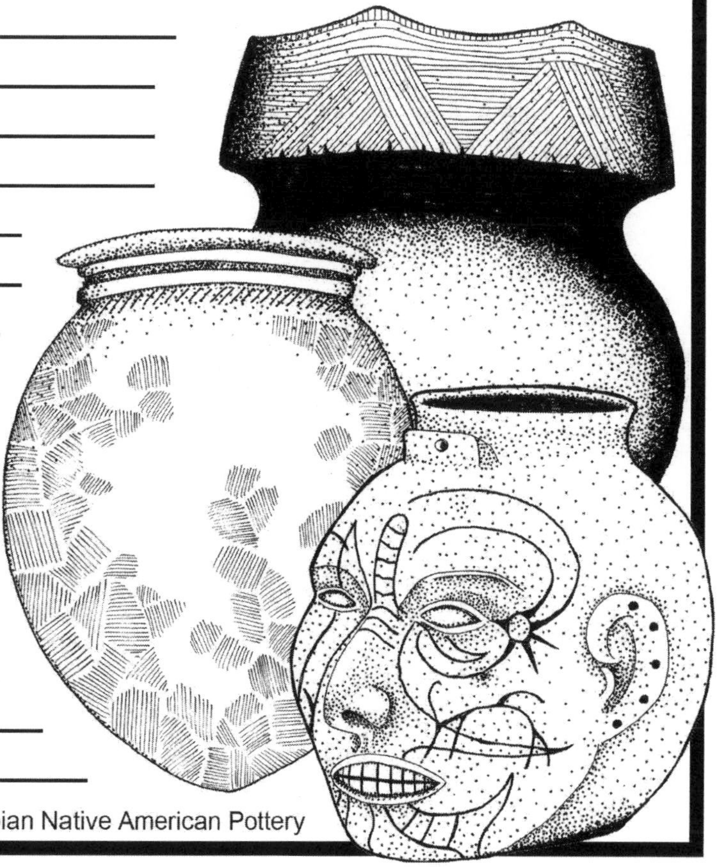

_____

_____

_____

_____

_____

_____

_____

_____

_____

_____

_____

_____

_____

_____

_____

_____

_____

_____

_____

_____

_____

_____

_____

_____

_____

_____

Illustration: Northeastern Woodland and Mississippian Native American Pottery

Name:_____ **Date:**_____

Essay

_____
_____
_____
_____
_____
_____
_____
_____
_____
_____
_____
_____
_____
_____
_____
_____
_____
_____

A Shawnee man spends quality time with his wife and young child. Nothing was more important to a Native American man than his family. When men were home from trading and hunting, and other jobs that took them away from the village for a while, they enjoyed spending time with the children of their family.

Wyandot men run after a deer they shot with an arrow and wounded. Hunting was an exhausting job that took husbands and fathers away from their families days to weeks at a time.

Question

_____
_____
_____
_____
_____
_____
_____
_____
_____
_____

Answer

_____
_____
_____
_____
_____
_____
_____
_____
_____
_____
_____
_____
_____
_____
_____
_____

Delaware men set a trap to catch a small animal, such as a raccoon. Both men and women were known to set and check animal traps.

Appendix B

Worksheets Specific to Mississippian, Fort Ancient, Hopewell, and Adena Cultures

Name_____ Date_____

The Mound Building People
of Indiana

Native American brother and sister, dressed in fiber woven clothes.

Name _____

Teacher _____ Grade _____

Name_____ Date_____

The Mound Building People
of Ohio

Native American
brother and
sister, dressed
in fiber woven
clothes.

Name _____

Teacher _____ Grade _____

What I Learned About Indiana's First People

_____
_____
_____
_____
_____
_____
_____
_____
_____

_____
_____
_____
_____
_____
_____
_____
_____
_____
_____
_____
_____
_____
_____
_____
_____

What I Learned About Ohio's First People

_____
_____
_____
_____
_____
_____
_____
_____
_____
_____
_____
_____
_____
_____
_____
_____
_____
_____
_____
_____
_____
_____
_____
_____

Some Pre-Contact Cultures & Sites in Indiana

Directions: Fill in the blanks under the map key descriptions with the correct culture or site from the word pool.

Map Key

△ This Fort Ancient site is located on both sides of the Indiana-Ohio border.

_____

▲ This mound, although naturally made, was still used as a Native American burial site.

_____

○ These village sites, named for the lake in their vicinity, was part of the Caborn-Welborn Culture - a variant of the Mississippian Complex.

_____

● This major Mississippian village featured earthworks and a palisade.

_____

■ This site features a group of mounds created by the Adena Culture.

_____

□ This site is attributed to the Crab Orchard Culture - a variant of the Hopewell Complex.

_____

 A cutural complex that flourished from about AD 900 to 1650/1700.

_____

Word Pool

Angel Mounds, Hovey Lake Sites, Mann Site, Mounds State Park, Oneota, Pyramid Mound, State Line Site.

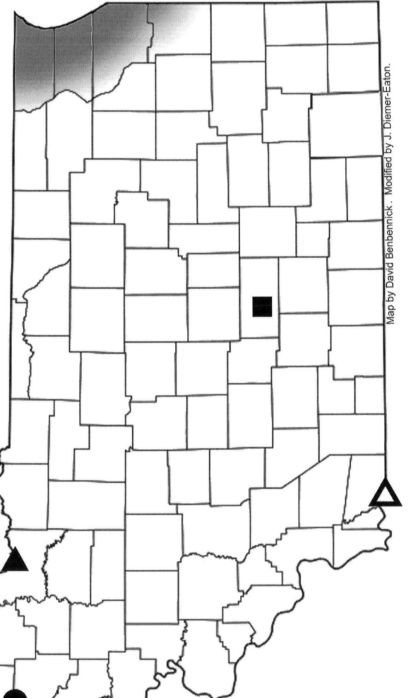

Map by David Benbennick. Modified by J. Diemer-Eaton.

An ancient Indian fortress existed on a high bluff overlooking the middle Wabash River, in present-day Sullivan County, late spring of 1205.

From "Natives Along the Wabash" by Sheryl Hartman & illustrated by Steve Tucker. http://piankeshawtrailsedu.org/

Men of
the village
fishing the
Tippecanoe River
where it flows into the
Wabash, summer 1227.

From "Natives Along the Wabash" by Sheryl Hartman & illustrated by Steve Tucker. http://piankeshawtrailsedu.org/

Young boys, in the
safety of their huge walled compound,
playing a game of skill with blunt spears
and a rolling target at Angel Mounds,
summertime 1421.

From "Natives Along the Wabash" by Sheryl Hartman & illustrated by Steve Tucker. http://piankeshawtrailsedu.org/

Great grandchildren of the Mounds people: this peaceful village of Native Americans was near the mouth of the Wabash River on Hovey Lake, 1531.

From "Natives Along the Wabash" by Sheryl Hartman & illustrated by Steve Tucker. http://piankeshawtrailsedu.org/

Name _____   Date _____

Ohio's First Engineers

Ohio has thousands of pre-contact Native American earthworks, and hundreds of enclosures and village sites have been identified within the state. Ohio was a mecca for the Hopewell and Fort Ancient peoples (among other cultures). Name a mound/site attributed to the Adena, a mound/site attributed to the Hopewell, and a mound/site attributed to the Fort Ancient cultures.

_____

_____

_____

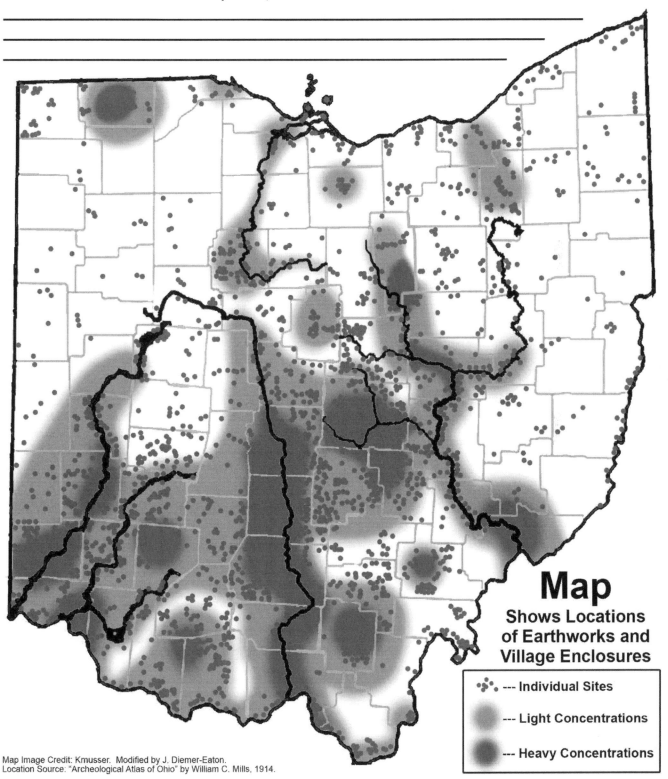

Map

Shows Locations of Earthworks and Village Enclosures

- •• --- Individual Sites
- --- Light Concentrations
- --- Heavy Concentrations

Map Image Credit: Kmusser. Modified by J. Diemer-Eaton.
Location Source: "Archeological Atlas of Ohio" by William C. Mills, 1914.

Leo Petroglyph

Leo Petroglyph in Leo, Ohio is thought to have been created by the Fort Ancient People. Nobody knows for sure as to why they were created in this place, or what every petroglyph is intended to depict. Some have been identified as human feet, fish, birds, and other small animals. What is a petroglyph?

The Fort Ancient Culture
Crossword Puzzle

The Fort Ancient People are thought to be, most likely, a separate society from the Mississippian. Still, the Fort Ancient and Mississippian had contact with each other, trading materials and ideas back and forth. Complete the crossword puzzle featuring 10 Fort Ancient culture-themed vocabulary words.

Word Pool

Alligator
corn
earthenware
Fort Ancient
plaza

Serpent
stockade
storage pit
SunWatch
wattle and daub

Down

1. A large fence constructed to protect a village's population from possible attacks by hostile invaders.
3. The Fort Ancient people cooked in _____ vessels made of clay tempered with crushed shell.
5. This Fort Ancient village was located on the Great Miami River, and served as the inspiration for the open-air museum that bears the same name.
7. A large hole dug into the earth, lined with mats or clay, that was used to store foods like corn for later consumption.
9. _____ Mound, thought to be constructed by the Fort Ancient people, is thought to be in the image of a snake with an egg in its mouth or a comet with a dust trail.

Across

2. The _____ culture flourished from about AD 1000 – 1650 in Ohio, southeastern Indiana, northern Kentucky, and western West Virginia.
4. Some Fort Ancient homes were constructed of _____ walls, while others were covered with bark or reed mats.
6. 50% to 75% of the Fort Ancient people's diet was comprised of this food crop.
8. Although called _____ Mound, the actual animal represented in the earthwork is more likely an opossum, salamander, or possibly the Underwater Panther deity so common among local Native American world-views.
10. The _____ at SunWatch Village was the "town square" that featured astronomical posts that corresponded with the solar calendar.

Name

Date

Find Your Way Through The
Mississippian Maze

Start

Finish

The Mississippian Marketplace

Word Search Worksheet

Mississippian traders were vital to sustain the Mississippian way of life. Vegetables, fruits, nuts, fish, and meat were traded daily. Locally made items such as chert (flint) tools, pottery, textiles, jewelry, carvings, and baskets were made by talented artisans and traded. The Mississippians were known for their trade routes that brought items from foreign regions to the Midwest. New varieties (seeds) of corn and other crops were probably traded from far away places. Many materials used for tools and adornment came from a distance: obsidian from the west, copper from the north, mica from the south, ocean shells and sharks teeth from the south and from the east. Find 22 of these trade items in the word search!

Tip: The words are across and down.

```
c g o u r d p i t c h e r s w a e b m
l b o n e n e e d l e s x e d o s f b
a a s h a r k t e e t h u r d b s m e
y s p i g m e n t s c a t e e s g i r
f k j e m c s g p u h e x o e i h b r
i e b m e d i c i n e s c w r d a c i
g t d h m p y c u e r r o y m i e s e
u s i f r e s h w a t e r p e a r l s
r t y w e a m i c a p e n d a n t s d
e t e x t i l e s w o d q u t k g n o
s h e l l b e a d s i m f i n n t d s
s t o n e p i p e s n a l o f i s h t
w a t e i f k j p o t t e r y v m a s
t o p b e a r f u r s v c u e f n l
c c o p p e r b r a c e l e t s s t g
```

Find All 22 Words!

- baskets
- bear furs
- berries
- bone needles
- chert points
- copper bracelets
- corn
- clay figures
- deer meat
- fish
- freshwater pearls
- gourd pitchers
- mica pendants
- medicines
- obsidian knives
- pigments
- pottery
- reed mats
- shark teeth
- shell beads
- stone pipes
- textiles

Name _____

Date _____

Design Your Own

Mississippian Pottery

Directions:

Color the 4 clays pots.

248

Design Your Own
Mississippian
Shell Pendant

Mississippian
Shell Pendant With
Woodpecker Design

Directions: Draw your own design on the shell pendant below. When finished, cut it out. Punch out the black holes. Put a string through the holes and wear as a necklace.

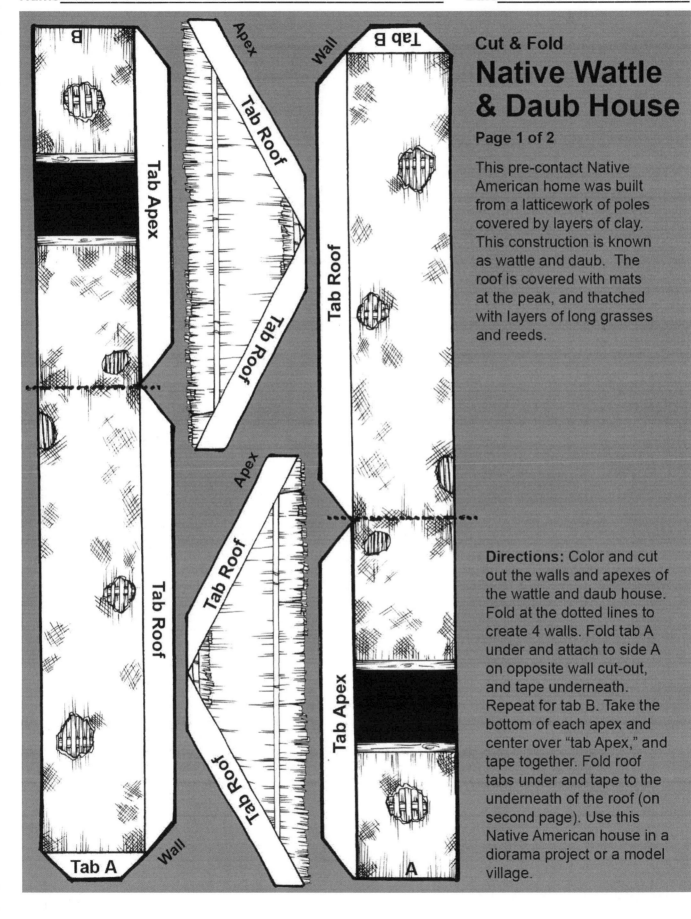

Cut & Fold
Native Wattle & Daub House
Page 1 of 2

This pre-contact Native American home was built from a latticework of poles covered by layers of clay. This construction is known as wattle and daub. The roof is covered with mats at the peak, and thatched with layers of long grasses and reeds.

Directions: Color and cut out the walls and apexes of the wattle and daub house. Fold at the dotted lines to create 4 walls. Fold tab A under and attach to side A on opposite wall cut-out, and tape underneath. Repeat for tab B. Take the bottom of each apex and center over "tab Apex," and tape together. Fold roof tabs under and tape to the underneath of the roof (on second page). Use this Native American house in a diorama project or a model village.

Cut & Fold
Native Wattle & Daub House
Page 2 of 2

This pre-contact Native American home was built from a latticework of poles covered by layers of clay. This construction is known as wattle and daub. The roof is covered with mats at the peak, and thatched with layers of long grasses and reeds.

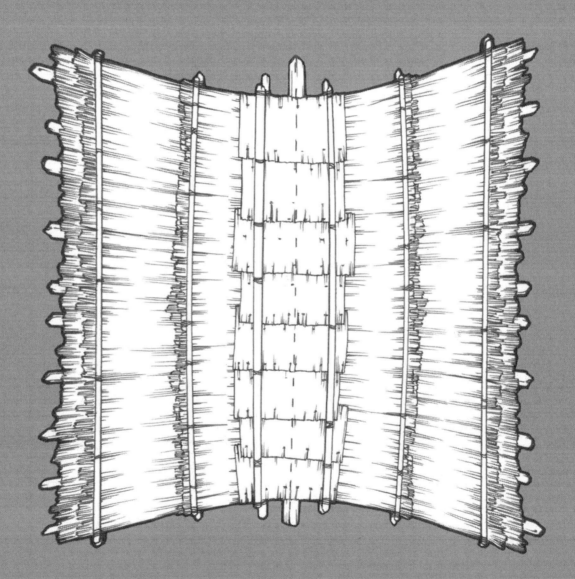

Directions: Color and cut out the roof of the wattle and daub house. Fold at the dotted line to create the peak. Attach this roof to walls (previous page). Use this Native American house in a diorama project or a model village.

Name _____ Date _____

Directions: Draw a Native American wattle and daub house.

Hopewell Trade Crossword

The Hopewell people established extensive trade routes that spanned across the Midwest. From all directions the Hopewell imported distant materials not local to the Indiana and Ohio areas. From the north around Lake Superior came copper. From the west in the Rockies came obsidian and grizzly bear teeth. From the south came alligator and shark teeth and shells from the Gulf of Mexico, quartz from the Arkansas Ozarks, and mica from the southern Appalachians. From the east coast came more shells, shark teeth, and pearls. Foreign varieties of chert (flint) and pipestone were traded to the Hopewell from every direction, and small amounts of silver and gold from sources not well known also ended up in the hands of Hopewell metalworkers. Hopewell trade routes were impressive and responsible for the moving of tons of foreign materials throughout more than half of the United States. To complete this crossword, find the trade materials from the word pool that fit the descriptions below (tip: there are two extra trade materials in the word pool).

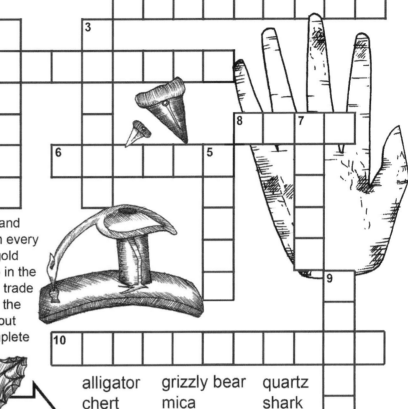

Word Pool

alligator	grizzly bear	quartz
chert	mica	shark
copper	obsidian	shells
gold	pearls	silver

Down

1. This metal was harvested from the Lake Superior region and used by Hopewell metalworkers to make jewelry and tools.
3. This precious metal, along with gold, was acquired in limited amounts through trade.
5. This protective "house" of a kind of saltwater creature was traded from the Gulf of Mexico to the Hopewell people, who then used it in decorative applications.
7. Commonly called flint, this rock variety, both found locally and obtained through trade, was fine-grained and suited for the flintknapping of sharp-edged tools like knives, scrapers, choppers, awls, spears, and arrowheads.
9. Many fossilized teeth from this large predatory sea animal have been drilled and worn as beads by the Hopewell people.

Across

2. This material, often called stone but more accurately described as volcanic glass, was traded from its origin in the west to Indiana and Ohio, where it was made into sharp cutting-edge tools by the Hopewell.
4. Teeth from this large reptile were traded to the Hopewell from its southeastern habitat.
6. These pea-size objects, valued for their decorative uses and often drilled and used as beads, were harvested from saltwater oysters and freshwater mussels.
8. This mineral, known for its thin transparent layers, was traded to the Hopewell in large quantities from the southern Appalachians.
10. Many teeth from this large land mammal were traded from its western habitat to the Hopewell where they were drilled and used to decorate clothing or worn as jewelry.

Color The Hopewell Indian Copper Cut-Outs!

Project: Make Hopewell Copper Cut-Outs

Subjects: Art, Social Studies (American History, Cultural Studies)
Grades 2-5

Description
Students will create Hopewell copper cut-outs from the provided templates.

Materials:
-Copper cut-outs templates on the next 6 pages
-Project foam sheets, thin cardboard, or heavy card stock paper
-Metallic copper craft or wrapping paper
-Markers
-Scissors

Preparation
Copy and cut out the copper cut-out templates on the next 6 pages. Trace them onto the project foam sheet, the thin cardboard, or the card stock paper. Cut these out to create the Hopewell copper cut-out stencils.

Procedure
Have students trace the Hopewell copper cut-out stencils onto the back of copper metallic paper. Cut out the tracing on the metallic paper to create the copper cut-outs. Decorate your classroom or bulletin board with the Hopewell copper cut-outs.

About Copper Cut-Outs
These Hopewell copper cut-outs are on permanent display at the Chicago Field Museum. Many were found in pairs, which is why some of the templates on the next 6 pages are doubled. It is believed that these were used for decoration as clothing or jewelry pieces. To make them, the Hopewell coppersmiths had to heat the copper and hammer it flat.

Learn more about the Hopewell Copper Cut-Outs and Exchange Networks on the Chicago Field Museum's Ancient Americas at http://archive.fieldmuseum.org/ancientamericas/index.html.

  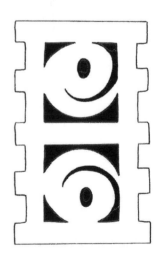

Notes

_____
_____
_____
_____

Project: Make Hopewell Copper Cut-Outs
Subjects: Art, Social Studies (American History, Cultural Studies)
Grades 2-5

Project: Make Hopewell Copper Cut-Outs
Subjects: Art, Social Studies (American History, Cultural Studies)
Grades 2-5

Project: Make Hopewell Copper Cut-Outs
Subjects: Art, Social Studies (American History, Cultural Studies)
Grades 2-5

Project: Make Hopewell Copper Cut-Outs
Subjects: Art, Social Studies (American History, Cultural Studies)
Grades 2-5

References

American Museum of Natural History. Anthropology Collections – North American Ethnographic Collection; New York City.

Angel Mounds State Historic Site and Museum. Evansville, Indiana.

Axtell, James. 2001. Natives and Newcomers: The Cultural Origins of North America. New York: Oxford University Press.

_____. 1981. The Indian Peoples of Eastern America: A Documentary History of the Sexes. New York: Oxford University Press.

Barreiro, Jose. 1988. Indian Roots of American Democracy. Cornell University - Northeast Indian Quarterly.

Beatty-Medina, Charles and Melissa Rinehart. 2012. Contested Territories: Native Americans and Non-Natives in the Lower Great Lakes, 1700-1850. East Lansing, Michigan: Michigan State University Press.

Blake, Leonard W. and Hugh C. Cutler. 2001. Plants From the Past. Tuscaloosa: The University of Alabama Press.

Brose, David C., C. Wesley Cowan, and Robert C. Mainfort Jr. 2001. Societies in Eclipse: Archaeology of the Eastern Woodlands Indians, A.D. 1400-1700. Washington: Smithsonian Institution Press.

Bruchac, Marge. 1999. Reclaiming the Word "Squaw" in the Name of the Ancestors. http://www.native-web.org/pages/legal/squaw.html

Chicago Field Museum. North American Indian Collections.

Conner Prairie Interactive History Park online article The Fall Creek Massacre. http://www.connerprairie.org/Learn-And-Do/Indiana-History/Original-Documents/Fall-Creek-Massacre.aspx

Cooke, Sarah E. and Rachel B. Ramadhyani. 1993. Indians and a Changing Frontier: The Art of George Winter. Indianapolis: Indiana Historical Society.

Culin, Stewart. 1975. Games of the North American Indians. New York, Dover Publications (originally published in the Twenty-Forth Annual Report of the Bureau of American Ethnology to the Smithsonian Institution 1902-1903).

Densmore, Francis. 1974. How Indians Use Wild Plants for Food, Medicine & Crafts. New York: Dover Publications (first published as "Uses of Plants by the Chippewa Indians" in the Forty-Forth Annual Report of the Bureau of American Ethnology to the Secretary of the Smithsonian Institution, 1926-1927).

Detroit Institute of Art. Africa, Oceania, and the Indigenous Americas Collections.

Drimmer, Frederick. 1961. Captured by the Indians: 15 Firsthand Accounts, 1750-1870. New York, Dover Publications.

Edmunds, R. David. 1984. Tecumseh and the Quest for Indian Leadership. Harper Collins Publishers.

_____. 1993. The Shawnee Prophet. Lincoln: University of Nebraska Press.

Ewing, Douglas C. 1982. Pleasing the Spirits: A Catalogue of a Collection of American Indian Art. New York: Ghylen Press.

Fort Ancient Archaeological Park. Oregonia, Ohio.

Greer, Allan. 2000. The Jesuit Relations: Natives and Missionaries in Seventeenth-Century North America. Bedford/St. Martin's Publishing.

Hartman, Sheryl. 2010. "Bison in the Ohio Valley." http://voices.yahoo.com/bison-ohio-valley-5822440.html?-cat=37

_____.1987. Indian Clothing of the Great Lakes: 1740-1840. Liberty, UT: Eagle's View Publishing.

Heckewelder, John. 1876. History, Manners, and Customs of the Indian Nations Who Once Inhabited Pennsylvania and the Neighbouring States. Philadelphia: Historical Society of Pennsylvania.

Indiana & The Old Northwest: An Exhibition. 1980. Indianapolis: Indiana Historical Society.

Jesuit Relations. Vol. 58

Johansen, Bruce E. 1982. Forgotten Founders: Benjamin Franklin, the Iroquois and the Rationale for the American Revolution. Ipswich, MA: Gambit Publishers.

Jones, David E. 2004. Native North American Armor, Shields, and Fortifications. Austin: University of Texas Press.

Jones III, James R. and Amy L. Johnson. 2012. Early Peoples of Indiana. Indianapolis: Department of Historic Preservation and Archaeology.

Jortner, Adam. 2012. The Gods of Prophetstown: The Battle of Tippecanoe and the Holy War for the American Frontier. New York: Oxford University Press.

Karklins, Karlis. 1992. Trade Ornament Usage Among the Native Peoples of Canada: A Source Book. Parks Canada Publication.

Kraft, Herbert C. 2001. The Lenape-Delaware Indian Heritage: 10,000BC – AD2000. Lenape Books.

Lang, Sabine. 1998. Men as Women, Women as Men: Changing Gender in Native American Cultures. Austin: University of Texas Press.

Leo Petroglyph State Memorial. Leo, Ohio.

Library of Congress. Primary Documents in American History: Indian Removal Act. http://www.loc.gov/rr/program/bib/ourdocs/Indian.html

Linemann, W.C. and C.R. Glover. 1990. Nitrogen Fixation by Legumes. New Mexico State University, College of Agriculture. http://www.csun.edu/~hcbio027/biotechnology/lec10/lindemann.html

Mancall, Peter C. and James H. Merrell. 2000. American Encounters: Natives and Newcomers From European Contact to Indian Removal, 1500-1850. New York: Routledge.

Mason, Otis T. 1990. Cradles of the Native Americans. Hammelstown, PA: Tucquan Publishing (originally published in the 1887 Annual Report of the Board of Regents of the Smithsonian Institution).

McKee, Irving. 1941. The Trail of Death: Letters of Benjamin Marie Petit. Indianapolis: Ind. Historical Society.

Merrit, Jane, T. 2003. At the Crossroads: Indians & Empires on a Mid-Atlantic Frontier, 1700-1763. University of North Carolina Press.

Nearing, Helen and Scott. 2000. The Maple Sugar Book. White River Junction, VT: Chelsea Green Publishing.

O'Neil, James F. 1995. Their Bearing is Noble and Proud. Dayton, OH: JTGS Publishing

Ohio History Central. http://www.ohiohistorycentral.org

Orchard, William C. 1971. The Technique of Porcupine-Quill Decoration Among the North American Indians. Museum of the American Indian, Heye Foundation.

Parker, Arthur C. 1968. Parker on the Iroquois. Syracuse University Press.

Rafert, Stewart. 1996. The Miami Indians of Indiana: A Persistent People. Indianapolis: Ind. Historical Society.

Speck, Frank G. 1995. Midwinter Rites of the Cayuga Long House. Lincoln: University of Nebraska Press.

Spencer, Oliver M. 1917. The Indian Captivity of O. M. Spencer. Milo M. Quaife, ed. The Lakeside Press: Chicago.

Spittal, W.G. 1996. Iroquois Women: An Anthology. Ohsweken, Ontario: Iroquois Reprints.

Stearns, Robert E. C. 1990. Wampum & Dentalium: A Study of Native American Shell Money. Hammelstown, PA: Tucquan Publishing (originally published in the 1887 Annual Report of the Board of Regents of the Smithsonian Institution).

Sturtevent, William C. and Bruce G. Trigger. 1978. Handbook of the North American Indians. Vol. 15 – Northeast. Smithsonian Institution.

SunWatch Indian Village and Archaeological Park. Dayton, Ohio.

Tanner, Helen Hornbeck. 1987. Atlas of Great Lakes Indian History. Norman: University of Oklahoma Press.

Utter, Jack. 2001. American Indians: Answers to Today's Questions. Norman: University of Oklahoma Press.

Weatherford, Jack. 1991. Native Roots: How the Indians Enriched America. New York: Ballantine Books.

_____. 1988. Indian Givers: How the Indians of the Americas Transformed the World. New York: Ballantine Books.

Where Two Worlds Meet: The Great Lakes Fur Trade. 1982. St. Paul: Minnesota Historical Society.

White, Richard. 1996. The Indian Tribes of the Upper Mississippi Valley and Religion of the Great Lakes. University of Nebraska, Bison Books.

_____. 2006. The Middle Ground: Indians, Empires, and Republics in the Great Lakes Region, 1650-1815. Cambridge University Press.

Willig, Timothy D. Prophetstown on the Wabash: The Native Spiritual Defense of the Old Northwest. Fall, 1997. Michigan Historical Review, Vol. 23, No. 2.

Zeisberger, David. 1999. David Zeisberger's History of the Northern American Indians in 18th Century Ohio, New York & Pennsylvania. Lewisburg, PA: Wennawoods Publishing.

Woodland Indian Educational Programs

Visit Us
www.WoodlandIndianEDU.com

Contact Us
info@woodlandindianedu.com

Made in the USA
San Bernardino, CA
23 October 2014